TWO
VIEWS
ON

THE DOCTRINE
OF THE TRINITY

Books in the Counterpoints Series

Church Life

Bible and Theology

TWO VIEWS ON
THE DOCTRINE OF THE TRINITY

Stephen R. Holmes

Paul D. Molnar

Thomas H. McCall

Paul S. Fiddes

Jason S. Sexton, general editor
Stanley N. Gundry, series editor

ZONDERVAN

Two Views on the Doctrine of the Trinity
Copyright © 2014 by Jason S. Sexton, Paul S. Fiddes, Stephen R. Holmes, Thomas H. McCall, Paul D. Molnar

This title is also available as a Zondervan ebook. Visit www.zondervan.com/ebooks.

Requests for information should be addressed to:

Zondervan, 3900 Sparks Dr. SE, Grand Rapids, Michigan 49546

Library of Congress Cataloging-in-Publication Data

Two views on the doctrine of the Trinity / Jason S. Sexton, general editor ; Stephen R. Holmes, Paul D. Molnar, Thomas H. McCall, Paul S. Fiddes.
    pages cm. — (Counterpoints)
Includes bibliographical references and index.
    ISBN 978-0-310-49812-4
    1. Trinity. I. Holmes, Stephen R. II. Molnar, Paul D., 1946- III. McCall, Thomas H. IV. Fiddes, Paul S. V. Sexton, Jason S., editor.
BT113.T89 2014
231'.044—dc23   2014016532

Cover design: Tammy Johnson
Cover photography: Masterfile
Interior design: Matthew Van Zomeren

Printed in the United States of America

HB 03.28.2024

For Fred

qui in trinitatis doctrina
optime de ecclesia meritus et meriturus est

CONTENTS

CONTRIBUTORS

Stephen R. Holmes — is Senior Lecturer in St. Mary's College, University of St. Andrews, UK. He is an ordained Baptist minister and holds the BA degree from the University of Cambridge, an MTh from Spurgeon's College, London, and a PhD from King's College, London. He is editor of the *International Journal of Systematic Theology* and author of *God of Grace and God of Glory: An Account of the Theology of Jonathan Edwards*; *Listening to the Past: The Place of Tradition in Theology*; and of *The Quest for the Trinity: The Doctrine of God in Scripture, History and Modernity*.

Paul D. Molnar — is Professor of Systematic Theology at St. John's University in New York. A Catholic theologian, he holds the BA from Cathedral College, the MA from St. John's University, and the PhD in Contemporary Systematic Theology from Fordham University. He is general editor of the Peter Lang Series: *Issues in Systematic Theology*, Editor of the *Karl Barth Society of North America Newsletter*, and Past-President, Member at Large of the Thomas F. Torrance Theological Fellowship, and consulting editor with the *Scottish Journal of Theology*. His publications include *Divine Freedom and the Doctrine of the Immanent Trinity*; *Incarnation and Resurrection: Toward a Contemporary Understanding*; and *Thomas F. Torrance: Theologian of the Trinity*.

Thomas H. McCall — is Associate Professor of Biblical and Systematic Theology at Trinity Evangelical Divinity School in Illinois, where he is also the Director of the Carl F. H. Henry Center for Theological Understanding. He holds the BA from Hobe Sound Bible College, the MA from Wesley Biblical Seminary, and the PhD from Calvin Theological Seminary. He is coeditor (with Michael C. Rea) of and a contributor to *Philosophical and Theological Essays on the Trinity*; coauthor (with Keith D. Stanglin) of *Jacob Arminius: Theologian of Grace*; and author of *Which Trinity? Whose Monotheism? Philosophical and Systematic*

Theologians on the Metaphysics of Trinitarian Theology; and *Forsaken: The Trinity and the Cross, and Why It Matters.*

Paul S. Fiddes — is Professor of Systematic Theology in the University of Oxford, and Director of Research at Regent's Park College, Oxford, having been Principal of the College from 1989 to 2007. He read for a double first in English Literature and Theology at St. Peter's College, Oxford, after which he completed a PhD at Oxford, while also preparing for ordination in the Baptist Union of Great Britain. After Postdoctoral work in the University of Tübingen, he returned to Regent's Park as Fellow and Tutor in Doctrine whilst also becoming Lecturer in Theology at St Peter's. Among his many publications are: *The Creative Suffering of God*; *Past Event and Present Salvation: The Christian Idea of Atonement*; *Freedom and Limit: A Dialogue Between Literature and Christian Doctrine*; *The Promised End: Eschatology in Theology and Literature*; *Participating in God: A Pastoral Doctrine of the Trinity*; *Seeing the World and Knowing God: Hebrew Wisdom and Christian Doctrine in a Late-Modern Context.*

Jason S. Sexton — is Research Associate at the Center for Religion and Civic Culture, University of Southern California, Los Angeles. He holds a BA in Theology from The Master's College, the MDiv and ThM in Systematic Theology from The Master's Seminary, and the PhD from The University of St. Andrews, UK; he has done postdoctoral work at Oak Hill College, London, and has taught theology at Ridley Hall, University of Cambridge, and also at Golden Gate Baptist Theological Seminary in California. He is author of *The Trinitarian Theology of Stanley J. Grenz*, and coeditor (with Derek J. Tidball and Brian S. Harris) of *Revisioning, Renewing, Rediscovering the Triune Center: Essays in Honor of Stanley J. Grenz.*

ABBREVIATIONS

ANF	*Ante-Nicene Fathers*
CD	*Church Dogmatics*, by Karl Barth
CT	*Christianity Today*
HeyJ	*Heythrop Journal*
IJST	*International Journal of Systematic Theology*
ITQ	*Irish Theological Quarterly*
JEH	*Journal of Ecclesiastical History*
JRT	*Journal of Reformed Theology*
JST	*Journal of Systematic Theology*
JTS	*Journal of Theological Studies*
MT	*Modern Theology*
MwJT	*Midwestern Journal of Theology*
NPNF²	*Nicene and Post-Nicene Fathers*, series 2
PG	Patrologia graeca
PL	Patrologia latina
SJT	*Scottish Journal of Theology*
ST	*Summa Theologiae*, by Thomas Aquinas

INTRODUCTION

JASON S. SEXTON

The doctrine of the Trinity stands front and center of the Christian faith and its articulation. Christians have always believed in the triune God, but they have not always confessed this doctrine uniformly. Early church controversies highlight this reality, with Hebrew and Greek mind-sets employing different concepts for understanding God's triune nature. Distinct Eastern and Western concerns then sought to add clarity to an ecumenical understanding of the doctrine through the early disputes. As the story goes, before long the doctrine came to be relatively settled, receiving little extensive engagement beyond the patristic era, with a few exceptions in the medieval and scholastic periods ... until recently.

The idea for this book arose as a result of recent trends within evangelical theology that underscored that the doctrine of the Trinity is not understood or appropriated consistently either within evangelicalism or within the wider Christian tradition. Explorations into the structure of this doctrine, while relatively reserved during most of the twentieth century, came with increased fervency in the last thirty years. Constructive effort continues, especially in English-speaking theology, often presenting views in lengthy, dense monographs not readily accessible to ordinary readers. Yet ordinary believers often wonder how the doctrine of the Trinity matters to the rest of Christian belief and practice. Before that matter can be addressed, however, the most significant available models of the Trinity must be considered.

Here is where this book enters the scene. It aims to clean up some of the discussion by providing clarity on the best ways of understanding the doctrine by four leading theologians working to articulate the doctrine of the Trinity today.

Background to the Debate

After a sustained drought of trinitarian engagement, largely assuming the doctrine rather than producing much reflection on it, and having used it largely for apologetic purposes in recent history, the doctrine of the Trinity has resurged to the center of Christian confession. This follows the widely acknowledged twentieth-century trinitarian revival commonly understood as led largely by Swiss theologian Karl Barth. Barth's work sets the backdrop and has been the catalyst for much trinitarian engagement over the past sixty years. Yet the second half of the twentieth century saw a different kind of trinitarian theology developing, giving way to what we will refer to broadly as the relational doctrine of the Trinity.

While relational models of the Trinity have at times commonly been referred to by the unfortunate term "the social Trinity," in this volume we are choosing the more appropriate terminology implied in the broader concept, "relational Trinity." This provides helpful distance between certain relational or "social" models that usually have been based deeply in anthropological or socio-political concerns. Jürgen Moltmann first harnessed the concept the "social Trinity" to address fundamental concerns in the world by both identifying God with and inextricably linking God to the world's affairs.[1] Moltmann's idea was developed by liberation theologians like Leonardo Boff and the feminist theologian Catherine Mowry LaCugna to produce a doctrine of God based on questions arising from human societal issues.[2] It has been further developed by evangelicals like Miroslav Volf[3] and, to some degree, Millard Erickson and John Franke.

In a way much less comfortable with the Marxist concerns of Moltmann and Boff, Wolfhart Pannenberg developed a kind of incipient model of the relational Trinity based on his futuristic theology and God's love for the world.[4] His model has been advanced by evangelicals like Stanley Grenz,[5] although innovative relational proposals by David

1. Jürgen Moltmann, *The Trinity and the Kingdom of God: The Doctrine of God* (trans. Margaret Kohl; Minneapolis: Fortress, 1981), 19.

2. See Leonardo Boff, *Trinity and Society* (trans. Paul Burns; Maryknoll, NY: Orbis, 1988); Catherine Mowry LaCugna, *God for Us: The Trinity and the Christian Life* (San Francisco: HarperSanFrancisco, 1991).

3. Miroslav Volf, "'The Trinity Is Our Social Program': The Doctrine of the Trinity and the Shape of Social Engagement," *MT* 14 (1998): 403–23.

4. Wolfhart Pannenberg, *Systematic Theology* (3 vols.; Grand Rapids: Eerdmans, 1991–98).

5. See the beginning of what was meant as a lengthy project in Stanley J. Grenz, *The Social God and the Relational Self: A Trinitarian Theology of the Imago Dei* (Louisville: Westminster John Knox, 2001); for an argument showing something of a reversal of his employment of the fashionable model of the doctrine Trinity, see Jason S. Sexton, *The Trinitarian Theology of Stanley J. Grenz* (New York: T&T Clark, 2013), chs. 4 and 5.

Cunningham and Paul Fiddes have done so more radically.[6] Additional relational models were derived from revisionist readings of patristic sources, including that of John Zizioulas[7] and, following Zizioulas while critical of Western trinitarianism, Colin Gunton.[8] Relational models have also been developed by those building on Barth's explicit reloca-tion of the doctrine of the Trinity as central to the systematic enterprise like Hans Urs von Balthasar, Thomas and James Torrance,[9] Robert Jenson, and arguably Elizabeth Johnson.[10] Analytic philosophers and philosophical theologians have also proposed relational models of the Trinity, including those by Richard Swinburne, Cornelius Plantinga, David Brown, Millard Erickson, Alan Torrance, and Thomas McCall.[11]

These innovations have led to a steady and increasing reaction and response from those holding to a classical doctrine of the Trinity— replete with features of divine simplicity, transcendence, ineffability, rejection of the hard East/West bifurcation, and nervousness toward any relational ontology. Some of this reaction has been accompanied by more careful readings of patristic sources, especially by Michel Barnes and Lewis Ayres on Augustine,[12] but also with more thor-ough readings of Nicaea and the Cappadocians by Khaled Anatolios

6. David S. Cunningham, *These Three Are One: The Practice of Trinitarian Theology* (Grand Rapids: Baker, 1998); Paul S. Fiddes, *Participating in God: A Pastoral Doctrine of the Trinity* (Louisville: Westminster John Knox, 2000).

7. John D. Zizioulas, *Being as Communion: Studies in Personhood and the Church* (Crestwood, NY: St Vladimir's Seminary Press, 1985).

8. Colin E. Gunton, *The One, the Three and the Many: God, Creation and the Culture of Modernity: The 1992 Bampton Lectures* (Cambridge: Cambridge University Press, 1993).

9. See Thomas F. Torrance, *The Christian Doctrine of God: One Being Three Persons* (Edin-burgh: T&T Clark, 1996); James B. Torrance, *Worship, Community and the Triune God of Grace* (Downers Grove, IL: InterVarsity Press, 1996).

10. Elizabeth A. Johnson, *She Who Is: The Mystery of God in Feminist Theological Discourse* (New York: Crossroad, 1993); for arguing for massive divergence of Johnson from Barth, see Cherith Fee Nordling, *Knowing God by Name: A Conversation between Elizabeth A. Johnson and Karl Barth* (New York: Peter Lang, 2010).

11. Cornelius Plantinga Jr., "Social Trinity and Tritheism," in *Trinity, Incarnation, and Atonement: Philosophical and Theological Essays* (ed. Ronald J. Feenstra and Cornelius Plantinga Jr.; Notre Dame: University of Notre Dame Press, 1989), 21–47; David Brown, *The Divine Trinity* (London: Duckworth, 1985); Millard J. Erickson, *God in Three Persons* (Grand Rapids: Baker, 1995); Alan J. Torrance, *Persons in Communion: An Essay on Trinitarian Description and Human Participation* (Edinburgh: T&T Clark, 1996); Thomas H. McCall, *Which Trinity? Whose Monotheism? Philosophical and Systematic Theologians on the Metaphysics of Trinitarian Theology* (Grand Rapids: Eerdmans, 2010).

12. Lewis Ayres, *Nicaea and Its Legacy: An Approach to Fourth-Century Trinitarian Theol-ogy* (Oxford: Oxford University Press, 2004); idem, *Augustine and the Trinity* (Cambridge: Cambridge University Press, 2010).

and Sarah Coakley,[13] bringing about not only a much more coherent reading of early trinitarian development but also a strong critique of relational trinitarian offerings. Evangelical scholars Keith E. Johnson and Brad Green have also given robust responses to the haphazard usage of Augustine by Gunton and others seeking to take Augustine in directions that his writings do not bear out. But the foremost pushback against the relational turn in theology proper has been sustained by sharp critiques from Catholic theologians like Paul Molnar and Karen Kilby.[14] Their critique has been accompanied by contributions from other significant figures in trinitarian theology, including efforts by John Webster, George Hunsinger, Kevin Vanhoozer, Fred Sanders, and the trenchant work by Stephen R. Holmes.[15]

The reach of development in trinitarian theology has spanned the spectrum of the Christian tradition, affecting even contemporary evangelicalism that had been especially known for its trinitarian paucity. Confusion remains, however. And as each tradition gets better at articulating the doctrine of the Trinity, and as the current and next generations of believers in all Christian traditions seek to be more explicitly and robustly trinitarian, the way forward for trinitarian theology must reckon with what are referred to in this book as the classical and relational views. Each view provides viable options equally vying for the church's attention as it seeks to hold forth the essence of the Christian faith as the hope of the world.

With pastoral discussions prompted by students and practitioners seeking to discern how best to understand the doctrine and appropriate its relevance in their ministries, the doctrine of the Trinity has garnered

---

13. Khaled Anatolios, *Retrieving Nicaea: The Development and Meaning of Trinitarian Doctrine* (Grand Rapids: Baker, 2011); Sarah Coakley, "Re-Thinking Gregory of Nyssa: Introduction—Gender, Trinitarian Analogies, and the Pedagogy of the Song," *MT* 18 (2002): 431–43; see also the other essays in that issue.

14. Paul D. Molnar, *Divine Freedom and the Doctrine of Immanent Trinity: In Dialogue with Karl Barth and Contemporary Theology* (Edinburgh: T&T Clark, 2002); Karen Kilby, "Perichoresis and Projection: Problems with Social Doctrines of the Trinity," *New Blackfriars* 81 (2000): 432–45.

15. See, e.g., Kevin J. Vanhoozer, *Remythologizing Theology: Divine Action, Passion, and Authorship* (Cambridge: Cambridge University Press, 2010); Fred Sanders, *The Deep Things of God: How the Trinity Changes Everything* (Wheaton, IL: Crossway, 2010); and Stephen R. Holmes, *The Quest for the Trinity: The Doctrine of God in Scripture, History and Modernity* (Downers Grove, IL: InterVarsity Press, 2012); in the UK: *The Holy Trinity: Understanding God's Life* (Milton Keynes: Paternoster, 2012).

much broader attention recently, evidenced in volumes from various Christian traditions. These include monographs, reference works, and popular books on the doctrine of the Trinity. In spite of the plethora of publications seeking to make sense of this doctrine, the models themselves are rarely overtly highlighted as of particular importance. Yet they represent critical differences between trinitarians. *Two Views on the Doctrine of the Trinity* enlists leading scholars, then, whose positions advocate different angles on the respective views, each view hosting one representative from within the evangelical tradition, and one representative from the Catholic or mainline Protestant tradition; each contributor gives a substantial account for his view and why it represents the best understanding of the doctrine of the Trinity.

The debate has not just been an evangelical one, of course, but has been held among most of the traditions in the West, and increasingly by those in the East. Indeed, evangelicalism has perhaps been less explicitly trinitarian than other ecclesial groups, which prompted Fred Sanders's recent work arguing that evangelicalism has been "tacitly trinitarian."

The Views

The views designated in this book are broadly conceived and maintained conventionally. There is a sense in which these could have been given as four distinct views, and a sense in which each of these could have been called classical (each drawing from ancient sources) or relational (each finding relations in the divine life). There is also an important sense in which these constructive proposals are in development—features of the views represented here have not always been held with the same degree of confidence in which they are presented, nor does each representation (although substantial) give an exhaustive treatment of its view. Nevertheless, in the present moment of trinitarian theology, we have assembled four of the most widely regarded thinkers to account for two broadly rendered views under consideration in this volume.

The Classical Doctrine of the Trinity

The classical view presents what is meant by a traditional doctrine of the Trinity, along with how and why it differs from the relational view. It develops an understanding of the traditional doctrine of the Trinity with two different essays, demonstrating critical features inherent to classical trinitarianism that are not resembled in relational models of the Trinity. These two essays highlight features essential to classical trinitarian theology. This view is represented by one evangelical theologian and one Roman Catholic theologian, highlighting similarities among their models and approaches along with a number of differences, especially regarding sources for developing this doctrine.

Stephen R. Holmes is the evangelical and Baptist theologian who studied for his PhD at King's College in London under one of our era's great relational trinitarians, the late Colin Gunton. This was a time at King's when John Zizioulas was visiting faculty member, Alan Torrance and Murray Rae were on faculty, and the best of imaginative thinking on the Trinity was in the air. However, embarking on his own career teaching theology alongside Gunton on the Strand, and later in St. Andrews, Holmes became convinced that much of what was being celebrated were innovations hardly resembling the tradition. His writings and work as editor of *International Journal of Systematic Theology* began to show this ahead of his "significant contribution to the debate"[16] that came with the 2012 volume, *The Quest for the Trinity: The Doctrine of God in Scripture, History and Modernity.*

Paul D. Molnar is the Roman Catholic theologian who once trained for the diocesan priesthood before completing the PhD at Fordham University in the same class as Catherine Mowry LaCugna. As general editor of the Peter Lang series *Issues in Systematic Theology*, Molnar maintains a keen eye on the contemporary theological landscape. His major contribution to trinitarian theology came with his 2002 book, *Divine Freedom and the Doctrine of the Immanent Trinity: In Dialogue with Karl Barth and Contemporary Theology.* As a ground-clearing exercise a decade ahead of Holmes's effort, this book called for a "shift away from a doctrine of the Trinity organized around an abstract principle of relationality or the primacy of historical experience towards a doctrine focused on the sovereignty and perfections of the triune God as the ground of his works."[17] In this way it was hailed as a major contribution illustrating the abandonment of the immanent Trinity by contemporary theology.

---

16. Robert Letham, "Old and New, East and West, and a Missing Horse," in *The Doctrine of the Holy Trinity Revisited: Essays in Response to Stephen R. Holmes* (ed. Thomas A. Noble and Jason S. Sexton; Milton Keynes, UK: Paternoster, forthcoming).

17. John Webster, "Review of *Divine Freedom and the Doctrine of the Immanent Trinity,*" *JTS* 56 (2005): 290.

The Relational Doctrine of the Trinity

This view sketches precisely what is and what is not meant by the term "relational Trinity" and how it may be straightforwardly rendered and itself deeply connected to the tradition. It accounts for features that have led to the elevation of relational doctrines, along with their promises and potential hazards (especially with forms of "the social Trinity"). It highlights sources for this doctrine, drawing from particular voices in church history (especially the Cappadocians), from the biblical text, and from ad hoc appropriation of analytic philosophy and critical theory—all the while being aware of various anthropological, societal, or other personalist findings in the social sciences that have been appropriated from other relational trinitarians.[18] It is represented by one evangelical theologian and one theologian from a mainline Baptist tradition, displaying a range of innovation and latitude for what relational models of the Trinity might look like.

Both scholars in this category argue for how a relational model is the best way to understand the doctrine of the Trinity. In one important sense, these models are different. Yet each employs new conceptual tools to discern more clearly the relationship between the threeness and oneness of the divine life, or to show how modernist (classical?) conceptions of the doctrine of the Trinity have limited what this doctrine could be. Thus they both fit under the broader heading of "relational" models of the Trinity and chart innovations for understanding the doctrine in the contemporary setting.

Thomas H. McCall is the evangelical theologian representing the relational doctrine of the Trinity. McCall is a Wesleyan theologian with a PhD from Calvin Theology Seminary and has contributed to the doctrine of the Trinity by playing an important role as part of the invigorating discussions from analytic theology, employing conceptual tools from analytic philosophy to better understand the doctrine's most problematic features. His 2010 book, *Which Trinity? Whose Monotheism? Philosophical and Systematic Theologians on the Metaphysics of Trinitarian Theology*,[19]

---

18. Some of these tools have been held at a critical distance by the contributors in this volume and have been more explicitly appropriated in the relational (or social) models of Zizioulas, Gunton, etc. However, we can note some of this in Alan J. Torrance, "Reclaiming the Continuing Priesthood of Christ: Implications and Challenges," in *Christology: Ancient and Modern* (ed. Oliver D. Crisp and Fred Sanders; Grand Rapids: Zondervan, 2013), 193–95; see also Gijsbert van den Brink, "Social Trinitarianism: A Defense against Some Recent Criticisms," *IJST* (forthcoming).

19. McCall, *Which Trinity?* ch. 8.

outlined theses for the way forward in trinitarian theology, which includes among other things conceiving the Trinity as three distinct "centers of consciousness and will" and maintaining that the three are indeed one. This volume provides space for clarifying some of these ideas.

Paul S. Fiddes comes from a mainline Baptist tradition and represents the radical relational doctrine of the Trinity. After the DPhil at Oxford, Fiddes undertook postdoctoral work in Tübingen, attending the seminars of Jürgen Moltmann and Eberhard Jüngel before returning to Oxford. His most significant contribution has perhaps come with his 2000 publication, *Participating in God: A Pastoral Doctrine of the Trinity*, whose innovation has been in developing an understanding of divine "persons" as nothing other than "relations," or as movements of divine relationship into which creatures are drawn. This move asserts that the doctrine of the Trinity cannot be developed apart from pastoral experience, which in turn demands retooling an understanding of the Trinity.

Other Views

It may be claimed that a number of other models on the doctrine of the Trinity are not represented in this volume. As already stated, the so-called "social Trinity" is absent, whether in its strong analytic shape or from its European, Latin American Liberationist, or North American proponents. An explicitly Eastern Orthodox representative is likewise not here. Of course, developments in trinitarian theology have run across ecclesial and denominational lines and so having all ecclesial traditions present is simply not necessary. But the robust appropriation of Thomas Torrance by Paul Molnar adequately ushers Athanasius into the discussion. And McCall's view will be seen as akin enough to a kind of social trinitarianism represented in the tradition of analytic theology/philosophy, with eternal I-Thou relations.

Other positions not addressed in this volume, of course, include the nontrinitarian ones, including oneness (modalist) views of the Trinity that various trinitarians have been inclined to engage recently.[20] In

20. E.g., "Oneness-Trinitarian Pentecostal Final Report, 2002–2007," *Pneuma* 30 (2008): 203–24; see also the situation with Mark Driscoll, James MacDonald, and T. D. Jakes in the 2012 Elephant Room (Michael Foust, "T. D. Jakes Embraces Doctrine of the Trinity, Moves Away from 'Oneness' View," *CT* [Jan. 27, 2012], available at www.christianitytoday.com/gleanings/2012/january/td-jakes-embraces-doctrine-of-trinity-moves-away-from.html (accessed Dec. 1, 2013).

these ways, the present volume has labored not to represent every imaginable view on the subject, but rather to gather the best representative voices from the most significant views being advocated on the Christian doctrine of the Trinity today. With the proposals on display, then, our goal is to move the conversation forward with the future of trinitarian theology considering the two views represented here.

The Approach

With this volume readers can look forward to having the four authors from orthodox Christian traditions establishing features of their models and approaches to the doctrine of the Trinity in relatively similar ways, which allows each writer to highlight the strengths of his view against the alternatives and to argue how it best reflects the orthodox or most appropriate perspective for understanding the Trinity.

In order to facilitate a genuine debate and ensure that the key issues are teased out, each essay addresses specific matters of concern related to methodology, trinitarian doctrine itself, and implications for each view.

Trinitarian Methodology

The views address where the doctrine of the Trinity originated and what sources are best for developing the doctrine: from Scripture, tradition, and culture; and from patristic, medieval, Reformation/Post-Reformation, and contemporary sources. Authors disclose whether their view finds an analogy between the triune life and anything in creation, and whether the triune God can be understood via a relational analogy or an analogy of being or faith. Consideration is also given to the role of the East/West division among historical and contemporary trinitarian thinkers, and to the role of the *filioque* clause in the Nicene Creed, denoting whether the Spirit proceeds from the Father or from the Father *and* the Son. Beyond this contributors reckon to some degree with what kind of ontology is posited for their views.

Trinitarian Doctrine

As it related to the trinitarian models themselves, authors consider what distinguishes the Father, the Son, and the Holy Spirit from one another, and how these distinctions and relations are to be understood in eternity and in the salvation economy. Attention is given to how God's tri-unity is constituted and how God can be three and yet one. Beyond this, each representative is asked to show how his view represents the relationship between immanent and economic Trinity, and how the divine presence is mediated to the creation. Questions about the nature of divine persons, relations, and the movements within God's own life are addressed, as well as matters of eternal generation, subordination, and hierarchy within the Trinity. The relationship between divine processions and missions is also addressed, as well as the matter of divine simplicity and temporality.

Trinitarian Implications

With any space that might remain, contributors address the matter of how his understanding of the doctrine of the Trinity matters in the articulation of the Christian faith, and how this doctrine might then shape Christian ethics, interreligious dialogue, civic engagement, and so on.

While each contributor has been given freedom to frame and develop his essay in ways deemed most fitting to represent his view of the doctrine of Trinity and its implications, special effort is given to highlighting the specific conceptual features of the represented view of the doctrine itself. Surely questions will remain for our readers, as these short chapters only represent some key features of the views at play, sufficiently highlighting differences in the views. Yet this book aims to bring the models in close-range dialogue between commentators capable of advancing the conversation regarding classical and relational trinitarianism, providing a helpful resource to enable the church to sort through some of the critical issues today.

Whether these questions have been adequately addressed we submit to our readers, hoping to spur them on further in the understanding of a hearty appropriation of the doctrine for their lives and ministries. It is impossible to address exhaustively the matter of God's triune life, not to mention being asked to do so in ten thousand words. And yet we commend each of these models to our readers as viable approaches from within the Christian tradition, each reflecting distinct conceptions that represent viable and compelling ways of understanding God the Trinity and in this way inviting our readers to think along with the four contributors in their ongoing reflection on the eternal Father, on the only begotten Son Jesus Christ, the Word, and on the Holy Spirit as the gift and giver of life.

On the way to generating the essays in this volume, we held a one-day conference at the University of St. Andrews on April 30, 2013. This conference was attended by scholars, pastors, and laypeople from throughout the UK, including leading figures in the theological world such as Alan Torrance, Iain and Morag Torrance, Joan O'Donovan, Don Wood, Ivor Davidson; biblical scholars like Scott Hafemann and Grant Macaskill; and very busy scholars outside the world of divinity in the larger University of St. Andrews community. Together with a host of postgraduate and undergraduate students in attendance, this earlier conference highlighted again how vibrant the community of St. Andrews is for theology today, and how significant the doctrine of the Trinity is for the life of the church and the academic community.

For support with this earlier conference, which allowed the contributors the time to enjoy personal interaction and friendship over meals as well as the formal, intense dialogue of the conference, we wish to thank Ivor Davidson, Head of School, St. Mary's College, Hodel's Development Corporation, the Foundation for the Advancement of Evangelical Theology in California, Mike and Amy Shane, David Garza, Eric Miller, and Andy Fossett. We acknowledge the contribution and keen insights of Heidi Sexton, Wendy Dixon, and Ursula Heise in the final stages of editing this book. We are also grateful for the wonderful support given by Jesse Hillman and Verlyn Verbrugge, and the enthusiastic backing for theology consistently shown by Katya Covrett and Zondervan Academic.

Jason S. Sexton
Advent 2013
Los Angeles, California

CHAPTER ONE

CLASSICAL TRINITY: EVANGELICAL PERSPECTIVE

STEPHEN R. HOLMES

By Way of Introduction

In a recent book on the doctrine of the Trinity,[1] I approached the subject from a historical perspective, and I want to do the same, at least initially, in this essay. I suggest that there is ground to be cleared before we can begin to work on how a constructive statement of the doctrine should be developed and articulated. We have inherited a number of historical claims that so confuse and obscure our thinking about the doctrine of the Trinity that, without some serious historical work, we will inevitably fail to make sense of it.

Perhaps I can demonstrate this need by illustrating from a different era of history. Anti-trinitarianism in England was common during the seventeenth and early eighteenth centuries. William Whiston and Samuel Clarke, among others, developed a biblicist anti-trinitarianism: rereading the Bible, particularly the New Testament, they found the inherited doctrine of the Trinity to be inadequate to the texts.[2] At the same time, or slightly earlier, Deists such as John Toland or Matthew

---

1. Stephen R. Holmes, *The Quest for the Trinity: The Doctrine of God in Scripture, History and Modernity* (Downers Grove, IL: InterVarsity Press, 2012); UK: *The Holy Trinity: Understanding God's Life* (Milton Keynes: Paternoster, 2012).

2. William Whiston, *Primitive Christianity Reviv'd in Four Parts* (London: n.p., 1712); Samuel Clarke, *The Scripture-Doctrine of the Trinity, in Three Parts* (London: James Knapton, 1712).

Tindal were developing a rationalist anti-trinitarianism, arguing that the doctrine of the Trinity made no logical sense.[3]

Both of these strands rested on the earlier work of John Biddle, who published a translation of the Racovian Catechism, the confession of faith of the anti-trinitarian Socinian Church of the Friars Minor. To analyze this sudden popularity of anti-trinitarianism, we may start with a revealing, albeit passing, comment from Biddle: "By Person I understand, as Philosophers do, *suppositum intelligens*, that is an intellectual substance compleat, and not a mood [*sic*, "mode"] or subsistence, which are fantastical & senseless terms, brought in to cozen the simple."[4] On this basis, he argues, to claim that the Son and the Spirit are persons distinct from the Father is to insist that they have a different will to the will of the Father, and, Biddle asserts, "he that hath a will distinct in number from that of God is not God."[5]

On the Meaning of Words

To grasp the importance of this marginal comment, we need to be aware of the standard English vocabulary of trinitarian doctrine: "subsistence" (a borrowing of a standard Latin term, *subsistentia*) and "mode of existence" (a translation of a standard Greek term, *hypostasis*) are both normal English words used for the three persons of the Trinity. But Biddle dismisses them. In his view, they are not even wrong; they are so obviously meaningless that no argument is needed to demonstrate the point. He bases this dismissal of standard vocabulary on an equally undefended definition of the word "person." This definition is borrowed, as he admits, from the "philosophers" of his day—presumably he means Descartes and those who followed.

So, Biddle redefined the word "person" to mean what philosophers mean by it. On the basis of this redefinition, the identification of "person" with "mode of being" or "subsistence" can simply be rejected as

3. John Toland, *Christianity Not Mysterious: Or, a Treatise Showing that There Is Nothing in the Gospel contrary to Reason Nor above It, and That No Christian Doctrine Can Properly Be Called a Mystery* (London: n.p., 1696); Matthew Tindal, *Christianity as Old as the Creation: or, The Gospel a Republication of the Religion of Nature* (London: n.p., 1731).

4. John Biddle, *XII Arguments Drawn out of Holy Scripture Wherein the Commonly-received Opinion Touching the Diety [i.e. Deity] of the Holy Spirit, Is Clearly and Fully Refuted* (London: s.n., 1647), 2–3, marginal note.

5. Ibid., 13.

meaningless—and this despite the fact that these identifications were standard in the tradition of English-language theology and directly related to scholastic Latin and patristic Greek theology as well. He is followed in this sort of redefinition by Whiston, Clarke, Toland, and Tindal—all of whom, writing after Locke, similarly also assume novel definitions of ontological terms used in standard trinitarian discourse, including "substance."[6]

These redefinitions were natural in that day. Every educated writer knew what "person" meant; good and careful contemporary definitions were available; without an acute awareness of the shape of philosophical history, there was no reason to think it meant anything different. With some historical perspective, however, we can see the nature of the problem here: if the meaning of key terms in an argument or statement is changed, then it is hardly surprising if the argument or statement begins to look incoherent or simply ridiculous. Almost the only writer of the day who saw through such terminological problems was the great Anglican bishop Edward Stillingfleet, whose 1697 *Discourse in Vindication of the Doctrine of the Trinity* traced the changes in meaning of various words with some care and attention.[7]

I mention such obscure early modern debates because, at our present historical distance from them, we can see clearly the way in which unthinkingly assuming a change of meaning of a word reshapes the entire discussion of a doctrine. This gives us a clue to where late twentieth-century thinking about the doctrine of the Trinity, and particularly the development of "social trinitarianism," has gone wrong.

This, it should be said, is not primarily a claim about analogies. I take it that there are no interesting analogies from creation to the Trinity, particularly not in the sphere of human sociality (on which more later)—but that is not the point here. My argument here is not that improper analogies were drawn from human personhood to divine personhood, but that the word "person" was assumed to mean something (an intellectual substance) that it had not meant in earlier formulations. This is a claim about the changing meanings of words, which must

---

6. I explore this in more detail in my *The Quest for the Trinity*, 173–80.

7. Edward Stillingfleet, *A Discourse in Vindication of the Doctrine of the Trinity: With an Answer to the Late Socinian Objections against It from Scripture, Antiquity and Reason* (London: Henry Mortlock, 1697).

be treated with great care if we are to make sense of ancient, or even early modern, documents.[8] That said, in this redefinition there was an assumption that the word "person" meant the same thing when applied to human and divine realities. Thus, the doctrine of analogy was denied in favor of a claim that words are univocal, and I do take this to be a problem (again, more on this later).

Words change their meaning over time, and if we want to understand what a writer is saying, we need to know what the words meant for that individual rather than reading our own meaning into the text. I suggest that most of (what I regard as) the misunderstandings of the doctrine of the Trinity in recent decades—and indeed, as the examples above show, in recent centuries—come from a failure to follow this rather obvious rule. Words like "person" and "relation" in particular have been redefined from their original, metaphysical meanings to some supposedly radical new ontological claims in the doctrine of the Trinity—the "social Trinity."

There are novel ontological claims in the classical development of the doctrine of the Trinity. The most obvious is the claim that a spiritual substance's logical relation to itself establishes a distinction that is real, but that does not prevent the substance being simple. But claims that the doctrine of the Trinity as it was established in the fourth century establishes a personalist or relational ontology are simply false, being based entirely on a reading of new meanings into old words.

On the de Régnon Thesis

A second methodological myth to be cleared is the so-called de Régnon thesis,[9] the proposal that the Greek-speaking Eastern church (most noticeably the Cappadocian Fathers) and the Latin-speaking Western church (most notably Augustine) developed visibly different doctrines

---

8. Examples of the problem are not hard to garner. One of Isaac Watts's hymns (and incidentally Watts suffered from all these problems when it came to trinitarian articulation) contains the line, "Let every creature rise and bring / Peculiar honours to their King." "Peculiar," of course, had the sense of "personal" or "particular" in the eighteenth century; it means something different now. Again, in the eighteenth century the term "enthusiast" carried the sense of "fanatic"; I have heard it claimed that somewhere there is a plaque celebrating a minister of a church who served for decades "without ever once showing any trace of enthusiasm in his ministry."

9. So called because first outlined in Theodore de Régnon, *Études de théologie positive sur la Sainte Trinité* (4 vols.; Paris: Victor Retaux, 1892–1898).

of the Trinity. In de Régnon's own presentation, the Greeks started with three persons and claimed they were one God, whereas Augustine started with one God and claimed God was tripersonal. For de Régnon, Augustine's approach was obviously better. In more recent formulations, the order of preference is reversed: the Cappadocian Fathers saw their way to this radically new ontology, the "social Trinity," in which persons in loving relationship were the basis of all things. It is said that Augustine, by contrast, missed this innovation completely and so returned to the older ontological scheme that focused on what a thing was, and which was as inadequate as it was pagan.

Against this, I would first note just how unlikely this seems. Augustine stood in a tradition of Latin trinitarian theology that had developed in active engagement with the Cappadocian pro-Nicene tradition, and which included many figures—most notably Ambrose and Jerome—to whom Augustine stood in close relation at various points in his life. There is no doubt that he knew the work of Hilary of Poitiers, Optatus, and Pope Damasus. I find virtually inconceivable the claim that he did not know the work of Ambrosiaster or Gregory of Elvira, along with many others. At what point, then, in this developing tradition of Latin pro-Nicene theology did the basic rupture with the Cappadocians occur? And why did no one notice? It seems virtually impossible to construct a plausible narrative of how the traditions could have suddenly divided—there is no time for a gradual growing apart.

Further, when one looks at the developments of the key concepts between Augustine and the Cappadocians, they often run in almost exact parallel. Consider the idea of relation. The idea is introduced by Gregory of Nazianzus in the third theological oration:

> "Father," they say, is a designation either of the substance or the activity; is it not?
>
> They intend to impale us on a dilemma, for if we say that it names the substance we shall then be agreeing that the Son is of a different substance, there being a single substance and that one, according to them, preempted by the Father. But if we say that the term designates the activity, we shall clearly be admitting that the Son is a creation not an offspring. If there is an active producer, there must be a production and they will declare themselves

surprised at the idea of an identity between Creator and created. I should have felt some awe myself at your dilemma, had it been necessary to accept one of the alternatives and impossible to avoid them by stating a third and truer possibility. My expert friends, it is this: "Father" designates neither the substance nor the activity, but the relationship, the manner of being, which holds good between the Father and the Son.[10]

Compare this to Augustine, in Book V of *De Trinitate*.:

With God, nothing is said modification-wise because there is nothing changeable with him. And yet not everything that is said of him is said substance-wise. Some things are said with reference to something else, like Father with reference to Son and Son with reference to Father; and this is not said modification-wise because the one is always Father and the other always Son.... Therefore, although being Father is different from being Son, there is no difference of substance, because they are not called these things substance-wise but relationship-wise; and yet this relationship is not a modification because it is not changeable.[11]

If these two theologians are using fundamentally different ontologies, it is remarkable that they can argue a technical point in exactly the same way.

I suggest, then, that to think adequately about the doctrine of the Trinity, we need to be careful about terminology, not letting historically accidental shifts in the meaning of certain words mislead us, and to resist the temptation to assume a fundamental difference between Eastern and Western approaches, unless such a difference can be demonstrated from careful reading of the texts. With these caveats in place, I turn to the origins and development of the doctrine.

The Origins of Trinitarian Doctrine in Reflection on the Bible

The set of conceptual distinctions and definitions that we refer to as "the doctrine of the Trinity" was largely formally defined as a result of

---

10. Gregory of Nazianzus, *On God and Christ: The Five Theological Orations and Two Letters to Cledonius* (trans. Frederick Williams and Lionel Wickham; ed. John Behr; Yonkers, NY: St. Vladimir's Seminary Press, 2002), 83–84.

11. Saint Augustine, *The Trinity* (trans. Edmund Hill, O.P.; ed. John E. Rotelle; Hyde Park, NY: New City Press, 1991), 192.

fourth-century debates, although inevitably those debates built on what had come earlier. The dispute between Arius and his bishop, Alexander of Alexandria, over the origin of the Son from the Father—is the begetting of the Son eternal, or in time?—led to the Council of Nicaea (AD 325). The failure of Nicaea to settle the broader issue of the relationship of the Son to the Father, and the later debate that involved the status of the Spirit, led finally to an ecumenical settlement generally reported to be enshrined at the Council of Constantinople (AD 381).[12]

That said, it would be wrong to suppose that trinitarian thought was a fourth-century novelty. Instead, I would argue that the worship of the church had been fairly consistently trinitarian, or "proto-trinitarian," from the earliest days of Christianity. The fourth-century developments were theological formulations that were adequate to making sense of how what was said and assumed in worship could properly be said/assumed. The ecumenical doctrine established by the Council of Constantinople, then, and developed by Augustine is a successful attempt to state theologically the things the churches had always tacitly assumed in their worship.

Israel's Monotheism and Early Church Worship

A proper statement of the doctrine must begin in Scripture. Again, however, I want to raise something of a protest against the way this has often been narrated in recent trinitarian theology. The powerful and lasting witness of the Old Testament to the oneness/uniqueness of Israel's God needs to be taken with at least as much seriousness as passages such as the gospel accounts of the baptism of Jesus. The contemporary fashion for an almost Marcionite assumption that everything the Scriptures have to say about God's life is found in the gospel narratives of the Father-Son relation must be resisted. These passages are important and are to be taken with the utmost seriousness (as is every Scripture), but they are not the only biblical witness to God's life.

---

12. For an authoritative history of the debates of the fourth century, see Lewis Ayres, *Nicaea and its Legacy: An Approach to Fourth-Century Trinitarian Theology* (Oxford: Oxford University Press, 2004). As Ayres notes, Constantinople is better considered "the *beginning* of the end of non-Nicene theology" (ibid., 260; emphasis original). The years that followed saw repeated imperial condemnation of groups who refused to accept the settlement. In the Western church, it is possible to trace anti-Arian polemic well into the fifth century.

The particular form of Israel's monotheism is important: famously, the Shema, the confession of faith from Deuteronomy 6, admits varying translations: "Hear, O Israel: The LORD our God, the LORD is one" (NIV) or "Hear, O Israel: The LORD is our God, the LORD alone" (NRSV). We do not need to decide between these translations—the Hebrew is ambiguous—but the very fact of ambiguity is significant. Ancient Israel, at least according to its Scriptures, would seem to have been rather uninterested in counting deities. We certainly do find powerful assertions that the Lord alone is God, and that the "gods" of the nations are idols, but we also find, sometimes in the next chapter, language about other gods bowing down to the Lord, which at least implies their real existence.[13]

If we read the Shema in context, we have to notice that the commitment demanded in the text appears to be fragile and in need of constant reinforcement. The people of Israel are instructed to talk constantly about these commands, to write them on the frames of their doors, and to bind them to their foreheads, in order to never forget the sole lordship of the God of Abraham. If what is being demanded is a philosophical conception that the number of deities who exist is an integer between zero and two, then these practices of reminder and recollection surely seem bizarre: the point may be believed or doubted, but once believed it is not a fragile or easily lost confession.

For reasons like this, it seems appropriate to suggest that Israel's "monotheism" is more properly classed as "monolatry."[14] It does not matter much whether other deities exist; Israel's worship and loyalty are to be offered to the Lord alone. We know, as they knew, that such loyalty is far more fragile than a philosophical position; there is a constant temptation to idolatry, and that temptation is there whether the idol is a real and powerful being or something we have carved out of a piece of firewood. Israel is to worship, adore, serve, and seek help from one God alone, the Lord.

New Testament Worship

When we come to the New Testament, worship is again—unsurprisingly, given this background in the Hebrew Scriptures—the crucial concept

---

13. See, e.g., Pss 96:5 and 97:7.

14. See extensively and convincingly on this point Nathan MacDonald, *Deuteronomy and the Meaning of "Monotheism"* (Tübingen: Mohr Siebeck, 2001).

in identifying the divine. Hebrews 1 does give us a theological account of the Son's superiority to the angels, but the decisive point is that the Son is properly worshiped, whereas angels and apostles are regularly pictured as refusing worship. The monolatry demanded by Israel's God is maintained with just as much jealousy, but is also opened up to permit worship of the Son.

Somehow, right at the beginning of the church, the exclusive loyalty and worship demanded by God alone in the Old Testament was assumed to be upheld and not violated by worship offered to Jesus.[15] For all the diversity we can discover in early Christian communities — and it is great — on this point they are remarkably united. Moreover, this commitment to worshiping Jesus is present and fully formed from the beginning, or at least from as early as we can know. The church knew from its birth, it seems, that offering worship to Jesus is not incompatible with exclusive loyalty to God. The doctrine of the Trinity is a set of conceptual distinctions and definitions that offer a theological account of the divine life that made sense of these primitive practices of worship. At the risk of oversimplifying, the church always knew how to speak *to* God. Yet it took four centuries or so to work out how to speak *about* God in ways that were compatible with this.

Although we know relatively little of pre-Nicene liturgical practices, it seems clear that there was a consistent pressure in certain doctrinal directions whenever early Christian writers addressed God's life, and it seems plausible to suppose that this pressure came from habits formed by the practice of worship. So, however much they may have struggled to articulate a doctrine of God adequate to all the points, the pre-Nicene theologians know, variously, that one God alone is to be worshiped and glorified; that Jesus is properly named alongside the Father; that there is a fundamental ontological gap between God and the created order; and so on. While many early attempts at (what we would now call) trinitarian articulation were judged to have failed to uphold one or another of these positions, it seems inescapable that there was broad agreement at what was being striven for.

---

15. This point is made powerfully by Larry Hurtado, *Lord Jesus Christ: Devotion to Jesus in Early Christianity* (Grand Rapids: Eerdmans, 2003); see also Hurtado, *One God, One Lord: Early Christian Devotion and Ancient Jewish Monotheism* (London: T&T Clark, 1998); and Richard Bauckham, *Jesus and the God of Israel: God Crucified and Other Studies on the New Testament's Christology of Divine Identity* (Grand Rapids: Eerdmans; UK: Milton Keynes, Paternoster, 2008).

To give one example, when Justin Martyr speaks of the Logos as "another God" (*Dial.* 56), not only do others in the tradition react with some horror at the term, but he himself immediately tries to qualify it to remove the offense. His articulation, however, is inadequate to the set of constraints within which he is trying to speak, and he is aware of that problem. So, here is the first point from the biblical texts: the doctrine of the Trinity is an attempt to speak about the relationship of Father, Son, and Spirit that makes sense of the church's worship, and that is responsible to the radical call to monolatry in the Old Testament.

For a second biblical point, we might look at the nature of the crucial debates around the councils of Nicaea and Constantinople. The definition of "the doctrine of the Trinity" in the fourth century can be viewed as an acceleration and intensification of the ongoing attempt to find a way of speaking that was adequate to the felt constraints I have been describing. It was also, increasingly, an attempt to find ways of speaking that were adequate to the text of Scripture. Beginning with Arius's criticisms of Alexander's preaching, a more-or-less continuous debate over what language was most adequate to speak of God's life developed, to which Constantinople brought some sort of end. Any reader of the primary texts will spot quickly a point that can easily be missed by readers of currently popular secondary texts: these debates were almost entirely exegetical. The Fathers formed the doctrine of the Trinity by debating the interpretations of texts. One of the reasons it is so hard for us to understand some of the patristic writings (e.g., Augustine's *De Trinitate*) is that much of the first half of that book is a series of interventions in long-running exegetical debates with which we are not familiar.

The Nature of the Doctrine of the Trinity

The crucial terms used in the orthodox formulations of the doctrine are not biblical terms, and the nature of the fourth-century exegetical debates bears examination. To state this briefly, each side had its set of proof texts, which seemed to support its view. After that, the major developments in debate tended to come as someone stepped back from the texts a little and offered a piece of theological conceptuality that allowed some texts to be read differently.

This is largely what happened with Augustine in *De Trinitate*. To take an easy example, the pro-Nicene theologians quickly developed what we might call a "two-state hermeneutic." Their description tended to draw on the language of Philippians 2 to insist that some texts spoke of the Son in the form of God, while others spoke of him in the form of a servant. This allowed the most obviously apparent subordinationist texts to be read without compromising the equality of Father and Son. Jesus indeed said, "The Father is greater than I," but he said this "in the form of a servant."

A Conceptual Framework, Not an Ontology

What we call "the doctrine of the Trinity" is, I suggest, a formal set of conceptualities developed like this: a set of conceptualities that finally allowed (or at least was believed to allow) every text to be read adequately. As such, it is not a "biblical doctrine" in the sense of being the result of exegesis; rather, it is a set of things that need to be believed if we are to be able to do exegesis adequately as we hold to the truth of every text of Scripture. The doctrine of the Trinity is a conceptual framework that allows us to read every biblical text (concerning God's life) with due seriousness, but without discovering contradictions between them.

Understood like this, it is clear that the doctrine of the Trinity is not primarily an ontology, nor does it depend on a particular ontology (although it does require certain ontological propositions, largely connected with divine simplicity, to be somehow defensible). Indeed, while one key ontological proposition — the idea that there are no gradations of being — was of some importance in the development of the doctrine, classical trinitarianism consistently refused to answer the ontological question concerning the divine. In a standard slogan, we can know "that God is, but not what God is." As we will see, this ontological modesty and the related denial of gradations of being were actually central in the development of the fourth-century doctrine.

In the fourth-century arguments, one area of debate concerned the then-standard idea of a "ladder of being," with God at the top and (usually) unformed matter at the bottom. Things higher up the ladder are more real than things lower down the ladder; ontology is a continuous variable. This view of ontology allowed the idea that the Son was divine, but a little less divine than the Father, to be held, and so allowed a variety of intellectually sophisticated anti-Nicene theologies to be developed. In response, Basil of Caesarea, in particular, articulated a different ontological assumption: there are two ways of being, divine and created. This is particularly clear when he offered the challenge concerning the being of the Holy Spirit that "either He is a creature, and therefore a slave, or else He is above creation, and shares the Kingship."[16] There is, as Basil insists, no middle rank.

This is, however, a modest claim concerning ontology: there is no suggestion here that the divine essence is knowable,[17] and so there is no claim to have a developed account of divine ontology. All that is being claimed is that divine existence is somehow different from created existence, and that the only ways to exist are to be divine or to be created. Eunomius tried to define divine essence (as "unbegotten") and to argue from his definition; Basil's response was to refuse the possibility of defining what God is, suggesting instead that the divine essence is ineffable and so in principle resistant to human definition. Words like "uncreated," "omnipotent," or "eternal" (or indeed "love") are partial and inadequate gestures toward the reality of the divine life, each of which points toward something real, but in a partial and inexact way. This is materially the same doctrine as Thomas Aquinas developed in his famous account of analogy in the *Summa*.[18]

At the heart of this ontological modesty is the recognition that our thought about God is inevitably limited in precisely this way: God's essence is simple, incomposite; our thought and speech about it are complex, multiple, discursive, and so inexact. One implication of this is that we cannot reason analytically about divine reality, or at least not with any confidence. Our terms have no sure referent but are instead in some degree metaphorical. They cannot bear the weight of precision needed for analytic reasoning.

The one ontological claim I find in the fourth century that appears to be novel (it may in fact be borrowed from middle platonic philosophy, but I do not know of the source if it is) concerns the introduction of the word "relation." Given the importance this word has come to bear in recent debates over "social trinitarianism," its origin is worth analyz-

---

16. St. Basil the Great, *On The Holy Spirit* (trans. David Anderson; Crestwood, NY: St. Vladimir's Seminary Press, 1980), 81.

17. This was claimed by Eunomius and denied in terms by Basil and Gregory of Nyssa in their responses to him; see Holmes, *The Quest for the Trinity*, 101–10.

18. Thomas Aquinas, *ST* Ia.13.

ing. The crucial argument is found in the two lengthy quotations from Gregory of Nazianzus and Augustine given earlier in this essay,[19] where both writers introduce the idea of "relation" to evade an apparent logical difficulty. They are alike faced with the question of the status of the hypostatic distinctions: what is "Fatherhood" or "Sonship"?

The force of the question is as follows: in a broadly Aristotelian ontology, there are two general categories of qualities: substantial, relating to what a thing necessarily is; and accidental, relating to qualities it possesses, which nonetheless could be different or absent.[20] If "Father" and "Son" are substantial terms, then Father and Son are different in substance, and so they are not one God — we are back with the unacceptable "another God" language of the apologists. If they are accidental terms, then divine simplicity is compromised, since there are qualities attached to God's being that could be removed or changed without changing that being — and God could be other than Trinity.

Relational Distinctions

Gregory and Augustine both refuse the dichotomy by proposing a third term, "relation."[21] Fatherhood and Sonship are relational terms, and so are neither substantial nor accidental. The claim here runs as follows: Father and Son are two existences of the same simple essence, distinguished by the relationship of begetting, and by that relationship only; that relational distinction is their difference from each other — the Father is not the Son — but it does not compromise the simplicity of the divine essence. Similar arguments are then made about the Father and the Spirit and the Son and the Spirit.

This argument is the heart of Cappadocian trinitarianism, so let me say several things about it. First, it is at least not obvious that the argument fails. Given the hesitancy with which we need to frame all claims about God, the proposal that there is a way of speaking of a real distinction that does not cause division such that simplicity is compromised is not demonstrably illogical. Indeed, in his *Tractates* Boethius tries to do the necessary logical work to establish it, precisely in relation

---

19. See above, pp. 29–30.

20. A red chair is substantially a chair, but only accidentally red, for example.

21. I assume Augustine knew of the prior Cappadocian use, either directly or mediately, and was consciously borrowing from it, but the genealogy is not important here.

to the Trinity, and John Duns Scotus's famous "*distinctio formalis a parte rei*" (usually rendered "formal distinction" in English) is an attempt to invent a similar idea in a very different context.[22]

Second, we can sit a little more lightly to the point than Gregory or Augustine—or indeed Boethius or Thomas—could. The substance/accident distinction is no longer a part of our assumed metaphysics and so does not have the power over our thought that it did over theirs. The broader points are enshrined: that God is what God is necessarily, and could not be different; that God is uncompounded, uncreated, and that there is no division in the perfect divine life; that being triune is essential to God being God. All these points we need to hold on to with just as much energy as the Fathers and the Schoolmen did. But we have less need than they did to be committed to logical claims about substance and accident. If we consider that Michael Rea's theory of relative identity (for example) works better,[23] we can cheerfully adopt that instead.

Third, and moving to more polemical points, the only properties that are properly ascribed to the persons rather than the essence are the relational names: the Father and the Son are identical in all respects except the relationship of begetting. If we speak of God's will, or God's power, or God's mind, or God's love, we speak of the simple divine essence.[24] The proposal in modern social trinitarianism to speak of three centers of consciousness—three "I's" in the Trinity—is excluded by this shared patristic doctrine.

Fourth, the common contemporary claim that the divine relationships are the divine essence, or similar, is not excluded here, but it is not demanded either. In the formal patristic logic, it is a claim to which it is difficult to give any sense or content.

This is because, fifth, the concept "relation" here is primarily logical, not personal. We are, crudely, talking about metaphysics, not about sociology, human or divine. A "relation" is a mode of distinction in a simple essence that establishes the simple unity of two distinct but not

---

22. Boethius, *Opuscula Sacra* 1; text and facing translation available in Boethius, *The Theological Tractates* (trans. H. F. Stewart and E. K. Rand; London: Heinemann, 1962).

23. Michael C. Rea, "Relative Identity and the Doctrine of the Trinity," *Philosophia Christi* 5 (2003): 431–45.

24. The extent to which this point was simply axiomatic for the Fathers can be seen from the progress of the Monothelite controversy, during which no one thought to suggest that the problems faced could be solved (as they could) by postulating a distinction between the will of the Father and the will of the Son.

different subsistences of that essence. To parse this in terms of "love," "gift," "otherness," "alterity," or any of the other popular contemporary words is inappropriate; to draw an analogy from this logical distinction to ways of ordering human society or the church is impossible. It happens that English uses the same word for a logical relation and for a personal relationship, but that is not adequate reason to imagine the Trinity to be any sort of model for human community.

The History of Trinitarian Doctrine

I have argued elsewhere that the doctrine of the Trinity, once developed, was taught remarkably consistently by all mainstream theologians from the close of the fourth century to the dawn of the eighteenth. The one possible exception to this is the *filioque* debate (dealt with below). My preferred historical sources for the doctrine, then, are based on style and clarity of expression, not on difference of doctrine — I simply do not see any substantial difference in doctrine between, say, Gregory of Nazianzus, Augustine, Boethius, John of Damascus, Thomas Aquinas, and John Calvin. For me, Thomas Aquinas reigns supreme as the most careful and exact expositor of the classical doctrine. That said, no doubt others will prefer a more discursive exposition, and that is a matter of no importance, turning only on preferences for rhetorical styles.

At the heart of this shared doctrine is a commitment to divine simplicity. From the close of the fourth century to the dawn of the nineteenth century, there is a universal assumption that the doctrine of divine simplicity and the doctrine of the Trinity are closely related, almost mutually entailed. When anti-trinitarianism becomes popular in the seventeenth century, the anti-trinitarians universally, as far as I have been able to discover, deny divine simplicity and assume that in so doing they have dispensed with the doctrine of the Trinity.

Simplicity is a property of the divine essence. A standard piece of logic in the Greek philosophical tradition, accepted without demur by the Fathers, claims that anything composite must have been composed by an agent; therefore, the claim that God is incomposite is to insist that God was not made by any more basic agent. Then if God is incomposite, God is necessarily simple — the two words are not quite synonyms, but they are certainly mutually entailed. There is no complexity in the divine nature; God is not separable into this bit and that bit.

This matter is coupled with the classical concern to avoid putting God into any class. The logic is once again easily described: if God is one example of a class of things—say, one merciful thing among many other merciful things—then the class as a whole is larger than God, and so something is greater than God. Similarly, the Christian solution to the Euthyphro dilemma is the doctrine of simplicity. The dilemma, in Christian theological terms, runs as follows. Is God good because we define good to mean what God is (which evacuates the term of any transcendental moral content)? Or is God good because God conforms to some external standard of goodness (which asserts the existence of something greater than God)? By identifying God's goodness with God's essence—divine simplicity—we are able to claim that God's own life is the transcendental standard of goodness, avoiding both unacceptable consequences.

I am conscious that contemporary analytic theology and philosophy of religion have developed a variety of different accounts of divine simplicity. In line with the ontological modesty that I have suggested is central to the development of classical trinitarianism, I want to deliberately sit fairly lightly to this work while acknowledging both the intellectual brilliance often on display and the potential apologetic helpfulness of some of the discussion in illustrating how claimed inconsistency in the doctrine may be refuted. It is not only not necessary on the account I am developing to choose between the different available versions of simplicity; it may even be improper, inasmuch as it may be a violation of the fundamental claim of divine ineffability. Historically, analytic precision about God's triune being was a feature of Eunomius's writing and was refused as theologically improper by the Cappadocians.

That said, simplicity is not primarily a claim about Father, Son, and Spirit but a claim about God's life. In classical doctrinal terms, we are here concerned with the doctrine of the divine attributes/perfections. Human narration of the divine life is inevitably partial and multiple: we say God is loving, just, merciful, omnipotent, and so on; but such descriptions are ours; they do not relate to any divisions in God's life. God is in no way composite, and so the divine mercy is strictly identical with the divine justice. That we cannot narrate how this makes sense is a limitation of our language, not a problem for God's existence.

Because our language is limited here, when we say "God is good," we are not claiming a strict logical identity. The reason for this is obvious and worked out with more patience than it deserves by, say, Thomas Aquinas, although this has not stopped various modern writers making the basic error. If such claims were strict logical identity claims, then saying "God is good" and "God is eternal" leads easily to the conclusion that "goodness is eternity," which seems nonsense. So we have to assert that our language about the divine nature is sufficiently loose (Thomas used the term "analogical") that it does not require or even permit such identity relations.

As I have noted, this point was at the heart of the fourth-century doctrinal development. Eunomius had advanced an argument that ran something like this: to be God is necessarily to be unoriginated. The Father is unoriginate, but the Son has his origin in the Father. Therefore the Father is truly God, whereas the Son is not. Eunomius combined this with a distinctively platonic theory of language in which words corresponded to things in a one-to-one mapping. "Unoriginateness" was the proper name, the true definition, of the divine essence.

The Cappadocian achievement, properly read, is nothing to do with redefining ontology in personal terms. Rather, it is the development of a theory of language that allows this problem concerning the divine names to be solved. The negative point was easy: as Gregory of Nyssa pointed out, Eunomius said the divine nature was simple as well as unoriginated. On his own doctrine, either there are two divine natures, or his theory of language must be wrong.

What of the positive, however? Basil argued that our words only inexactly refer to the divine; our language about God is an example of an *epinoia*— a Greek word meaning something like "mental construction." Eunomius mocked this, suggesting that Basil was saying his theology was mere imagination, a point Eunomius was prepared gladly to concede! Basil's point was in fact subtle and curiously modern: there is, necessarily, a gap between what we can say about a thing and what it is *in se*. In the case of the ineffable divine nature, this gap is yawning; our language has only weak purchase. In particular, we can only speak of the divine nature by piling up multiple inexact terms: God is simple, ineffable, eternal, unoriginate, and so on. But if the divine nature is simple—something all agreed on—then it is not, in principle, divisible into these various different attributes. Eunomius's strict logical formulations are inadequate because they presume too much about the ability of our language to refer to God. He was right to assert that there is one single perfect divine life, but wrong to think he could name it exhaustively and reason on the basis of that naming.

What of the doctrine of the Trinity? The divine essence is unrepeatable and so, in crude terms, "one." But the divine essence is beyond our numeric classes as well as all other classes, and so to speak of the oneness of God is again to deploy an *epinoia*. There are, however, three divine subsistences. How do we make sense of this? Basil proposed that the relation of subsistence to essence is the relation of the particular to the common. The simple life of God exists three times over.

Two comments here: first, why three? The primary answer must be, because that is what we find in the New Testament. Father, Son, and Holy Spirit are each properly named to be God, and no other thing is. The history of the doctrine of the Trinity is full of attempts to make the triunity of God something more than this, a necessary logical proposition. So Augustine: God is love, and in a relationship of love there is a lover, a beloved, and the love they share—so the Trinity can be derived from the claim that God is love.[25]

Again, a common medieval Western line, originating in Anselm, noted that there is one divine person who originates but is not originated, the Father; one who both originates and is originated, the Son; and one who is originated but does not originate, the Holy Spirit. There is no other possible existence alongside these three, and so God must be triune.[26] I see no great harm in such speculations, but neither do I find them particularly convincing. I cannot help feeling that if Scripture had spoken to us of four divine persons, we would have found it just as easy to discover reasons why it must have been four.

Second, my definition above deliberately echoes a common scholastic slogan, the maxim that God's essence is God's existence (which is another, this time medieval scholastic, definition of the crucial idea of divine simplicity). The slogan is, properly understood, trinitarian. God's existence is the eternal divine life of Father, Son, and Spirit—and this is, precisely, the divine essence. If God's essence is the eternal triune life, then the existence of the three subsistences is necessary and eternal:

---

25. To be fair to Augustine, he did not propose this as a "proof" for God. That idea was first advanced, I believe, by Richard of St. Victor.

26. Again, I suspect that this was championed less as a proof of the triunity of God and more as a polemical argument for the *filioque*.

this is what it is to be God. And this—being Father, Son, and Holy Spirit—is all that it is to be God. There is no residue, no divine nature behind the three persons. The eternal life of the three persons just is the divine nature. The eternal, simple, ineffable life of God is, just, being Father, Son, and Spirit. The best definition we can give of God's eternal being is, in fact, "Trinity" (but Trinity rightly understood!).

Essence and Subsistences

When we hear a claim about God—a biblical, and so true, claim—how do we decide whether to relate it to the unrepeatable ineffable divine essence or to (one of) the three divine subsistences? There is a simple principle at play: because God's essence is his existence, all language that refers to God's life necessarily refers to Father, Son, and Spirit together as well as severally. As the so-called Athanasian Creed has it, "the Father eternal, the Son eternal, and the Holy Spirit eternal. And yet they are not three eternals but one eternal."[27] This is, as can be seen, a necessary consequence of the logic I have been developing thus far. God's life is simple; and God's life is to be Father, Son, and Holy Spirit.

The single, and very limited, exception to this is language that names the relations of origin of the three persons—necessarily so, as these relations are the only distinctions there are in the simple, ineffable divine essence. So the Father is not the Son, and Father is not the Spirit, and the Son is not the Spirit, and the Father begets and the Son is begotten, and the Spirit proceeds from the Father and the Son—this language is particular and hypostatic. All other language, without exception, qualification, or reserve, refers to the unrepeatable divine essence.

There are two relations of origin in the eternal life of God: the Son is begotten of the Father, and the Spirit proceeds from the Father (and the Son? As I will argue later, the point is not especially important). These relations are necessarily eternal, in that these relations are what

---

27. The "Athanasian Creed" (or *Quicunque Vult*) has nothing to do with Athanasius, being a bringing together of two sixth-century Western documents (on the origins, see J. N. D. Kelly, *Early Christian Creeds* [Harlow: Longman, 1972]). Although currently out of fashion, the document provides a capable summary of orthodox doctrine on the Trinity and Christology; the "damnatory clauses" are, however, unfortunate.

it is for God to be God.[28] These eternal relations are also the content of God's life, insofar as we can speak that phrase with any meaning at all. The Father is eternally begetting the Son; the Father and the Son together are eternally spirating the Spirit. That, according to Cappadocian doctrine, is what it is to be the God of the gospel.

So, when we use our partial and figurative language about the divine essence, what we are referring to is this account of the triune life: the Father is eternally begetting the Son; the Father and the Son together are eternally spirating the Spirit. This is the eternal reality we gesture toward when we say things like "God is love" or "God is omniscient" (or, indeed, "God"). Of course we cannot explain exactly how these two forms of language interact. The simple perfection of the eternal divine life is not accessible in any interesting sense to our understanding or language — God is ineffable. That said, both forms of language are required by the biblical text, as is the claim that the referent of both forms of language is the same unrepeatable divine life.

Alongside this, we need to be careful — and here, again, I suggest contemporary theology has often failed — to maintain the difference between trinitarian and christological language. This begins with, but is not exhausted by, the form of God/form of a servant distinction I noted above. A claim about the incarnate Son — particularly a claim about the relationship of the incarnate Son to the Father — may be a trinitarian proposition, but it may also be a christological assertion. To take a classic example, well worked through in patristic thought, when we hear Jesus pray, either in Gethsemane or in the high-priestly prayer of John 17, we necessarily hear the authentically human voice of the incarnate Son pleading with God, not an internal triune dialogue between the eternal Father and the eternal Son.

I say "necessarily" here for several reasons. First, prayer is an authentically human act. It is the priestly task of human beings to hold the creation in all its beauty and pain before the Father in intercession. Second, prayer (explicitly in the case of Gethsemane) assumes an at-least-potential difference in desire or will. The divine will, however, being a property of the divine essence, is one and undivided. So pleading

---

28. On this basis we should insist that the recent fashion for denying eternal generation in certain strands of North American evangelicalism is extraordinarily poor theology, and indeed formally heretical.

before the Father for the alignment of desires and volition ("not my will but yours be done") is properly understood to be an act of the human nature. Third, prayer inevitably implies subordination and so cannot be a feature in inter-triune relations. More will be said on this below with reference to the question of "eternal functional subordination."

More broadly, there is a contemporary tendency, which may perhaps be traced back to Hegel, to find in the Father-Son relationship the fundamental alterity that defines divine transcendence. As indicated above, my reading of the classical tradition shared by the Fathers, the Scholastics, and the Reformers is that transcendence, the ontological gap that divides creation from its Creator, is bridged in the hypostatic union, not in the triune relationships. Confusing trinitarian and christological claims is always a mistake.

The *Filioque*

I have several times postponed discussion of the *filioque* on the grounds that it was not of great importance. It is now time to explain this position. To borrow the careful logic of Thomas Aquinas, there are two processions in the Trinity—begetting and proceeding—which means that there are four relations: paternity and filiation (the two directions of begetting) and spiration and procession (the two directions of proceeding). The Cappadocian/Augustinian doctrine specified that paternity was the property of the Father, filiation the property of the Son, and procession the property of the Spirit. Spiration, however, was left undefined. In the Nicene Creed it is the property of the Father, until the addition of the *filioque* in the West. In patristic literature, the phrase "proceeds from the Father through the Son" was regularly used.

In the West, apparently as a result of a desire to combat lingering Arianism, the procession of the Spirit from the Father and the Son became standard doctrine, regularly confessed in the creed.[29] In the East, almost certainly in reaction, Photius of Constantinople proposed the formula "proceeds from the Father alone." For two centuries or so after Photius's time, however, the two sides existed in communion with each other, although aware of the debate. Clearly the difference in doctrine was not then perceived as church-dividing.

---

29. Kelly, *Early Christian Creeds*, is again useful on the history.

The point of division, historically, was not over the doctrine, but over the Pope's attempt to insist on its acceptance by all churches and to insert it into the creed. That division, that is, was not over the *filioque*, but over the Pope's claimed jurisdiction over the Greek churches and the Pope's claimed ability to decide on the correct text of the creed. The *filioque* was standard in the West by this point, and the historical fact that it was not in the original creed was probably not well known, particularly given the creed is not contained in the extant proceedings of the Council of Constantinople.

In Thomas's terms, the Eastern claim is that spiration, like paternity, is the proper personal property of the Father. The easy Western criticism against this would be that a divine person is a subsistent relation, and so this doctrine seems to imply two Fathers, or to violate trinitarian logic. It is not hard to respond to this criticism, however: spiration and paternity may be two words we find it necessary to use to describe the ineffable subsistence of the Father, just as goodness and eternity are two of the words we find it necessary to use to describe the ineffable essence of the Trinity. The Western claim, by contrast, is that the Father and the Son together (in developed doctrine, "acting as a single principle") spirate the Spirit. Again, there is an easy criticism: this apparently makes Father and Son together into a fourth divine person/subsistence. Again, the best response to the criticism relies on divine ineffability and a profound awareness of the limits of our language concerning the divine.

On this argument it will be seen that the two sides of the *filioque* debate are two appropriate ways of giving precision to a point left unclear in the patristic doctrine. Furthermore, history suggests that the difference was not found to be of significant moment—certainly not church dividing—for many years. On these grounds, I maintain that, as suggested above, the *filioque* is not a decisive, or even an important, point of dispute.

That said, is there a solution to this problem? Contemporary attempts to recover patristic language of "through the Son" as a mediating position tend to lack any precision as to what this means in terms of the standard sorts of logic described above. It might be possible, however, to parse such language in an adequate way as well as to capture some of the reciprocity ("the Father begets the Son through the Spirit") sometimes demanded.

If we reflect on identifying both the relationship of paternity and the relationship of spiration with the subsistence of the Father, we can see that it is, necessarily, only as the Father of the Son that the Father spirates the Spirit. This preserves both the primacy of the Father's role in spiration demanded by the East and the involvement of the Son demanded by the West. Equally, we can see that it is necessarily only as the spirator of the Spirit that the Father begets the Son, addressing the reciprocity point. If, as is common, we admit a logical order to the eternal processions, begetting then has priority over proceeding. Thus, there is a sense in which it is more appropriate to focus on the Son's role in the spirating of the Spirit, and so, if we wish to say more than "proceeds from the Father," to add "and/with the Son." This is all rather speculative, however.

The Use of the Doctrine

What use is the doctrine of the Trinity? In the sense in which the question is usually put, my answer is robust and required. The doctrine of the Trinity is necessarily and precisely useless, and that point must never be surrendered. The doctrine of the Trinity is an account—a careful and spare account, paying as much or more attention to what cannot adequately be said as to what might, hesitantly, be said—but an account nonetheless of the divine life. Now, to gaze on the beauty of God's eternal life is, according to medieval tradition, our highest end—the doctrine of the beatific vision. In a different strand of the tradition, the chief end of humanity is asserted to be "to glorify God and enjoy him forever." Whichever strand we follow, we are led to confess that knowledge of the divine life is necessarily our highest end.

Now, Jonathan Edwards does the analysis,[30] but the point is easy enough: it is of the essence of a highest end that it has no use. A highest end is of value in itself, not an instrumental step to some other end. If the doctrine of the Trinity is taken—as on the account I have given, it must be—to be an anticipation, partial and hesitant, but still an anticipation, of this eschatological vision, then it can have no instrumental use.

---

30. "Concerning the End for Which God Created the World," in *The Works of Jonathan Edwards*, vol. 8: *Ethical Writings* (ed. Paul Ramsey; New Haven, CT: Yale University Press, 1989), 403–526; esp. 417–64.

If the doctrine has any use, it is in clarifying errors about its own articulation. So the doctrine of the Trinity is useful in confronting Arianism and "social trinitarianism"; it is also useful in correcting narrower errors, such as the strange idea becoming prevalent in certain evangelical circles of "eternal functional subordination." To be brief and straightforward, the language of "function" is necessarily meaningless in narrating the eternal life of God. There is one will, one activity, one life, that is the divine Trinity. So language of "functional subordination" is either a logically confused attempt to reintroduce Arianism, or is simply meaningless.

Fundamentally, however, the doctrine serves no end. It offers us a glimpse — spare and austere, certainly — but a glimpse nonetheless, of the beauty and the glory of the eternal divine life. And for us to see the beauty of the divine life and to respond with awestruck worship is not something that serves another, higher, end, not something of use. Instead, it is, simply and bluntly, what we were made for.

PAUL D. MOLNAR

Stephen Holmes makes a number of extremely important points in his essay, demonstrating what classical trinitarian theologians were trying to say and why. He clearly opposes the so-called "social doctrine" because it does not intend to say the same things that Christians were trying to say when they developed the doctrine of the Trinity on the basis of the biblical witness. Holmes makes this point initially by showing how the meaning of terms can change, and he explains that it is important to understand how the early theologians used terms such as "person" with respect to their knowledge of the Trinity. For instance, Holmes points out that the anti-trinitarians of the early modern period rejected the doctrine of the Trinity as illogical based on a philosophical and not a theological understanding of the word "person."

While Holmes makes it clear that "there are no interesting analogies from creation to the Trinity" (p. 27), his main point is that when the word "person" was given a different meaning (an intellectual substance), it could no longer refer to a "mode of being" or a "subsistence" as it should have. Holmes gives another example of how words change their meaning: in the eighteenth century "the term 'enthusiast' carried the sense of 'fanatic'." But he notes that there was a plaque "celebrating a minister of a church who served for decades 'without ever once showing any trace of enthusiasm in his ministry'" (p. 28 n.8). This is an amusing example of how and why it is important to pay attention to the way words change their meaning over time.

There is much to admire in Holmes's essay. He explains nicely why he thinks "social trinitarians" improperly use analogies "univocally," thus, for instance, applying the word "person" to divine and human realities to mean the same thing. There is a twofold danger here: (1) loss of the Creator/creature distinction, which was pivotal to classical trinitarian theology; and (2) the assumption that we can use the doctrine of the Trinity as a model for social behavior. One issue that is nicely developed concerns the importance of seeing and maintaining the divine simplicity. This is a central insight of all classical trinitarian thought. From this, Holmes rightly concludes that "claims that the doctrine of the Trinity as it was established in the fourth century establishes a personalist or relational ontology are simply false, being based entirely on a reading of new meanings into old words" (p. 28).

Holmes rightly questions the "de Régnon thesis," according to which the Eastern church fathers began their reflections with the three persons while the West began with God's oneness; de Régnon, of course, preferred starting with what was claimed to be an Augustinian move from the one God toward the three persons. More recently, he noted, it is said that the Cappadocians came to see a "radically new ontology, the 'social Trinity,' in which persons in loving relationships were the basis of all things," so that Augustine is then supposed to have "missed this innovation completely" by focusing on an older "ontological scheme" that concentrated on "what a thing was," and that this was "as inadequate as it was pagan" (p. 29).

Holmes carefully and convincingly argues against this thinking that both East and West operated with fundamentally different ontologies (one relational and the other substantialist), showing that Gregory Nazianzus and Augustine really were saying similar things about the relations of the trinitarian persons in the one divine substance, so that it is improbable that there ever was a rupture between Eastern and Western "pro-Nicene" developments. This leads him to downplay the significance of the *filioque* as well and to conclude that we need "to resist the temptation to assume a fundamental difference between Eastern and Western approaches, unless such a difference can be demonstrated from careful reading of the texts" (p. 30).

Holmes is also right to insist that the original context for reflection on the Trinity was the church's worship so that the fourth century developments of the doctrine were seen to be attempts to make sense of "how what was said and assumed in worship could properly be said/ assumed" (p. 31). He likewise explains with clarity how and why proper trinitarian doctrine must begin with Scripture by showing why it is important to hold together Old and New Testament assertions about God's oneness. While I found his use of the term "monolatry" a bit jarring (pp. 32–34), I did see his point, namely, that Christians who worshiped the Lord Jesus Christ were not in any way compromising their belief in the unique oneness of God confessed in Israel.

Holmes helpfully explains that many of the debates surrounding Arius's thinking "were almost entirely exegetical" (p. 34). His example of what he called a "two-state hermeneutic" was helpful, where Augustine, for instance, distinguished between the Son in the "form of God" and in the "form of a servant" to avoid a subordinationist reading of Philippians 2. From this analysis Holmes concludes that "what we call 'the doctrine of the Trinity' is ... a formal set of conceptualities ... that finally allowed (or at least was believed to allow) every text to be read adequately" (p. 35). Hence the doctrine is not the result of exegesis but "a conceptual framework that allows us to read every biblical text (concerning God's life) with due seriousness, but without contradictions between them" (p. 35).

There is truth in this assertion. But it would be important here to counterbalance such a statement with a firm and often repeated assertion of T. F. Torrance that what God is toward us in his saving actions, he is eternally in himself, and what he is eternally in himself he is toward us.[31] In other words, while the point of the doctrine was to identify who God is as the eternal Father, Son, and Holy Spirit, this very knowledge led to an understanding of what this God did and was doing for us in the economy, that is, acting as our savior, helper, and friend in the incarnation and outpouring of the Holy Spirit.

I make this statement here because while Holmes is right in stressing God's incomprehensibility, even as we know him through his Word and Spirit, some of what he says verges on a way of thinking that could lead toward an agnosticism, which suggests that we never really know who God is in himself. Hence, he refers to Basil of Caesarea's argument against the idea that the Son was divine, "but a little less divine than the Father," by emphasizing that "there are two ways of being, divine and created" (p. 36). From this, Holmes concludes that "there is no suggestion here that the divine essence is knowable" (p. 36). But if the divine essence is unknowable, how can we affirm that what God is toward us he is eternally in himself? Of course God's essence is and remains a mystery to us in that we do not know God as God knows himself, but

31. Thomas F. Torrance, *The Christian Doctrine of God: One Being Three Persons* (Edinburgh: T&T Clark, 1996), 130; idem, *The Trinitarian Faith: The Evangelical Theology of the Ancient Catholic Church* (Edinburgh: T&T Clark, 1988), 130.

in our knowledge of God as Father, Son, and Spirit, it must be true that we know God in his internal relations, or we don't have true knowledge of God's essence and existence.

I agree with Holmes's reticence to think "analytically about divine reality" (pp. 36, 67) because God does indeed remain incomprehensible to us even in his revelation; this excludes attempts to "name" the perfect divine life of the Trinity "exhaustively and reason on the basis of that naming."[32] And I agree with his continued discussion of the divine simplicity and of his presentation of the distinctions within the unity of the divine essence as it relates to the begetting of the Son and the procession of the Spirit. I also agree with his assertions "that God is what God is necessarily, and could not be different" (p. 38) and that "the proposal in modern social trinitarianism to speak of three centers of consciousness—three 'I's' in the Trinity—is excluded by this shared patristic doctrine [of the divine simplicity]" (p. 38).

At this point I would like to request that Stephen Holmes clarify several issues I will note related to his essay. First, when he says that the concept of relation is "primarily logical, not personal," it seems that he is rejecting any attempt on our part to project our human understanding of persons onto the uniquely related divine persons, for he says, "We are, crudely, talking about metaphysics, not about sociology, human or divine" (p. 38). While I agree that we are not speaking about sociology in speaking about the trinitarian relations, I wonder if it is helpful to say that we are talking here about metaphysics. Metaphysics is not bound to the unique personal being in relation of the Father, Son, and Holy Spirit who are perichoretically one in relations of mutual knowledge and love (Matt 11:27; John 17:23–26). I agree with Holmes's depiction of this, but I think the eternal begetting of the Son and spirating of the Spirit is not some impersonal occurrence.

We are in fact talking about personal relations based on the scriptural witness to revelation. These are therefore uniquely divine personal relations into which we are drawn by the Holy Spirit of the risen Lord; they are not abstract metaphysical relations, but personal acts of God's free love in himself and toward and with us. I agree with Holmes that we should not "imagine the Trinity to be any sort of model for human community"

---

32. The discussion of Eunomius in this regard (p. 42) was interesting and helpful.

(p. 39), and I certainly agree with his firm rejection of those who would deny the eternal generation of the Son. But that hardly means that the relations of the Father, Son, and Spirit are not deeply personal relations.[33]

Second, I agree that contemporary theology "has often failed ... to maintain the difference between trinitarian and christological language" and that this means (contra Hegel) that "transcendence, the ontological gap that divides creation from its Creator, is bridged in the hypostatic union, not in the triune relationships" (pp. 44–45). Confusing trinitarian and christological claims lead to the historicization of the eternal Son, which then opens the door to subordinationism and modalism. This thinking might have carried over into his discussion of the *filioque*, so that instead of simply dismissing it as something unimportant, he might have consulted T. F. Torrance's work on that subject on the basis of which he claims that if theologians followed Athanasius and held that the Spirit proceeds from the being of the Father (as was held at Nicaea), instead of simply from the person of the Father, then the whole reason for conceptualizing the *filioque* itself never would have arisen in the first place.[34]

Third, Holmes claims that "the doctrine of the Trinity is necessarily and precisely useless" because it is no more and no less than an account of the divine life (p. 47). If he means that it is useless in the sense that we can take the doctrine and use it as a model for how we think we should behave, I agree. But he seems to mean that the sole end of the doctrine is contemplation of God or "the beatific vision." Hence, he concludes that "knowledge of the divine life is necessarily our highest end" (p. 47). Yet, knowledge of the divine life is not simply meant to leave us contemplating God, but necessarily involves our service of God in worship and action.

Here I agree with Colin Gunton, who once stated that everything looks different in light of the Trinity.[35] But by this he meant that we

---

33. T. F. Torrance attempted to present this with his notion of "onto-relations." See Paul D. Molnar, *Thomas F. Torrance: Theologian of the Trinity* (Burlington, VT: Ashgate, 2009), 44, 61, 63. Torrance also rightly insisted that God's being is intrinsically personal.

34. See, e.g., Paul D. Molnar, *Divine Freedom and the Doctrine of the Trinity: In Dialogue with Karl Barth and Contemporary Theology* (Edinburgh: T&T Clark, 2002), 325–30; *Torrance: Theologian of the Trinity*, 65–67 and *passim*.

35. See Colin E. Gunton, *The Promise of Trinitarian Theology* (Edinburgh: T&T Clark, 1991), 7.

are different because, as we come to know God in truth, we do so only because of God's reconciling grace and so we come to know the truth and thus to live as God intended us to live. Hence, it seems to me, we must agree with Karl Barth, who insisted that knowledge of God means service of God; there must be a connection between dogmatics and ethics. If that is so, then the doctrine is, as Torrance famously asserted, the ground and grammar of theology.[36] Theology could never simply mean contemplation of God since knowledge of the truth means knowledge of the truth that God is for us, in the incarnate and risen Lord, as the one who enables us to live here and now and in the world to come, as his good creatures precisely by being united to him through faith (which means knowledge of the truth which is self-involving). As such:

> Knowledge of God is obedience to God. Such knowledge becomes actual by man's becoming a new man through faith in Jesus Christ as his Lord. This newness ... consists in relying upon his Lord and not upon himself ... and in his serving his Lord and not himself ... in the freedom of the Holy Spirit who awakens him to this obedience, and not in any freedom of his own. Thus the true knowledge of God is already service of God and the true service of God can only consist in true knowledge of God.[37]

I agree with Holmes that the doctrine of the Trinity helps to clarify errors. But I think it also teaches us who God is in himself and for us in the life, death, and resurrection of Jesus himself. So the doctrine does have a function. Through it we are able to make some sense of who we are in relation to God, because God has and does enable that in his grace and mercy. The doctrine does serve an end as well. It teaches us who this God is one who has loved us and loves us even now in his Word and Spirit, and it shapes our understanding of all the important doctrines that concern God's activities toward us and for us in the economy. Most of all it tells us that it is only in serving God that we live in and from the truth of our new being in Christ and through his Spirit.

---

36. See Thomas F. Torrance, *The Ground and Grammar of Theology* Charlottesville: University Press of Virginia, 1980).

37. Karl Barth, *The Knowledge of God and The Service of God According to the Teaching of the Reformation* (trans. J. L. M. Hare and Ian Henderson; London: Hodder and Stoughton, 1949), 114–15.

THOMAS H. MCCALL

I appreciate a great deal of what Stephen R. Holmes has to say in his essay. His work is erudite and careful. There is a lot to learn from in this work (and from Holmes's broader corpus), and I find we are close in many significant ways.

He begins with historical observations that contain some salutary notes of caution. Especially important are his concerns about the possibility of changes in the meaning of important theological terms (particularly with respect to talk of "persons"), and he is exactly right to point out that unnoticed changes (however subtle) may be misleading and may produce problematic misunderstandings. It is, of course, also easy to exaggerate any differences or to confuse development with departure (again, particularly with respect to talk of "persons"). But I agree with Holmes that "great care" must be taken "if we are to make sense of ancient, or even early modern, documents" (p. 28).

Turning from methodological issues to more substantive matters, I am in full agreement with Holmes when he says that the Old Testament (and especially the affirmations of monotheism) is vitally important; indeed, I think that just as it is true that we wouldn't have the doctrine of the Trinity if we did not have the New Testament, so also we probably wouldn't have the doctrine if we did not have the Old Testament. I agree with him that the "worship of the church had been fairly consistently trinitarian, or 'proto-trinitarian,' from the earliest days of Christianity" (p. 31). Holmes helpfully observes that many of the debates in the early church were exegetical in nature, and that the "two-state hermeneutic" is crucial for understanding these debates (p. 35). In addition, I judge Holmes to be right in his insistence that the doctrine of divine simplicity was important in patristic (as well as medieval) theology. In all these ways—and many more—Holmes does great work in narrating important aspects of the history of the doctrinal development as well as raising some important criticisms and cautions.

I am not entirely sure why Holmes cordons off "analytic reasoning" as he does (p. 36). Indeed, I'm not sure what Holmes means by this. He insists that "we cannot reason analytically about divine reality," but he does not specify just what this claim means. In standard usage, "analytic theology" refers generally to concern for clarity and rigor of argument and more specifically to careful attention to logical and metaphysical matters.[38] It is hard to think that this is really what Holmes can mean when he says that it cannot and should not be done, for Holmes appears to have no actual scruples about *this* kind of analytic reasoning. After all, he insists that what "God is God is *necessarily*, and could not be different," that "being triune is *essential* to God being God," that the "Father and the Son are *identical* in all respects except the relationship of begetting," that "simplicity is a *property* of the divine *essence*," and so on (italics added). Meanwhile, he criticizes contemporary efforts to deal with the problem of the *filioque* on the grounds that such efforts "tend to lack any precision as to what this means" in terms of logic (pp. 38–39, 46). But these issues—necessity and contingency, identity, etc.—are standard topics in analytic theology, and concern for logical precision and coherence is a hallmark of it. So it is hard to think that Holmes intends this when he lays a moratorium on "analytic reasoning" in trinitarian theology. Exactly what he does mean, however, is not as obvious as it might be.

The doctrine of divine simplicity plays a leading role in Holmes's discussion. In such a historically grounded discussion, this is understandable (and I agree with Holmes that the doctrine of divine simplicity is prevalent throughout the "East" as well as the "West"). Holmes is right to see that the doctrine of simplicity is closely related to the doctrine of the Trinity, but it isn't clear (from what he says here) that he recognizes either the diversity within the tradition on this point or the significant challenges to the doctrine of simplicity. He does see that "contemporary analytic theology and philosophy of religion" distinguishes between different versions of simplicity doctrine (p. 40). But the diversity is not limited to contemporary work; in point of fact, this variety can be found in the tradition as well. Holmes characterizes the

---

38. See Michael C. Rea and Oliver D. Crisp, eds., *Analytic Theology: New Essays in the Philosophy of Theology* (Oxford: Oxford University Press, 2009).

doctrine so that "the divine mercy is strictly identical with the divine justice" (p. 40), but this only accounts for *parts* of the Christian tradition. Notably, Gregory of Nyssa (arguably) takes a different view. As Andrew Radde-Gallwitz says, for Gregory "we are far from holding that divine simplicity entails that God only has a single property or has no properties—so far, in fact that, in his hands, the doctrine of simplicity actually comes to entail that God has *multiple* properties."[39]

More importantly, Holmes does not wrestle with the challenges to the doctrine of simplicity. Here is one such challenge: on some versions of simplicity doctrine, the Father, the Son, and the Holy Spirit are each said to be identical to the divine essence but not—on pain of modalism—identical to one another. If we take identity in the classical sense (as an equivalence relation that satisfies "Leibniz's Law" of the Indiscernibility of Identicals, as reflexive, symmetrical, and transitive), then we have the following:

(1) The Father is not identical to the Son (on orthodox Trinity doctrine);
(2) The Father is identical to the divine essence (on the doctrine of simplicity in view); and
(3.) The Son is identical to the divine essence (on this account of simplicity).

Given the fact that identity is symmetrical and transitive,

(4) the Father is identical to the Son.

is strictly entailed by the conjunction of (2) and (3). But (4) is the direct denial of (1), and as such it is in direct contradiction to orthodox trinitarianism.[40] This entailment is heretical, of course, but (on standard accounts of identity) it follows inexorably from the identity of both the Father and the Son with the divine essence. To be clear, I'm not charging Holmes with this problem, and I don't disagree with Holmes's conviction that the doctrine of simplicity can be consistent with the doctrine of the Trinity. Indeed, I am optimistic that *some versions* (although probably not *this* version) of the doctrine may cohere well with trinitarian

---

39. Andrew Radde-Gallwitz, *Basil of Caesarea, Gregory of Nyssa, and the Transformation of Divine Simplicity* (Oxford: Oxford University Press, 2009), 212.

40. See William Hasker, *Metaphysics and the Tri-Personal God* (Oxford Studies in Analytic Theology; ed. Michael C. Rea and Oliver D. Crisp; Oxford: Oxford University Press, 2013), 59–61.

theology. My point is only that any defender of the doctrine should face the challenges to it.

Holmes sharply rejects any doctrine according to which there are "I-Thou" relationships within the triune life on the grounds that this is "excluded by this shared patristic doctrine" of divine simplicity (p. 38). Unfortunately, he does not offer an argument for this conclusion, and we are left to wonder why this would be so (again, it may be true on some versions of the doctrine of simplicity but not others). With respect to the patristic theologians themselves, while Holmes is correct to caution us against reading distinctly modern notions of "person" into the patristic doctrine, he does not demonstrate that the patristic theologians were opposed to just any understanding of an "I-Thou" relation between the eternal Father and the eternal Son. As I have argued in my essay in this volume, Michel R. Barnes shows that Gregory of Nyssa thought of "the Spirit *like the Son* [as] a psychological entity with a distinct existence."[41]

Similarly, Khaled Anatolios argues that although it "has become fashionable to deny that early Christian theology conceived of divine 'personhood' in terms anywhere resembling our contemporary understanding of this notion," nonetheless, we should "not overlook the ways in which a theology like Athanasius's, in its careful adherence to the narrative biblical patterns of identifying Father, Son, and Spirit, finds itself depicting the relation between Father and Son in terms that intersect with some aspects of our modern notion of personhood."[42] He demonstrates that Athanasius "affirms conscious intentionality" of the divine persons "because he is beholden to the patterns of biblical narrative and symbol," and that he depicts the "oneness of trinitarian being as a oneness of mutual love and reciprocal willing."[43] Similarly, Gilles Emery demonstrates that Thomas Aquinas holds that the Father loves the Son and indeed that "the Father and Son know each other in a mutual comprehension."[44]

Holmes denies that we should think of the relation between the Father and Son "in terms of 'love.'" (p. 39). Going behind the historical

---

41. Michel R. Barnes, "Divine Unity and the Divided Self: Gregory of Nyssa's Trinitarian Theology in its Psychological Context," *MT* 18 (2002): 476. Cf. Khaled Anatolios, *Retrieving Nicaea: The Development and Meaning of Trinitarian Doctrine* (Grand Rapids: Baker, 2011), 220.

42. Anatolios, *Retrieving Nicaea*, 153.

43. Ibid.

44. Gilles Emery, *The Trinitarian Theology of St Thomas Aquinas* (Oxford: Oxford University Press, 2007), 155.

issues to the biblical basis, it is difficult to see how Holmes might be right about this. Doesn't the high priestly prayer of Jesus (John 17) show exactly this? Well, maybe not. Holmes remonstrates that this prayer is "necessarily . . . the authentically human voice of the incarnate Son pleading with God, not an internal triune dialogue between the eternal Father and the eternal Son" (p. 44). He says "necessarily" because prayer is "an authentically human act" (as well as entailing subordination). Of course I do not deny that prayer is an authentic human act, but I do reject the notion that it cannot be a divine action. After all, does not the Holy Spirit also "intercede" for us (Rom 8:26)? Does this imply that the Spirit is human (or subordinate)? I fail to see how this follows. Moreover, I struggle to see how Holmes's view really fits with the prayer of Jesus at all, for the Son refers to his relationship to the Father "before the world began" (John 17:5, 23–24). This is, after all, the incarnate Christ speaking to the Father of his relation as the *preincarnate* Son.

In conclusion, I find that Holmes's own view is close to my own proposal in some important ways. We are in substantial agreement on the biblical roots of the doctrine; we agree about the importance of the Hebrew Bible/Old Testament, about the centrality of worship in the "proto-trinitarianism" of earliest Christianity, and much more. We agree that contemporary trinitarian theology should come through the broad Christian tradition. More specifically, we agree that the doctrine of simplicity cannot be ignored in work in trinitarian theology, and we agree further that the venerable doctrine might be a resource rather than an impediment to the future of trinitarian theology. I share his concern about lack of historical sensitivity in reading the tradition, and I applaud his cautions.

Actually, I think that even *more* historical sensitivity would help Holmes's account, for at a few points he appears to lump various traditional views together and pit them all against everything deemed "modern." In reality, I think that the situation is rather more complicated, and that issues of continuity-discontinuity as well as consistency-inconsistency need a bit more nuance. I think that a careful reading of the tradition demonstrates both a substantial, stable theological core *and* some truly remarkable diversity (regarding both simplicity and Trinity). What I see emerging from the biblical basis and historical formulations differs from Holmes's theology in some ways. To summarize, I am convinced that we should affirm that the divine persons are really and relationally distinct (as depicted in Scripture and the creedal tradition as distinct lovers and agents), that they are fully and thus equally divine, and that there is exactly one God. While I'm sure that Holmes would agree with much of this, we do seem to differ about what it means to affirm the distinction of the persons.

Without a definition of "person" from Holmes (and I don't find one), it is hard to know exactly how far apart we remain (it is also, by the way, hard to know how one might rule out Sabellianism or Nestorianism without such a definition). Since the biggest area of difference between us seems to be the issue of divine personhood, I will conclude with a query: *Is there mutual love between the divine persons within the immanent Trinity?* I believe that the answer should be unflinchingly affirmative: Scripture teaches (e.g., John 17:23–24), and tradition (e.g., Thomas Aquinas) affirms, that there is love between the persons within the triune life.[45] Can Holmes's view affirm this much? If so — if the Father loves the Son — then why deny that the divine persons are distinct enough that one can say "I love the Son?" Or if not, just how deeply does his theology cohere with Scripture and the Christian tradition (the label "classical" notwithstanding)? Despite these remaining questions, I find much to appreciate and applaud in his well-informed and well-written essay.

---

45. Aquinas, *ST* 1a.37.2.

PAUL S. FIDDES

My first note of response must be appreciation for what Stephen Holmes rightly calls his "serious historical work" (p. 25), which sets the scene for all our discussions. I am also grateful for the two weighty caveats in his first section. I agree with his first opening point that we must be sensitive to change of meaning of theological terms, and that the words "person," "*hypostasis*," and "subsistence" have been wrongly understood in recent social trinitarianism as implying an individual center of consciousness, just as they were wrongly understood by John Biddle in the seventeenth century as a "complete intellectual substance." I also agree with his second opening point, that we must resist the temptation to assume a fundamental difference between Eastern and Western approaches, unless such a difference can be demonstrated from careful reading of the texts, which he shows in fact to be ruled out. In particular, we should reject the rather crude opposition often made between the Cappadocian Fathers and Augustine, and here he offers a telling comparative example from Gregory of Nazianzus and Augustine on the meaning of the word "person."

However, in this example it seems to me that Holmes misses what I would call an "experimental" aspect of redefining "*hypostasis*" as relationship, in the face of the Arian challenge. Where Gregory declares that "'Father' designates neither the substance nor the activity, but the relationship, the manner of being, which holds good *between* the Father and the Son" (p. 30, my italics), Augustine similarly proposes that "the names, 'Father' and 'Son,' do not refer to the substance but to the relation (*non secundum substantiam dicuntur, sed secundum relativum*)." Here, it seems, both Gregory and Augustine are not just envisaging a subsistence *distinguished* from others by their relationship, but in some (perhaps playful) way regard a divine "person" *as* a relationship. Holmes blunts the force of this identification by using the English version of

Augustine's "On the Trinity" by Edmund Hill, which translates *secundum relativum* more vaguely as "relationship-wise."

Later, in dealing with the *filioque*, Holmes refers to the Western concept that "a divine person is a subsistent relation" (p. 46), but in fact Holmes himself is arguing not for a subsistent relation at all but for a subsistence that is merely *distinguished* by relation. In my own chapter I make the case for understanding "person" or "*hypostasis*" as nothing more or less than a relationship, thus preventing us from thinking of the Trinity as any kind of object, and compelling us to speak of God only in the context of actually *participating* in God in such relational activities as praying, suffering, living in community, and assisting the dying.

These very texts from Gregory and Augustine that Holmes so aptly cites give us reason to doubt his sweeping condemnation that "claims that the doctrine of the Trinity as it was established in the fourth century establishes a personalist or relational ontology are simply false, being based entirely on a reading of new meanings into old words" (p. 28). Later on he asserts similarly, "The Cappadocian achievement, properly read, is nothing to do with redefining ontology in personal terms" (p. 41). There are surely different kinds of "relational ontology," or a thinking about "being" in terms of relationships. I altogether agree with his criticism that we cannot create this from the notion of three divine centers of consciousness in relation together. Yet being sensitive to change of meaning in terms should not stand against doctrinal development, against a deliberate development of meaning for our day in an intended continuity with tradition. There might, then, be another kind of relational ontology, developing the experimental ventures by Gregory and Augustine, and remembering that language about God cannot be literal or univocal but is to be tested for appropriateness.

Here Holmes is right to resist the assumption that "the word 'person' meant the same thing when applied to human and divine realities," so that "the doctrine of analogy was denied in favor of a claim that words are univocal" (p. 28). Rather, he is properly concerned throughout for "appropriate" language about God. But his principle cannot in itself rule out the making of appropriate analogies of relationship, as long as they are not based on a strict univocality of persons. Again, I raise the possibility that we might consider a divine person *as* a relationship (unlike a human person), which exactly does not treat human and divine persons as the same kind of reality. It follows that I will be opposed to his conclusion that "I take it that there are no interesting analogies from creation to the Trinity, particularly not in the sphere of human sociality" (p. 27). He himself affirms the appropriateness of talk about the "generation" of the Son from the Father, but this itself of course is an analogy from creation to Trinity, in the sphere of relationality and sociality.

Holmes goes on to discuss in a highly illuminating way the relation between the doctrine of the Trinity and Scripture. He makes two key points. First, the doctrine of the Trinity is an attempt to speak about the relationship of Father, Son, and Spirit that makes sense of the church's worship, and especially the worship we find portrayed in the Bible. Second, "what we call 'the doctrine of the Trinity' is . . . a set of conceptualities that finally allowed (or at least was believed to allow) every text to be read adequately" (p. 35). His conclusion is: "Understood like this, it is clear that the doctrine of the Trinity is not primarily an ontology, nor does it depend on a particular ontology" (p. 35). His word "primarily" and denial of dependency are surely right, but he seems to be making the point with the aim of ruling out *any* "relational ontology," while at the same time he immediately qualifies it by saying that the doctrine of the Trinity "does require certain ontological propositions, largely connected with divine simplicity." An ontology of simplicity is thus allowed where an ontology of relations is not, and also approved is another ontological requirement, that of an "ontological gap" between God and the world. While he regards these requirements as "ontologically modest," we might well question how modest they actually are.

With regard to simplicity, there is surely no controversy in holding to divine simplicity in the sense that "God's essence is . . . incomposite," or that "God is not separable into this bit and that bit" (pp. 36, 39). However, it is another matter to conclude that "there is no complexity in the divine nature." Holmes also goes on to reflect the view of Aquinas that simplicity means that God's being cannot be affected by anything external to God. The identity of divine essence with existence is taken to mean that "God is what God is necessarily, and could not be different." We should ask: different in all respects? To say that God is uncreated is to affirm that "God *is*, necessarily," which is not exactly the same as the affirmation, "*All that* God is, God is necessarily." Aseity is not the same as self-sufficiency, since a God who exists only from God's own self (*a se*) can be free to choose not to be self-sufficient and to be affected by God's own creation. Ideas are being smuggled into divine simplicity here.

The significance of this criticism will emerge in a moment, with regard to my concern for our participation in God. The same considerations apply to Holmes's assertion (based on Basil) that "divine existence is somehow different from created existence, and that the only ways to exist are to be divine or to be created" (p. 36). We should agree with Holmes (and Basil) that the great difference is between the uncreated and the created. But this does not inevitably mean a gap between two separate ontological spheres that has to be bridged by a mediator, excluding analogies of relationship between created beings and the triune life of the Creator.

We now come to the central point that Holmes bases on his particular notions of simplicity and the ontological gap. With regard to the Trinity, he asserts:

> ... the concept "relation" here is primarily logical, not personal. We are, crudely, talking about metaphysics, not about sociology, human or divine. A "relation" is a mode of distinction in a simple essence that establishes the simple unity of two distinct but not different subsistences of that essence. To parse this in terms of "love," "gift," "otherness," "alterity," or any of the other popular contemporary words is inappropriate. (pp. 38–39)

Clearly Holmes wants to oppose the (social trinitarian) imagining of "the Trinity to be any sort of model for human community," and with this concern I am thoroughly sympathetic. However, there could be another reason for wanting to affirm the appropriateness of personal language for the "relations" in God, namely, to encourage a human *participation* in the life of Trinity here and now.

In fact, Holmes's exclusion of the personal dimension from divine relations in favor of a purely "logical" meaning seems decidedly odd. Later he criticizes Augustine for the trinitarian analogy of "lover," "loved," and "the love they share," but refrains from criticizing the appropriateness of language of love relations between persons, which is regularly used by the church fathers. Moreover, as I previously noted, he does allow the analogy of "generation," which is a personal analogy drawn from created reality. His argument is that since the divine life is simple, descriptive language such as "goodness," "eternity," and "love" can only be attributed to the one divine essence, not to the distinct persons:

> The single, and very limited, exception to this is language that names the relations of origin of the three persons.... So the Father is not the Son, and Father is not the Spirit, and the Son is not the Spirit, and the Father begets and the Son is begotten, and the Spirit proceeds from the Father and the Son — this language is particular and hypostatic. All other language, without exception, qualification, or reserve, refers to the unrepeatable divine essence. (p. 43)

The assertion that only relations of origin are distinctions in the divine being rules out understanding the indivisible divine being *as* the relations of Father, Son, and Spirit. It also seems to run into the problem of the scriptural accounts of the personal quality of the relations between Jesus and the one he calls "Father." Holmes is obliged to confine these relations to the human nature of Christ, so that, for example, "in the high-priestly prayer of John 17, we necessarily hear the authentically human voice of the incarnate Son pleading with God, not an internal triune dialogue between the eternal Father and the eternal Son" (p. 44). This isolation of a "human voice" makes it difficult to establish "one person" and "one son" in Christ, presumably also to be applied to such other important New Testament themes as the obedience of Christ to his Father, the glorifying of the Father by the Son, and the giving of honor to the Son by the Father (e.g., in baptism and resurrection). Holmes's approach seems to diminish the possibility of receiving the incarnation as a revelation of the very nature of God.

My own argument, by contrast, is that our participation in God allows us to use other analogies than those of origin. Indeed Scripture and our experience *require* us to do so, showing us a divine simplicity that is also a complexity of relations, in which the triune God freely submits to enhancement of divine fellowship and joy by creation. Holmes strikingly affirms that "the doctrine of the Trinity is necessarily and precisely useless," since "the doctrine serves no end. It offers us a glimpse — spare and austere, certainly — but a glimpse nonetheless, of the beauty and the glory of the eternal divine life" (pp. 47–48). But this glimpse does in fact serve an end, not ours, but God's end or purpose: as a means of worship it enables us to find ourselves participating in God. I agree with Steve Holmes that we should not seek to *use* the Trinity as a mere model for human community—but the doctrine does enable us to find ourselves in God in everyday life and experiences.

REJOINDER COMMENTS AND CLARIFICATION

STEPHEN R. HOLMES

I am grateful to my three colleagues for this fascinating and helpful conversation, and particularly for the careful and serious responses each has made to my initial contribution. Many of the points raised are matters I addressed in my own responses to their contributions, and I see no need to address them here; in this category I include, for instance, Paul Molnar's comment about the procession of the Spirit from the Father's essence, Paul Fiddes's reflections on participation, and Tom McCall's argument concerning simplicity. That said, there are two issues I would like to take further, both relating to relatively passing phrases in my initial essay that my colleagues have helped me see might be occasions for confusion; certainly they demand further clarification.

The first concerns my comment that "we cannot reason analytically about divine reality" (p. 36). Tom McCall connects this sentence to the new school of "analytic theology," which I acknowledge in retrospect is an obvious connection, but not one I intended. I take it that the virtues that analytic theologians would particularly celebrate are those of precision in statement and clarity in argument; and I take it as a given that these are goals for which every theologian should strive. To the extent that the methodologies of analytic theology can help us achieve them, they are always appropriate to use, including when we reflect on the doctrine of the Trinity.

That said, in more general English usage "analysis" refers to a mode of reflection in which we examine an object by breaking it down into constituent parts; when we speak of "analyzing a poem" or of "chemical analysis," this is the root meaning. My claim is simply that God — I think uniquely among possible subjects of human reflection — is not available to this process of reflection. I could defend this in a number of ways but, most straightforwardly, it is relatively obvious that a commitment to divine simplicity precludes analysis in this sense of the divine being.

Second, all of my colleagues picked up another comment I made, that "the concept 'relation' here is primarily logical, not personal. We are, crudely, talking about metaphysics, not about sociology" (p. 38). In defending this comment, I stress the words "here" and "crudely." On the first ("here"), this was a claim only about the use of the word "relation" (or rather about the use of the Latin and Greek words translated "relation") in Gregory of Nazianzus and in Augustine; on the second ("crudely"), the contrast between "metaphysics" and "sociology" is, I acknowledge, a rhetorical device intended to make clear my distance from those recent approaches to the doctrine of the Trinity that go by the name "social trinitarianism."

What of the broader point? I want to continue to insist that "relation" is, in English as in Latin and Greek, not a term that can apply only to persons (contrast "love"). We can imagine a relation "being to the left of," which might apply to two persons, but might equally apply to two houses or two snooker balls. That said, in English the word "relation," without qualification, is most usually understood as personal; when coupled with the (as I have argued, unhelpful) use of the word "person" to translate *hypostasis*, it becomes difficult not to read into the fourth-century texts a "personalist" ontology that was never in fact there; there was no necessary specification of "relation" as "personal relationship." Paul Fiddes's account of participation and Tom McCall's exegesis of the Gospels each give them reasons for so specifying, reasons whose validity we may discuss, and which I have addressed at some length in my responses to their essays. My point is that if we are attentive to fourth-century language, it does not, despite appearances, provide any *a priori* reason to assume that their side of the debate is more plausible than mine.

With those two clarifications, I end; the conversation has, it seems to me, helpfully illuminated methodological convergences and differences, and illustrated at least something of what is at stake in contemporary debate about the Trinity. I am grateful for it.

PAUL D. MOLNAR

What are some of the hallmarks of classical trinitarianism? Once identified, what insights of classical trinitarianism might help contemporary theologians think through our human relations with God and with each other in a way that will not only respect divine and human freedom, but will see that human freedom is indeed based on and insured by God's freedom for us, which itself is grounded in the eternal freedom of the Father, Son, and Holy Spirit?

Classical Trinitarian Theology and Epistemology

Thomas F. Torrance provides some helpful clues about what constitutes the hallmarks of classical trinitarianism.[1] His thinking, of course, is shaped by the councils of Nicaea (AD 325) and Constantinople (AD 381), which teach that in the Father, Son, and Holy Spirit there is *"one Godhead, Power and Being of the Father, of the Son, and of the Holy Spirit, equal in Honour, Majesty and eternal Sovereignty in three most perfect Subsistences [ἐν τρισὶ τελειοτάσεσιν ὑποστάσεσιν], that is, in three perfect Persons [ἤγουν τρισὶ τελείοις προσώποις])."*[2] Citing Ephesians 2:18 Torrance notes that it is *"through the Son [that] we have access to the Father in one Spirit"* and concludes from this that it is the teaching of the gospel

---

1. See Thomas F. Torrance, *Trinitarian Perspectives: Toward Doctrinal Agreement* (Edinburgh: T&T Clark, 1994), ch. 7, "Agreed Statement on the Holy Trinity," 115–22, and chs. 8–9, which discuss the significant features of the common agreement between Reformed and Orthodox theologians.

2. Ibid., 115 referring to *Ep. Syn. Constantinopolitanae* (AD 382).

that God indeed has revealed himself "in the Father, the Son and the Holy Spirit."[3]

It is important to realize that the New Testament witness to God's revelation refers us to the Father, the Son, and the Holy Spirit, which are "unique and proper names denoting three distinct Persons or real Hypostases which are neither exchangeable nor interchangeable while nevertheless of one and the same divine Being."[4] This means, of course, that it is impossible to believe in the unity of God "apart from the Trinity" as it is impossible to believe in the divine Trinity without the unity. It is imperative, however, in Torrance's understanding that we acknowledge the words of Matthew 28:19 as the words of the risen Lord himself. Otherwise the basis of baptism in the name of the Father, Son, and Holy Spirit could be construed as the ecclesial community and not a command derived from the risen Lord.[5]

In other words, without this acknowledgment, there would be a confusion of the church with its Lord, which could lead to the idea that there is more than one source of revelation — that is, in addition to Jesus Christ and the Holy Spirit, one might also appeal to the experience of the present and the witness of the past.[6] Any such thinking could open the door to

---

3. Ibid.

4. Ibid., 116.

5. See Thomas F. Torrance, *Space, Time and Resurrection* (Edinburgh: T&T Clark, 1998), 7; *Reality and Evangelical Theology* (Philadelphia: Westminster, 1982), 80; and *Conflict and Agreement in the Church* (Eugene, OR: Wipf & Stock, 1996), 2:115–16.

6. John Macquarrie argues for this problematic position in his book, *Jesus Christ in Modern Thought* (Philadelphia: Trinity Press International, 1990), 21, when he claims that "there is no sharp dividing line between Jesus and the community," and that the Christ event must refer to "something larger than the career of Jesus of Nazareth. In that larger reality there were joined inseparably the career of Jesus and its impact on the believing community" (ibid., 20). This thinking highlights his belief that there are "two sources for the knowledge of Jesus Christ — the testimony of the past and the experience of the present" (ibid., 6). This tendency to confuse Christ and the church under the category of the "Christ-event" leads Macquarrie to advance an adoptionist Christology in the form of an explicit degree Christology, which causes him to espouse belief in more than one savior figure and to wonder why Christians have to believe that the incarnation happened only once in Jesus of Nazareth. My point here is simply this: when one's thinking about the relationship between Christ and the church is not shaped by the truth affirmed in the classical doctrine of the Trinity, then a different avenue is opened for knowledge of God that bypasses the need to see that all true knowledge of God takes place from the Father, through the Son, and in the Spirit and therefore it cannot be based in the experience of the present, even though of course there can be no knowledge in the present without experience. Yet, when it is the triune God who is known, it is always the case that one also knows that such knowledge comes to us as a revelation of the Trinity, and thus it cannot be based on our experiences but only on that act of God that meets us in our experiences of faith. Hence the source of our knowledge of God is and always remains God, who meets us in his incarnate Son and frees us to know him through his Spirit.

what has been referred to as social or relational doctrines of the Trinity. An example of such a fashionable view is sometimes presented as follows: "the so-called social analogy ... takes the human experience of life-in-relationship as the best clue to an understanding of the triune life of God."[7]

Once one assumes that "life-in-relationship" is indeed "the best clue" for understanding God's triune life, one of the prime ingredients of classical trinitarianism is disrupted. One might then conclude, with Ted Peters, that "relationality—a social psychological concept" could unlock "newer understandings of the divine life" such that we might then link Trinity and eschatology to understand God's life

> as one in which the divine undergoes self-separation [which] requires us to think about a reunion, an eschatological reunion [that] involves more than just Jesus alone.... It involves the whole of creation. The trinitarian life is itself the history of salvation ... the fullness of God as Trinity is a reality yet to be achieved in the eschatological consummation.[8]

One might even suggest that "God's eternity is gained through the victory of resurrection and transformation,"[9] so that "the relationality God experiences through Christ's saving relationship to the world is constitutive of trinitarian relations proper,"[10] or even that the resurrection itself is God's *ousia* so that one no longer needs to acknowledge the *Logos Asarkos* in order to assert Jesus' unmitigated divinity.[11] One might conclude that

---

7. Daniel L. Migliore, *Faith Seeking Understanding: An Introduction to Christian Theology* (2nd ed.; Grand Rapids: Eerdmans, 2004), 78. Unfortunately, by shifting the analogy from the analogy of faith, that is, from the knowledge of the Father that we have exclusively from the Son and Spirit and not from our experiences of life in relationship, Migliore is misled into thinking he can and must search for alternative language for the eternal Trinity (ibid., 75) because he believes that the reference to God as Father, Son, and Holy Spirit, while offering what he calls a "biblical baseline," cannot be "absolutized" in the church's theology and worship. Hence he claims there is a depth-grammar to the doctrine that sees that God is community-forming love and that where such love is experienced, there God is also experienced. The problem with this is that it suggests that one then has an understanding of God that can be had without specifically allowing one's thinking to be shaped by the eternal Father, Son, and Holy Spirit, into whom Christians are baptized and whom they worship and adore. Put another way, this thinking allows a prior conception of God that is not tied to the revelation of the Father in the Son and through the Spirit to determine our understanding of the Trinity.

8. Ted Peters, *GOD as Trinity: Relationality and Temporality in Divine Life* (Louisville: Westminster John Knox, 1993), 15–16.

9. Ibid., 175.

10. Ibid., 96.

11. Robert W. Jenson, *The Triune Identity: God according to the Gospel* (Philadelphia: Fortress, 1982), 168, 140–41.

Jesus' divinity is to be understood as the outcome of his human life on earth rather than as a reality that always was within the eternal Godhead.[12]

Each one of these assertions runs counter to the main ingredients of what I take to be vital for the classical doctrine of the Trinity:

- that each of the three divine persons is fully God as one being, three persons in a *perichoresis* that nothing can disrupt;[13]
- that God is perfectly one and three and would have been triune even if he never decided to create, reconcile, and redeem the world;[14]
- that the relations of the trinitarian persons are inherent to God's eternal being and that God cannot be rightly conceived if the Trinity is thought to exist solely for the sake of creation, if the Trinity is in any way reduced to what God does as creator, reconciler, and redeemer;
- that God is in no way or at no time constituted by what he does for us within the economy since all of God's actions *ad extra* are sovereign acts of grace expressing God's eternal love for us;
- that "what God the Father is toward us in Christ and in the Spirit he is inherently and eternally in himself, and what he is inherently and eternally in himself he is toward us in the Incarnation of his Son and in the Mission of the Spirit."[15]

Nonetheless, without acknowledging the freedom of God's love within the immanent Trinity, anything said about God acting for us within the economy becomes little more than a projection of human experience and

---

12. See ibid., 140; also Wolfhart Pannenberg: *"God, through the creation of the world, made himself radically dependent on this creation and on its history"* ("Problems of a Trinitarian Doctrine of God," *Dialog* 26 [1987]: 255, italics in original).

13. As Torrance states: "While the three Divine Persons differ from one another precisely as Father, Son and Holy Spirit, they are nevertheless conjoined in all their distinctiveness, for the entire and undivided Godhead resides in each Person, and each Person dwells in or inheres in the Other; so that the whole of one Person is imaged in the whole of the Other.... Each and all reveal the whole Godhead, and thus none can be regarded as being partial in any way as compared with the other two: each Person is '*whole God*' and the '*whole God*' is in each Person. Since '*God is Spirit*' (John 4:24) the '*whole God*' and '*each Person*' and relations within the Holy Trinity are to be understood in a completely spiritual way" (*Trinitarian Perspectives*, 117–18).

14. Yves Congar, *I Believe in the Holy Spirit* (trans. David Smith; New York: Crossroad, 1997), 3:13, writes: "As the Fathers who combated Arianism said, even if God's creatures did not exist, God would still be a Trinity of Father, Son and Spirit, since creation is an act of free will, whereas the procession of the Persons takes place in accordance with nature, *kata phusin*." Karl Barth agrees: "His Word will still be His Word apart from this becoming [incarnation], just as Father, Son and Holy Spirit would be none the less eternal God, if no world had been created" (*CD* I/2:135).

15. Torrance, *Trinitarian Perspectives*, 117.

relationality into God in an overt or unwitting attempt to define God *by* our experiences of relationality as is clearly evident in the statements noted above that depict the eternal divine relations of the Trinity in categories borrowed from social psychology and from historical analysis.

In addition, it was and remains a crucial insight of classical trinitarian theology that the processions within the immanent Trinity are an ineffable mystery. We cannot explain *how* the Son is begotten of the Father or *how* the Spirit proceeds from the Father through the Son. It is not right, Athanasius says, to "seek how the word is from God, or how He is God's radiance, or how God begets, and what is the manner of His begetting."[16] Such questions demonstrate our ignorance of God because they mistakenly seek to "measure God and His Wisdom by our own nature and infirmity." It is better, Athanasius says, "to be silent and believe, than to disbelieve on account of the perplexity: for he who is perplexed may in some way obtain mercy."[17] In his mind those who think of the Word as external to God clearly were trying to explain doctrine in their own way and not in faith. For with the explanation given in faith, "God's Word is proper to Him and from Him, and is not a work; and yet is not like the word of man, or else we must suppose God to be a man."[18] The element of mystery here was crucial for classical theologians[19] and remains crucial to us today.[20]

---

16. Athanasius of Alexandria, *Contra Ar.* 2.36 (*NPNF²* 4:367).

17. Ibid.

18. Ibid. See also *The Letters of Saint Athanasius concerning the Holy Spirit* (trans. C. R. B. Shapland; London: Epworth, 1951), 1.20, 113–14, where Athanasius opposes any idea that would suggest that the "Triad" is "diverse in nature." He then asserts that anyone who asks "how, when it is truly a Triad, the Triad is described as one" is mistaken because the "Godhead" is not declared to us "by demonstration in words, but by faith and by pious and reverent use of reason."

19. See Lewis Ayres, *Nicaea and Its Legacy: An Approach to Fourth-Century Trinitarian Theology* (Oxford: Oxford University Press, 2004), 236, where he notes three principles that characterize what he calls a "pro-Nicene" theology: (1) "a clear vision of the person and nature distinction, entailing the principle that whatever is predicated of the divine nature is predicated of the three persons equally and understood to be one (this distinction may or may not be articulated via a consistent technical terminology)"; (2) "clear expression that the eternal generation of the Son occurs within the unitary and incomprehensible divine being"; and (3) "clear expression of the doctrine that the persons work inseparably" (see also ibid., 336–37).

20. While Torrance insists that we cannot remain agnostic when it comes to knowing the triune God, still we must use the concepts we have "with apophatic reserve and reverence," Thomas F. Torrance, *The Christian Doctrine of God, One Being Three Persons* (Edinburgh: T&T Clark, 1996), 194. On this point see also Thomas F. Torrance, *Divine Meaning: Studies in Patristic Hermeneutics* (Edinburgh: T&T Clark, 1995), 202, and *Theology in Reconciliation* (London: Geoffrey Chapman, 1975), 224. Torrance rejects what he deems "fatal" forms of apophaticism (*Theology in Reconciliation*, 221).

Barth himself followed Augustine here and insisted that "we must accept the fact that these three who delimit themselves from one another are antecedently a reality in God Himself. We can state the fact of the divine processions and modes of being. But all our attempts to state the How of this delimitation will prove to be impossible"[21] because "what has to be said will obviously be said definitively and exclusively by God Himself, by the three in the one God who delimit themselves from one another in revelation."[22] Explicitly following Barth at this point, T. F. Torrance adds that when we speak of the begetting of the Son or the proceeding of the Spirit, "we have to suspend our thought before the altogether inexpressible, incomprehensible Nature of God and the onto-relations of the Communion of the Father, the Son, and the Holy Spirit, which the Holy Spirit eternally is."[23] Citing Athanasius, he concludes: "Thus far human knowledge goes. Here the cherubim spread the covering of their wings."[24]

When this is not respected, rationalistic attempts are made to explain what God alone can reveal to us in his Word and Spirit. While we know the fact that God is one being, three persons from our encounter with Jesus Christ and through his Holy Spirit, and while we know that the order of the trinitarian relations cannot be arbitrarily changed without compromising the fact that there can be no subordinationist, modalist, or tritheist understanding of God's being and action, it is impossible for us to define and delimit the distinction of persons in the one being of God from the human side without reading back into the immanent Trinity the limitations associated with our human attempts to apprehend the mystery of the triune God. Whenever this reversal is introduced into trinitarian thinking, the distinction of persons and the unity of God's actions *ad extra* are also obviated by generating a construction that finds God in some sense dependent on the world for the development of his being.

The viewpoint expressed by the social doctrine is best contested by the kind of thinking offered by Sarah Coakley when she carefully

---

21. Barth, *CD* I/1:476.

22. Ibid.

23. Torrance, *The Christian Doctrine of God*, 193.

24. Ibid. In other words, we cannot pry into the inner being of God but must rely on God to reveal himself to us and to include us in his own self-knowledge and love.

presents Gregory of Nyssa's analogy of the three men, Peter, James, and John, who have one essence, and correctly notes that those who would use this analogy to argue that we must begin with the three and then attempt to understand God's oneness are mistaken.[25] Beyond that, she rightly notes that it is a mistake to import the modern concept of person as an individual consciousness and will into the discussion because this inevitably leads to tritheism. Gregory never employed the analogy this way. In fact this was not Gregory's analogy at all but one suggested by Ablabius, to whom he was responding concerning the problem of tritheism. Yet Gregory emphasized the unity of the trinitarian persons, and he questioned the analogy itself because of the great difference between human and divine persons.[26]

In other words, Gregory believed the divine persons are ineffably one and three in a way that does not apply to human persons and cannot be read off from human experience apart from revelation. Hence, "in the case of the Divine nature we do not [as in the case of men] learn that the Father does anything by Himself in which the Son does not work conjointly, or again that the Son has any special operation apart from the Holy Spirit."[27] This is a crucial insight of classical trinitarian theology because, as Coakley rightly notes, there is reference to the *communion* or *koinonia* of the persons but not to the community of the persons, since for Gregory there is no thought of attempting to unify separate individuals with their own wills and consciousness; instead, "'there is apprehended among these three a certain ineffable and inconceivable communion [*koinonia*] and at the same time distinction'" that in no way compromises their one divine nature.[28]

---

25. See recent attempts to do this in Stanley J. Grenz, *Rediscovering the Triune God* (Minneapolis: Fortress, 2004), x, drawing from Pannenberg; also Veli-Matti Kärkkäinen, *The Trinity: Global Perspectives* (Philadelphia: Westminster John Knox, 2007). Lewis Ayres, however, makes a strong case that the common assumption that Eastern theologians began with the three persons and moved toward the unity of God while Western theologians began with the divine unity and moved toward the three persons was mistaken (*Nicaea and Its Legacy*, 52). T. F. Torrance also rejects this view, insisting we must begin with God as one God, three persons (*Trinitarian Perspectives*, 113–14).

26. Sarah Coakley, "'Persons' in the 'Social' Doctrine of the Trinity: A Critique of the Current Analytic Discussion," in *The Trinity: An Interdisciplinary Symposium on the Trinity* (ed. Stephen T. Davis, Daniel Kendall, SJ, and Gerald O'Collins, SJ; Oxford: Oxford University Press, 1999), 132.

27. Gregory of Nyssa, cited in ibid., 132.

28. Ibid., 134.

Recently, this problem was addressed in an interesting analysis and critique of the trinitarian theology of Colin Gunton. While Gunton asserted that everything looks different in light of the Trinity and while he clearly wanted to avoid individualism and collectivism as well as projectionism, in the end he was led to subvert the function of *ousia* within the being of God by elevating the concept of relationality to a position of dominance. According to Bernhard Nausner,

> substance, for Gunton, does not indicate another underlying principle of deity but rather is constituted by three persons in communion. This shift leads him to the sublation of substance-talk in relationality-talk with the result that the notions of oneness and substance are derived solely from the perspective of the particular as constituted by the whole.[29]

By abandoning the notion of *ousia* Gunton was "forced to anchor the notion of God's oneness in the universal notion of relatedness. Each person is therefore constituted by relationality and hence eternal relatedness becomes the substance of God."[30] This happens because the important dialectical relationship that classical trinitarian theology intended to maintain between *ousia* and *hypostasis* was compromised by an overemphasis on relationality, which itself was not defined solely from revelation but from human experience within history.[31]

For a classical doctrine of the Trinity, the best clue for an understanding of the triune life of God, then, is the revelation of God himself in his Word and Spirit. For instance, Gregory of Nyssa appeals to revelation:

> once for all we have learned from the Lord ... to what we ought to look with the eyes of our understanding, — that is, the Father, the Son and the Holy Spirit ... it is a terrible and soul-destroying thing to misinterpret these Divine utterances and to devise in their stead

---

29. Bernhard Nausner, "The failure of a laudable project: Gunton, the Trinity and human self-understanding," *SJT* 62 (2009): 413.

30. Ibid.

31. Ibid., 413–14. In an extreme form that Gunton certainly would reject, this type of thinking is captured in the statement that "person, not substance is the root (*radix*) of all reality" (Catherine Mowry LaCugna, *God for Us: The Trinity and Christian Life* [San Francisco: HarperSanFrancisco, 1991], 398).

assertions to subvert them,—assertions pretending to correct God the Word.[32]

Hilary insists that "the action of God must not be canvassed by human faculties; the Creator must not be judged by those who are the work of his hands,"[33] while Athanasius maintains that we must not ask "why the Word of God is not such as our word, considering God is not such as we."[34]

This means that although we meet and know God in our experiences of faith, we also know that it is God alone who frees us for such knowledge through the reconciling action of his Son and in and through the action of his Holy Spirit, which can never be confused with the human spirit.[35] This certainly is one of the main reasons why T. F. Torrance followed Athanasius and insisted that it is "more godly and true to signify God from the Son and call him Father, than to name God from his works alone and call him Unoriginate."[36] Repeatedly Torrance asserts that if we are to think rightly about God and about human freedom, we can do so only by thinking from a center in God and not from a center in ourselves. The classical doctrine of the Trinity upholds thinking from a center in God while social and relational doctrines clearly tend to begin by thinking from a center in us.

---

32. Gregory of Nyssa, "Against Eunomius," 2.2 (*NPNF²* 5:101–2).

33. Hilary, *Trinity* 3.26 (*NPNF²* 9:70)

34. Athanasius, *Contra Ar.* 2.36 (*NPNF²* 4:367).

35. Torrance impressively notes that it is our minds that need healing so that we might have the mind of Christ. And that indeed is what happens when we know the Father through the Son and in the Spirit. See Thomas F. Torrance, *Atonement: The Person and Work of Christ* (ed. Robert T. Walker; Downers Grove, IL: InterVarsity Press, 2009), who follows the thought of the Greek fathers and argues that "they put their finger on the twisted state of affairs in the depths of the human mind. It is in the heart of our mental reality which governs and controls all our thinking and culture that we have become estranged from the truth and hostile to God. And it is right there, in the ontological depths of the human mind, that we desperately need to be redeemed and healed" (ibid., 439). That is why Apollinarianism was such a threat. For Apollinaris, the Son of God did not take on our alienated and twisted mind in the incarnation, that mind in which sin had "become rooted and entrenched," because if he had, then he himself would have been a sinner and perhaps even "an original sinner." Thus he concludes that in the incarnation Jesus' human mind was "displaced by the divine mind." Hence, by thinking that the Word assumed some sort of neutral humanity, and not the "actual humanity in which we sinners all share" he undercut the full incarnation of God in Christ and also undermined the fact that our reconciliation actually took place in the divine and human mediation of Christ himself in that he truly healed our minds and enabled us to know God in his internal relations through the power of his resurrection and in the Spirit (ibid., 439–47).

36. Thomas F. Torrance, *The Trinitarian Faith: The Evangelical Theology of the Ancient Catholic Church* (Edinburgh: T&T Clark, 1988), 49.

That is why Torrance so vehemently opposed the approach of such thinkers as Rudolf Bultmann, John A. T. Robinson, and Paul Tillich. Each of these theologians in his own way conceptually let go of the God who revealed himself in his incarnate Word and through his Spirit by refusing to think from a center in God and instead proceeded to think from a center in himself. Bultmann, of course, did this by existentializing the gospel and substituting the disciples' faith experience for the objective event of the resurrection of Jesus Christ, and in Torrance's mind this occurred because Bultmann did not think from a center in God, which is to say he did not allow his concept of God to be shaped by the objective revelation of God in the history of Jesus of Nazareth. Not only is it impossible to try to think about God by leaving the sphere of history and of space and time, but it is also unnecessary just because what God is toward us in the incarnation and outpouring of the Holy Spirit, God is eternally in himself. That is what it means to think from a center in God — it means to allow our concepts about who God is in time and in eternity to be shaped by who God is for us in his Word and Spirit. Instead of doing this, Bultmann detached his concepts from the empirical correlates of faith by locating them in people's existential reactions to the story of Jesus;[37] this finally led Torrance to claim that in Bultmann's view, Jesus' death on the cross was no different from a fatal accident in the street.[38]

Robinson thought about God in pictorial images and therefore was unable to detach God's actions for us in history from the ground of being he conceptualized and so thought of God as involved in the same turmoils we face in a way that made even God helpless to act on our behalf.[39] Tillich virtually equated God with our experiences of depth and argued that if the traditional meaning of the word "God" did not appeal to people, then they should translate the word and speak of the

---

37. See Rudolf Bultmann, *Jesus Christ and Mythology* (New York: Charles Scribner's Sons, 1958), 73, where he writes: "we cannot speak of what God is in Himself but only what He is doing to us and with us." But, as Torrance astutely points out, "if we can say nothing about God in himself or about what he does objectively, can we still give any content to his actions in relation to ourselves, and can we really say anything at all of God, even in analogical language?" Thomas F. Torrance, *Incarnation: The Person and Life of Christ* (ed. Robert T. Walker; Downers Grove, IL: InterVarsity Press, 2008), 288.

38. Thomas F. Torrance, *Theology in Reconstruction* (London: SCM, 1965), 277.

39. See ibid.

depths of their own lives or of what they take seriously as of ultimate concern.[40] Each of these approaches to knowledge of God led in reality to the God these theologians wanted instead of to God as he actually exists as the eternal Father, Son, and Spirit.

Torrance consistently applied the doctrine of justification by faith to his epistemology when thinking about the Trinity and thus always claimed that, although everyone has some knowledge of God, when one comes to know God the Father in and through his Son Jesus Christ, that natural knowledge must be set aside as a way to know God scientifically, that is, in accordance with his true nature. So, the point to be made here is that one of the hallmarks of classical trinitarian theology is that God, who is inherently one being, three persons can only be known through God himself and in faith. And since that is true, a social doctrine of the Trinity will always be seen as more than a little problematic because its first major premise is that we can use an analogy other than the analogy of faith (the knowledge of God that comes to us through the Son and in the Spirit and thus in faith). And that other analogy is, as was just noted, the experience of being in relationship.

To put it more pointedly, such thinking allows relationality as we experience it to be the starting point for our reflections on the Trinity. It is one of the crucial implications of the classical doctrine of the Trinity that once that occurs, then in reality God becomes the predicate in the sentence instead of the subject and thus becomes whatever we describe using religious and even biblical categories based on the experiences of human relationality that are most important to us. Some obvious examples can be seen in the thinking of representative social trinitarians such as Jürgen Moltmann, Elizabeth Johnson, and Catherine LaCugna. This, however, is not the place to discuss those examples. That will come later.

Implications of the Full Equality and Identity of Nature of the Trinitarian Persons

Because God traditionally has been understood to be one being, three persons by Athanasius, Hilary, Augustine, Thomas Aquinas, Gregory

---

40. See Paul D. Molnar, "'Thy Word Is Truth': The Role of Faith in Reading Scripture Theologically with Karl Barth," *SJT* 63 (2010): 85–86.

Nyssa, Gregory Nazianzus, and others in the tradition, this insight led early church theologians to insist that "to believe in the Unity of God apart from the Trinity is to limit the truth of divine Revelation. It is through the divine Trinity that we believe in the divine Unity, and through the divine Unity that we believe in the divine Trinity."[41] Hence, as Gregory the Theologian insisted, "'*One is not more or less God, nor is One before and after Another,' for there is no greater or less in respect of the Being in the consubstantial Persons.*'"[42] This insight ruled out all forms of subordinationism as well as tritheism and modalism. Since the persons of the Trinity are coeternal and coequal, one must recognize that "they are all perfectly one in the identity of their Nature and perfectly consubstantial in their Being."[43]

As noted above, this is a crucial insight of classical trinitarian theology. Without it trinitarian thinking becomes arbitrary; that is, it becomes a way of using trinitarian categories to describe our experiences within the economy of salvation. Again, we look to the thinking of Ted Peters. It should be noted that Peters regards the thinking of Catherine LaCugna as "a real jewel" precisely because she collapses the immanent into the economic Trinity and thinks that "the life of God is not something that belongs to God alone. *Trinitarian life is also our life*."[44] This confusion of God's life with ours is evident in Peters's own understanding of the task of trinitarian theology:

> The task of trinitarian theology is to explicate the biblical symbols in such a way as to gain an increasingly adequate set of ideas for conceiving of God's creative and redemptive work. There is no inherent reason for assuming that the three persons have to be identical or equal in nature.... The notion of one being in three persons is simply a conceptual device for trying to understand the drama of salvation that is taking place in Jesus Christ.[45]

A classical doctrine of the Trinity that holds to the identity and equality of nature of each of the divine persons stands flatly opposed to

---

41. Torrance, *Trinitarian Perspectives*, 116.
42. *Or.* 31.14; 40.43, quoted in ibid., 116–17.
43. Ibid., 117.
44. Peters, *GOD as Trinity*, 122, 125–26.
45. Ibid., 70.

this thinking, as we have noted above. This is no idle chatter because unless one recognizes the truth of this traditional assertion, one is likely to reduce the doctrine of the Trinity to a description of what takes place in the economy.[46]

Both Karl Barth and T. F. Torrance recognized the danger here. Barth insisted that the point of the doctrine was not to describe God as creator, mediator, and redeemer but rather to recognize who God eternally is as Father, Son, and Holy Spirit.[47] He further asserted that "we cannot say anything higher or better of the 'inwardness of God' than that God is Father, Son, and Holy Spirit, and therefore that He is love in Himself without and before loving us, and without being forced to love us."[48] What this meant to him was that if anyone were to suppose that the point of trinitarian theology was simply to describe the events of salvation, that person had already misunderstood the doctrine because such thinking necessarily reduces the immanent to the economic Trinity. Once that happens, then and to that extent God is seen as a dependent deity who is in reality indistinguishable from history;[49] in this thinking God once again cannot be seen as able to act decisively for us within history as our Savior in a way that does not depend on us for its validity. T. F. Torrance rightly insists that

> "Father," "Son" and "Holy Spirit" are not just ways of thinking about God, for there is no other God but he who IS Father, Son and Holy Spirit. "Trinity" is not just a way for us to think about God, for the one true God IS actually and eternally triune and cannot be conceived properly otherwise.[50]

This statement categorically opposes the thinking advanced by those who think symbolically rather than in a significative way; the

---

46. Ted Peters is not alone in thinking this way. Roger Haight insists that "the doctrine is not intended to provide information about the internal life of God, but is about how God relates to human beings" (*Jesus: Symbol of God* [Maryknoll, NY: Orbis, 1999], 485).

47. Barth, *CD* I/2, 878–79.

48. Ibid., 377.

49. Even if one were to say that God has chosen to make his existence dependent on history, that would not overcome the difficulty here because the God who becomes incarnate for us in Christ never makes his actions for us in Christ or in the Spirit dependent on history—they always remain free sovereign acts of grace even in the humility and obedience of the Son on the cross.

50. Torrance, *Trinitarian Perspectives*, 133.

former refers to thinking that allows our imaginations and experiences to shape and reshape our concepts of who God is, while the latter refers to a kind of thinking that is formed by allowing the objective reality of God revealed by his Word and Spirit to determine what is thought and said. The contrast here can be seen starkly by observing what those who think symbolically have to say about the doctrine of the Trinity:

> the symbol of the Trinity is not a blueprint of the inner workings of the godhead, not an offering of esoteric information about God. In no sense is it a literal description of God's being *in se*. As the outcome of theological reflection on the Christian experience of relationship to God, it is a symbol that indirectly points to God's relationality.... God is *like* a Trinity, *like* a threefoldness of relation.[51]

Thinking symbolically thus leads one away from a statement that God IS the eternal Father, Son, and Holy Spirit to a kind of nonconceptual thinking that maintains we must think symbolically about what we take to be our own experiences of relationship to God and then conclude that God is not a Trinity of persons but that God is only *like* a Trinity! Nothing could be further from the truth as understood in the classical doctrine of the Trinity.

A doctrine of the Trinity that relies on our experiences of relationality to understand the unique relations of the trinitarian persons inevitably ends up projecting human experiences of relationality into God by thinking symbolically about the Trinity, thus obviating any true objective knowledge of God grounded in his internal relations in favor of a kind of subjectivism that supposes that the most we can say is that God is *like* a Trinity, *like* a threefoldness of relation. This thinking leaves the door open to conceptualizing God using any number of notions that are then thought to help us to use our symbols in ways that create the kind of human relations we presume are appropriate today.

But such thinking is both unscientific and unrealistic. It is, as Torrance never tires of reminding us, dualistic in that it will not allow the reality of God present to us within history in his Word and Spirit to shape

51. Elizabeth A. Johnson, *She Who Is: The Mystery of God in Feminist Theological Discourse* (New York: Crossroad, 1992), 204–5.

our understanding. Such thinking once again ends up undermining the truth of who God is as recognized in the Nicene-Constantinopolitan creed by thinking from a center in ourselves instead of from a center in God; it ends up advancing some form of self-justification that bespeaks the fact that one has not yet begun to think on the ground of God's own self-revelation in his Word and Spirit and thus in faith.

Furthermore, trinitarian theology expressed along the lines of Ted Peters's thinking in which he assumes that relationality as understood in social psychology should inform our view of the Trinity, leads him to conclude that God is in the process of becoming who he will be precisely by relating with us in history. While this thinking is manifestly modern in the sense that it is clearly influenced by Hegelian dynamics,[52] this is exactly what the ancient doctrine was meant to deny. A God who depends on history is indistinguishable from history. And a dependent deity could only be conceptualized when and where the persons of the Trinity are not seen in their full coequality and identity of nature.[53]

Here it is important to restate the classical affirmation that "the whole Being of God belongs to each divine Person as it belongs to all of them and belongs to all of them as it belongs to each of them, and thus does not detract from the truth that the Monarchy is One and indivisible, the Trinity in Unity and the Unity in Trinity."[54] This crucial insight that rules out all subordinationism also reaffirms the simplicity and the indivisibility of the triune being of God. It likewise means that the monarchy cannot be limited only to a single person because the monarchy is found in the perichoretic relations of the three persons in the one being of God. As we will see toward the end of this essay, it is this insight that enables a view of the Spirit's procession from the Father in the Son or from the being of the Father rather than simply the person of the Father and so avoids the problems long associated with the *filioque* and those who oppose it.

---

52. For a clear presentation of Hegel's influences, see Stephen R. Holmes, *The Holy Trinity: Understanding God's Life* (Milton Keynes: Paternoster, 2012); published in the US as *The Quest for the Trinity: The Doctrine of God in Scripture, History and Modernity* (Downers Grove, IL: InterVarsity Press, 2012), 184–86.

53. Peters, *GOD as Trinity*, 15–16, 72, 82. See also Paul D. Molnar, "Experience and Knowledge of the Trinity in the Theology of Ted Peters: Occasion for Clarity or Confusion?" *ITQ* 64 (1999): 219–43.

54. Torrance, *Trinitarian Perspectives*, 125.

The Importance of Recognizing the Priority of the Father/Son Relation over the Creator/Creature Relation

It is a historical fact that Origen, who was a great theologian in his own right,[55] nonetheless at an important juncture failed to give priority to the Father/Son relation over the Creator/creature relation. In other words Origen "was unable to think of God as *Pantokrator* ... or the Almighty except in a necessary eternal conjunction with all things ... for Origen the creation had to be regarded as concomitant with the being of God and as eternally coexisting with him."[56] According to Georges Florovsky, this was typical for the Greek mind:

> The Greek mind was firmly addicted to the conception of an Eternal Cosmos, permanent and immutable in its essential structure and composition. This Cosmos simply existed. Its existence was "necessary," it was an ultimate or first *datum*, beyond which neither thought nor imagination could penetrate.[57]

This thinking led to Origen's failure to distinguish clearly both ontological from cosmological dimensions in his view of God as Father and as Creator and between the eternal generation of the Son from the Father and the creation of the world by the Father's Word. As Torrance would have it, Origen maintained a "logical link" between the Son's eternal generation and creation. In that logic Athanasius detected "a depreciation of the nature and status of the Son" and "precisely because of his eternal generation" Origen mistakenly advanced "a doctrine of the eternity of the world."[58]

It is exactly here, where the classical doctrine of the Trinity affirms the fact that while the Father was always Father and not always Creator and that the Son was always Son but not always incarnate, that the importance of stressing the priority of the Father/Son relation over

---

55. See Khaled Anatolios, *Retrieving Nicaea: The Development and Meaning of Trinitarian Doctrine* (Grand Rapids: Baker, 2011), 16. See also Holmes, *The Quest for the Trinity*, 74–81. Strangely, while Holmes recognizes the greatness of Origen and the problem of subordinationism in his thought, he never mentions the problem of Origen's belief in the coeternity of the world with God that follows from Origen's inability to distinguish God's internal and external relations clearly and consistently.

56. Torrance, *The Trinitarian Faith*, 85.

57. Georges Florovsky, *Aspects of Church History: Volume Four in the Collected Works of Georges Florovsky* (Belmont, MA: Nordland, 1975), 39.

58. Thomas F. Torrance, *Theology in Reconciliation*, 220. On this point see esp. Florovsky, *Aspects of Church History*, 55–56.

the Creator/creature relation illuminates the insights that flow from this distinction. First, affirmation of this priority means that one must clearly acknowledge that the eternal generation of the Son from the Father is without beginning or end just because it is an eternal begetting of God from God and Light from Light. Thus, there never was a time when the Father was Father without his begotten Son.

Furthermore, since the Son is begotten and not made, that must mean that the Son does not receive his deity from the Father because the Son is just as much divine, and eternally so as is the Father, even though the Son is begotten and not the one who begets. This suggests that one cannot confuse the order of the personal relations within the Trinity with the being of the persons. And one certainly cannot maintain this unity of nature and being between the Father and Son if one supposes that the Son's existence results from an act of will on the part of the Father. As Khaled Anatolios has shown, Arius, Asterius, Eusebius, and Eunomius, in spite of their differences, diverged from Alexander, Athanasius, and the Cappadocians, who had their own different emphases, specifically with regard to this point. The former theologians insisted that the "relations between Father and Son pertained to will, not to being," while the latter "designated the relation between Father and Son in terms of unity of being."[59]

Moreover, since the Spirit proceeds from the being of the Father and not simply from the person of the Father—as long as this insight is maintained, in virtue of the doctrine of *perichoresis* (where the Spirit proceeds from the Father through the Son)—there is no need even to raise the question of the *filioque* at all since there would have been no perceived need to ward off the threat of subordinationism with its notion of a derived deity flowing from the misperception that the Spirit proceeds only from the Father as person. So if the Spirit proceeds from the being of the Father, since Father and Son have their being in and with each other, the Spirit could not be thought of as proceeding only from the Father. Of course, this eventually led to misunderstanding and division between the Eastern and Western churches and is a point T. F. Torrance finds in Athanasius and develops to great effect in his theology.

Athanasius insisted that creation must be understood in a trinitarian way by seeing that the Father created all things through his Word so that there would be no act of the Creator if the Word was not intrinsic to the

---

59. Anatolios, *Retrieving Nicaea*, 31.

being of God. In other words, the internal relations of the Father and Son had priority over God's free act of will in creating something outside the divine being. It should be noted, however, that this important statement placed his thinking dangerously close to the erroneous thinking of Origen. Athanasius was clearly aware of this as he deployed two vital distinctions that obviated the possibility of claiming that creation was indeed coeternal with the existence of the Father and the Son. First, he insisted that the Son's generation from the Father was "impassible, and eternal, and worthy of God" and that this could not be understood by comparing it to the way that human beings beget other humans:

> the divine generation must not be compared to the nature of men, nor the Son considered to be part of God, nor the generation to imply any passion whatever; God is not as man; for men beget passibly, having a transitive nature, which waits for periods by reason of its weakness. But with God this cannot be; for He is not composed of parts, but being impassible and simple, He is impassibly and indivisibly Father of the Son.[60]

Second, Athanasius maintained that "although God always had the power to make, yet the things originated had not the power of being eternal."[61] This, because "a work is external to the nature, but a son is the proper offspring of the essence"; consequently, "it follows that a work need not have been always, for the workman frames it when he will; but an offspring is not subject to will, but is proper to the essence."[62]

---

60. Athanasius, *Contra Ar.* 1.28 (*NPNF²* 4:322–23). While the subject of God's impassibility and passibility has become a burning issue in contemporary theology, I think it is perfectly appropriate to hold that God can be both passible and impassible precisely because God became incarnate in Jesus Christ without ceasing to be God and without being transformed into a human being. In the incarnate Word, therefore, God could take our suffering and pain into himself while exercising his divine impassiblity in order to overcome the weakness and transitoriness of our human existence by overcoming sin and death in the human history of Jesus for us.

61. Athanasius, *Contra Ar.* 1.29 (*NPNF²* 4:323).

62. Ibid. See Florovsky, *Aspects of Church History*, 55–56. Since the power to create could not have come *to* God, and since God was *Pantokrator* (where God and the universe are deemed belonging necessarily and logically together), Origen concluded that the world was eternal. But the Arians used just this argument to conclude that nothing that came from God, including the *Logos*, could be eternal. Athanasius responded that while God always had the power to create, he did not create of necessity but by a free act of will. Yet, the Son is of the Father's "substance" and so is not the product of the Father's will and deliberation but of his nature. That is the difference between the begetting of the Son and creation.

T. F. Torrance captures the gist of Athanasius's thinking perfectly and understands the weakness of the Origenist idea that creation could be conceived as eternal when he asserts that the Arians could appeal to Origen's thinking but drew a different conclusion. "Since all God's works were eternal, what would be wrong, they asked, in saying that they did not exist before they were generated?"[63] In Torrance's understanding this means that the Arians attempted to equate "the kind of 'eternity' attributed to creatures brought into existence by the will of God with the kind of 'eternity' they attributed to the Son in the light of their notorious statement that 'there was once when he was not.'"[64] Athanasius responded that there is an enormous difference between things that are brought into being from nothing by an act of God's will and as works "'external to his nature' and the Son who 'is the proper offspring of the being of God' and is internal to his nature. Compared to the Son, therefore, who is as eternal as God the Father is, created things (things made, not begotten) do not eternally coexist with God."[65]

So, while God was always Father and always had the power to create and did actually create because he was and is the Father of the Son, it is important to realize that, in the words of Athanasius, "'for God to create is secondary, and to beget is primary.'"[66] Hence, God created things outside himself out of nothing when he willed to do so and when it was good for them. And in light of what God has done in creation and redemption and in light of what God has revealed to us of his eternal purpose, we may speak this way.

But the all-important point here is that "*while God was always Father, he was not always Creator or Maker.*"[67] Following Athanasius, Torrance could say that creation was in God's mind before he created.[68] But because he consistently maintained the priority of the Father/Son relation over the Creator/creature relation, he not only rejected the idea that God is eternally the Creator, but he also rejected the associated notion that "the creation eternally exists in the mind of God, for

---

63. Torrance, *The Trinitarian Faith*, 86.
64. Ibid.
65. Ibid., 86–87.
66. Athanasius, *Contra Ar.* 2.2 cited in Torrance, *The Trinitarian Faith*, 87.
67. Torrance, *The Trinitarian Faith*, 87.
68. Ibid.

the creation of the world out of nothing meant that it had an absolute beginning."[69]

Hence Torrance could never say with Moltmann, that "if God's eternal being is love, then the divine love is also more blessed in giving than in receiving. God cannot find bliss in eternal self-love if selflessness is part of love's very nature."[70] And Torrance could never agree with Moltmann that "the idea of the world is already inherent in the Father's love for the Son."[71] Because Moltmann was unable to distinguish clearly God's internal and external relations, he believed that "the economic Trinity not only reveals the immanent Trinity; it also has a retroactive effect on it."[72] This led him to think that God *needs* to suffer in order to love;[73] that "God 'needs' the world and man. If God is love, then he neither will nor can be without the one who is his beloved";[74] and that "creation is a part of the eternal love affair between the Father and the Son."[75]

Each of these statements manifests the kind of mutual conditioning between Creator and creation that Athanasius sought to avoid and that must be avoided in any classical account of the trinitarian actions *ad extra* as grounded within the internal relations of the Father, Son, and Holy Spirit. Each of these statements eradicates the crucial distinction between Creator and creatures that was critical to classical trinitarianism just because of its failure to distinguish the immanent and economic Trinity.[76] And this thinking leaves Moltmann exposed to charges of tritheism, modalism (Patripassianism), and pantheism.[77] All of these

---

69. Thomas F. Torrance, *The Ground and Grammar of Theology* (Charlottesville, VA: University Press of Virginia, 1980), 66.

70. Jürgen Moltmann, *The Trinity and the Kingdom: The Doctrine of God* (trans. Margaret Kohl; New York: Harper and Row, 1981), 106.

71. Ibid., 108.

72. Ibid., 160.

73. Ibid., 19–20, 32–33, 197.

74. Ibid., 58.

75. Ibid., 59.

76. Moltmann, of course, famously declared that he did not want to cling to any distinction between the immanent and economic Trinity (*The Trinity and the Kingdom*, 160). And while he did make statements that suggest he recognized the importance of maintaining the freedom of God implied in *creatio ex nihilo* such as when he said, "Without the difference between Creator and creature, creation cannot be conceived of at all" (Jürgen Moltmann, *God in Creation: A New Theology of Creation and the Spirit of God* [trans. Margaret Kohl; New York: Harper and Row, 1985], 89), his panentheistic reinterpretation of the doctrine made it impossible actually to do so in any consistent way.

77. See Paul D. Molnar, *Divine Freedom and the Doctrine of the Immanent Trinity: In Dialogue with Karl Barth and Contemporary Theology* (London: T&T Clark, 2002), chs. 2 and 7.

difficulties plague Moltmann's doctrine of the Trinity because he says his social doctrine will enable him to think relationally, precisely "by taking up pantheistic ideas from the Jewish and the Christian traditions."[78] In reality panentheism never escapes the dilemma of pantheism.

Moltmann's own panentheism leads him to adopt the kabbalistic doctrine of creation with its inherent emanationist overtones and the espousal of the doctrine of the *zimsum*, which asserts that there is a shrinkage process in God so that the nothingness from which God creates the world emerges as the condition for God's creating the world. Yet, this thinking makes nothing into something and thus misses the point of the doctrine of creation from nothing. Moreover, Moltmann continually espouses the idea that God needs the world because all panentheistic conceptions in one way or another require that in some sense God's eternal being is dependent on the development of history for its own existence.[79]

All of these insights seem required by Moltmann's social doctrine of the Trinity but are excluded by a doctrine that ascribes priority to the Father/Son relation over the Creator/creature relation. Emphasizing the priority of the Father/Son relation over the Creator/creature relation therefore leads to the true idea of the contingency of creation. This is a difficult concept. But it means that creation might never have existed or might have existed differently had God willed that to be the case. It also means that the meaning of the universe cannot be found within the created realm but can be understood only from the one who created the world and maintains it in existence.

Even more importantly, it is only when the priority of the Father/Son relation is properly understood that human freedom is truly appreciated as a freedom that comes to us only from God in such a way that we are enabled to live by grace through faith in and through our own free acts of obedience to the Word heard and believed. Inability to distinguish clearly between Creator and creature is one of the hallmarks of Moltmann's panentheistic reinterpretation of the Trinity; this feature of this thinking sets it off sharply from the classical insistence on such a distinction.

---

78. Moltmann, *The Trinity and the Kingdom*, 19.

79. For extended critical engagement with Moltmann on these points, see Molnar, *Divine Freedom*, 197–216.

Additionally, a classical doctrine of the Trinity is able to state with clarity that "gender may not be read back into the Nature of God as Father, Son and Holy Spirit."[80] But this can only be done with clarity and consistency when Athanasius's stress on the priority of the Father/Son relation over the Creator/creature relation is respected. Gender belongs only to creatures and not to God, as all Christian theologians theoretically admit, even though some claim that because the Son of God became incarnate in the man Jesus, therefore "a certain leakage of Jesus' human maleness into the divine nature" takes place so that "maleness appears to be of the essence of the God made known in Christ."[81]

This muddled thinking once again stems from a starting point in human experience rather than in revelation and leads to the problematic notion that analogies for speaking about the triune God are drawn not only from our experience of human fatherhood and sonship but from the experiences of women.[82] In reality all true analogies are developed within faith in the Son or Word who reveals the true nature of God to us so that we must indeed think from a center in God and not at all from a center in ourselves. Thus "human fatherhood may not be used as a standard by which to judge divine Fatherhood, for it is only in the light of the Fatherhood of God that all other fatherhood is to be understood."[83]

The Importance of Recognizing the Full Deity and Distinct Personhood of the Holy Spirit

Before concluding this discussion, I think it would be helpful to consider one further significant aspect of classical trinitarian theology, namely,

---

80. Torrance, *Trinitarian Perspectives*, 129–30.

81. Johnson, *She Who Is*, 152. Of course the only way that one might think this way is if one had already ceased allowing God himself to be the starting point and criterion of what is said about God. The moment experience, whether male or female, becomes the starting point for reflection on the being of the triune God, it becomes impossible to think about God's nature on the basis of revelation alone because one will always assume that gender could be projected into the divine being. The attempt to offset this mistake by arguing that what is needed is a "creative 'naming toward God,'" as Mary Daly so carefully calls it, from the matrix of their own [women's] experience" (ibid., 5) only makes matters worse!

82. Elizabeth Johnson therefore asserts that "analogy … means that while it [human naming of God] starts from the relationship of paternity experienced at its best in this world, its inner dynamism negates the creaturely mode to assert that God is more unlike than like even the best human father…." (*She Who Is*, 173).

83. Torrance, *Trinitarian Perspectives*, 130. See also Barth, *CD* I/1:392.

the importance of upholding the full divinity of the Holy Spirit and of distinguishing the Holy Spirit from the human spirit.

It has sometimes been suggested that the relative neglect of the Holy Spirit early on during the developments of Nicene theology was due to the fact that "Christ's divinity had a logical priority and had to be settled first."[84] Yet, as Khaled Anatolios notes, the Spirit was not totally neglected before the debates of the fourth century, as could be seen in the thinking of Irenaeus, Tertullian, and Origen. Still, Anatolios thinks the question of the Son's divinity did engender a certain forgetfulness of the Spirit because the main question centered on how God and creation were related and how Jesus Christ as divine could be both Creator and creature.

Nevertheless, the pressure to assert the fact that the Spirit also was *homoousion* with the Son and the Father came from the need to clarify trinitarian thinking over against the *tropici* and the Macedonians. The *tropici* consisted of a group of Egyptian Christians who held that the Spirit was subordinate to the Father and to the Son and concluded that "the Spirit was created as an angel, the chief of God's 'ministering spirits.'"[85] Apparently they were so named by their opponents because of the way they used scriptural figures or "tropes" in their thinking. T. F. Torrance rejects what he calls "tropical" argumentation from Scripture because he thinks it amounts to a mythological reading that does not respect the reality of God attested in the texts and thus becomes arbitrary.[86] Unfortunately, the *tropici* claimed that since the Spirit could not be related to the Father by way of generation as in the case of the Son, therefore the Spirit had to be "external to the divine nature."[87] They argued that if the Spirit were integral to the divine nature, "it would have to be another Son, as a brother of the Son, or even a son of the Son, and thus grandson of the Father."[88]

The very idea that the Son might have a brother or that the Father might have a grandson and thus be a grandfather was simply an indication of the kind of mythological thinking that Athanasius furiously rejected in rejecting Arianism. For Athanasius, "the traditions of the faith are not

---

84. Anatolios, *Retrieving Nicaea*, 133.

85. Ibid., 24.

86. Torrance, *Divine Meaning*, 230–32, 263–64, 275.

87. Anatolios, *Retrieving Nicaea*, 24.

88. Ibid., 24–25.

to be known by impertinent scrutiny."[89] The disciples simply believed when they heard the words of the baptismal formula and did not ask why the Son was second and the Spirit third or why the whole was a Triad. Rather, "as they heard, so they believed. They did not ask ... Is the Spirit then a son? ... Is the Father then a grandfather? For they did not hear 'into the name of the grandfather,' but 'into the name of the Father.'"[90]

In Athanasius's trinitarian understanding one could not simply project an understanding from our limited human experience mythologically back into the Godhead, but must allow all of one's thinking to be transformed in light of the unique relations that exist within the eternal Trinity as revealed by the incarnate Son and through the Spirit. Thus one could easily see why Torrance rightly insisted that all our thinking about the Spirit must be controlled by our thinking about the Son since both the Son and Spirit are equally *homoousion* with the Father. The Spirit therefore is the Spirit of the Son and can never be detached from or subordinated to the being of the Father or the Son. The Macedonians, who were named after the bishop of Constantinople, Macedonius, believed in the Son's full divinity but expressed that belief by speaking of a similarity of essence and would not confess the Spirit's full divinity. They also used arguments similar to the *tropici* to oppose the full deity of the Spirit.

Athanasius and Basil of Caesarea both strongly opposed any subordination of the Spirit and affirmed the Spirit's full divinity. The Spirit's full divinity was later affirmed by the Council of Constantinople in AD 381, and the first record of this was documented at the Council of Chalcedon in AD 451.[91] Without getting into a lengthy discussion of the issue here, let it be said that the doctrine of the Spirit's full divinity was and remains crucial to a properly understood classical doctrine of the Trinity.

There are practical implications that follow from this. Whenever the full divinity of the Spirit is damaged, serious difficulties arise, such as: (1) the confusion of the Holy Spirit with the human spirit or with the spirit of the cosmos; and (2) the separation of the Spirit from the Word or Son. With regard to the second point, the idea is frequently

---

89. Athanasius, "Letters to Serapion, IV.5," in *The Letters of Saint Athanasius concerning the Holy Spirit*, 185.

90. Ibid.

91. Anatolios, *Retrieving Nicaea*, 26.

expressed today that since the Spirit can be present beyond Christ and the church in other religions, it must be possible to find the saving Spirit in other religions and thus without acknowledging that salvation comes only from the Father and through the Son. The main problem here is self-evident, for any such assertion is in conflict with the heart of the Christian faith because it denies that it is through union with Christ that we know the Father in and through the Holy Spirit.

With respect to the confusion of the Holy Spirit with the human spirit one might ask: How and when does such confusion occur? The answer is simple and straightforward. Since the Holy Spirit is the Spirit of the Father and the Son *ad intra*, the Spirit acting *ad extra* is the act of the triune God opening us to God by uniting us with his Word and thus with the Father. The Spirit enables creatures through faith to know and love God and to live their justification and sanctification that comes to them in and through the humanity of Christ and thus through their union with him. Hence, any claim that we can know God or relate with God without relying on Christ would necessarily mean a confusion of the Holy Spirit with our response to Christ through the Spirit. In Torrance's view, whenever people are thrown back on their own resources to live the Christian life whether in knowledge, love, or worship, there and then the Holy Spirit has been confused with the human spirit and some form of self-justification will always follow. Hence, the hallmark of such confusion is embodied in attempts to know God while bypassing Christ as the way, the truth, and the life.

With respect to the *filioque*, it is worth commenting that in a classical doctrine of the Trinity, if the doctrine of *perichoresis* is rightly understood, then it will be seen, as Torrance proposes, that the Spirit who proceeds from the Father according to John 15:26 does not proceed from the *person* of the Father *only*, but from the *being* of God the Father in unity with the Son and Spirit in line with the teaching of the Council of Nicaea, which held "that the Son is from the *Being* of God the Father and is of one and the same Being as the Father."[92] This, according to Torrance,

> transcends the rift between the teaching of the Western Church that the Spirit proceeds from the Son as well as the Father [problematically implying two ultimate Principles in God], and the

---

92. Torrance, *Trinitarian Perspectives*, 113.

teaching of the Eastern Church that the Spirit proceeds from the Father only [creating the need for the *filioque* to avoid any hint of subordinationism].[93]

The being of the Father, of course, refers to the perichoretic inter-penetration, mutual indwelling, and coinhering of the Father, Son, and Holy Spirit within the one being of God such that there is no unity without Trinity or Trinity without unity. Since this is the case, one cannot see the monarchy or oneness of God only in the Father as the supposed source of the divine being of the Son and Spirit, where Son and Spirit are understood as "derived Deities"[94] because it is a question of order within the Trinity when reference is made to the Father as the one who begets the Son and when the Spirit is said to proceed from the Father.[95] It is not a question of the Son and Spirit deriving their deity from the Person of the Father because they are fully God and coequal with the Father from all eternity even as there is a clear order within the trinitarian life inasmuch as they are begotten and proceed in their eternal perichoretic relations.

Thus, there can be no subordinationism as would be implied if the Spirit is thought to proceed from the Person of the Father only, and there can be no undercutting of the *homoousion* of the Spirit with the Father and the Son as would happen if the Spirit is thought to proceed from the Father alone as Person and not from the being of God as the Father, since Son and Spirit never exist except in relation to each other as the one God. Hence, one could say that "the Holy Spirit proceeds from the Father, but because of the unity of the Godhead in which each Person is perfectly and wholly God, he proceeds from the Father through the Son for the Spirit belongs to and is inseparable from the Being of the Father and the Son."[96] In this sense Torrance rightly maintains: "It is precisely with the doctrine of the consubstantiality and Deity of the Holy Spirit that the proper understanding of the Holy Trinity is brought to its completion in the theology and worship of the Church."[97]

---

93. Ibid.
94. Ibid., 112.
95. Ibid., 119.
96. Ibid., 121.
97. Ibid.

The purpose of this essay was to explore some of the hallmarks of classical trinitarianism with a view toward seeing that human freedom is indeed based on and insured by God's freedom for us, which itself is grounded in the eternal freedom of the Father, Son, and Holy Spirit. To accomplish this we have presented the ancient councils and early Fathers to appreciate what was believed to be central to the Christian understanding of the doctrine of the Trinity. Then we contrasted the classical view with some contemporary views in an effort to assist modern theologians in developing positions that truly respect divine and human freedom as grounded in God's freedom *in se* and *ad extra*. It is hoped that this study will continue to assist our present generation in our common quest for understanding this most important doctrine of the faith.

RESPONSE TO PAUL D. MOLNAR

STEPHEN R. HOLMES

I am grateful to Paul Molnar for his careful demonstrations of the real dogmatic dangers of departing from classical trinitarianism (as mediated through T. F. Torrance, in particular) in various directions. In general, I simply agree with his various warnings and assessments and would want to echo almost all of them. Some response is here required, however, and so I focus on two concerns with Molnar's exposition: one regarding the source of the doctrine, and the other regarding what seems to me an unfortunate conclusion concerning the autotheotic nature of the Son and the Spirit.

On the former, Molnar begins by expressing the utter necessity of understanding the baptismal formula of Matthew 28:19 as the *ipsissima verba* of the risen Christ. I certainly would not want for a moment to suggest that they are not, but Molnar's stress on this point puzzles me slightly for two reasons — one, a minor point of theological logic; and the other rather more serious, at least in my estimation.

On the minor point, Molnar seems to suggest that if we do not understand these words as dominical, we can only regard them as the words of the early community, which words are necessarily lacking in adequate authority for the establishment of trinitarian doctrine. The point is drawn from Torrance and makes some sense in his historical context, where a particular emphasis on form criticism made the assumption that a non-authentic text must be the product of the community, a standard one. But the point is perhaps not logically tight and seems theologically misconstrued: inspiration is properly a pneumatological category, not a christological one, and the words of Scripture derive their authority from being inspired by the Spirit, not from being spoken by Christ. Romans, after all, is unquestionably a product of the early community, specifically of one member of that community, the apostle Paul, but loses nothing in authority because of that (and, if we understand the doctrine of inspiration properly, the proposal that Ephesians might not be by Paul, but instead a product of some other member or members of the community, does not affect our account of its authority). As I say, between Molnar and me this is a distinction without a difference, in that I do not doubt the dominical provenance of Matthew 28:19 — or indeed the Pauline provenance of Ephesians — but the point is worth making.

More seriously on this point, Molnar seems to suggest in his piece that the developed doctrine of the Trinity he describes may be derived from this single text in Matthew 28. This I do not accept; indeed, I find the proposal rather surprising. The point, however, is suggested in at least two places in his essay. In the opening section on the Matthean baptismal formula we first find an assertion that "the New Testament witness to God's revelation refers us to the Father, the Son, and the Holy Spirit, which are 'unique and proper names denoting three distinct Persons or real Hypostases which are neither exchangeable nor interchangeable while nevertheless of one and the same divine Being.'"[98] This seems to me to be potentially overstated; it may be that doctrine of this precision and clarity can be derived from exegesis of the New Testament alone, but the point would seem to require demonstration, not mere assertion (historically, of course, the exegetical basis for the fourth century decisions involved regular and decisive appeal to the Old Testament, which was sometimes read in ways that would make a responsible modern exegete at least pause). That said, Molnar's immediate turn to an exclusive focus on the single text containing the triune baptismal formula rather suggests that he would like to find this entire doctrine in that one text, a point seemingly supported by the — remarkable — comment: "the disciples simply believed when they heard the words of the baptismal formula and did not ask why the Son was second and the Spirit third or why the whole was a Triad."[99]

Now, I take it from the context that this comment is intended as a summary of a point made by Athanasius, but it is a point cited with apparent approval by Molnar, and it echoes a regular theme of his essay, often connected with Athanasius, that we should simply believe what is

---

98. See p. 70; the embedded quotation is from Torrance.
99. See p. 92.

revealed. (Admittedly the specificity of reference to the baptismal formula is lacking elsewhere.) I do not, of course, disagree that we should believe what is revealed, but I struggled to share Molnar's apparently unruffled confidence that what is revealed in the New Testament/whole Bible is no more, no less, and no other than the doctrine he finds taught in T. F. Torrance.

There may be a confessional difference between myself and Molnar on this point, in that Roman Catholic theology does receive the developed tradition as an authentic hearing and amplifying of the biblical revelation, whereas my Baptist/evangelical tradition is rather less ready to assume this point. If Molnar's appeal is indeed to a confessional account of doctrinal development, it is surprising to see him citing Barth and Torrance—both Reformed theologians—as his sources for the Catholic tradition (St. Thomas, conciliar definitions, or indeed the Catechism would seem to be more obvious choices).

All that said, Molnar's developed argument concerning the baptismal formula, as far as I can reconstruct it, runs something like this: if we do not accept Matthew 28:19 as originating with Christ, then we must ascribe it to the Christian community; in so doing, we inevitably embrace communal reflection as a locus of revelation, which opens us to the various projectionist moves he goes on to criticize. While heartily agreeing on the undesirability of each of those moves, I find this argument inadequate to the task of rejecting them, for reasons sketched above: Romans is clearly—in the terms in which Molnar constructs the question—a product of the early community (particularly an apostle named Paul and his amanuensis); I nonetheless hold it to be authoritative for the construction of Christian doctrine. (I note that Molnar's seemingly exclusive focus on the Matthean baptismal formula does make his argument consistent at this point, but it also seems rather eccentric.)

All this is methodological. As I have indicated, I agree on almost every doctrinal point, positive and negative, that Molnar makes. There are two exceptions, one of which I suppose to be merely a result of unfortunate phrasing. On p. 87, we read, first, that "creation was in God's mind before he created." (Again this is a paraphrase of Torrance, but it seems to be a position Molnar wishes to assert.) I certainly want to agree with Molnar's insistence on the distinction between eternal generation and creation and with his assessment that the blurring of this distinction is a significant problem in contemporary theology. That said, I am genuinely unsure what speaking of creation being "in God's mind before" the act of creation means. If we take the standard orthodox position that God created time in the act of creation, to speak of something happening "before" that act is unhelpful and confusing; to speak of existence in "God's mind" might be a reference to a Molinist middle knowledge, but without further specification it must be unclear. And when we read a few lines later that Torrance rejected the idea that "the creation eternally exists in the mind of God" (p. 87), we are left with an uncomfortable impression that God changed his mind. As I say, I suppose these two phrases to be chance, but I find them unhappy.

My one point of substantial doctrinal difference with Molnar concerns my commitment to the autotheotic life of the Son and the Spirit. The question—which he raises on a number of occasions—concerns the source of the deity of the Son and Spirit. History suggests three possibilities: the Son and Spirit may derive deity from the *hypostasis* of the Father, from the *ousia* of the Father, or from their own being as themselves divine *hypostases*.

Molnar clearly rejects the first of these, and equally clearly affirms the second, at least twice in his essay: on p. 85, where we read "the Spirit proceeds from the being of the Father and not simply from the person of the Father"; and on p. 93, which states: "the Spirit who proceeds from the Father according to John 15:26 does not proceed from the *person* of the Father *only*, but from the *being* of God the Father in unity with the Son and Spirit." (This is claimed to be the teaching of Nicaea, although I am not sure on what basis; so sophisticated a distinction seems far from the relatively crude anti-Arian formulae of AD 325.) The problem with this affirmation is that, given that the *ousia* is common to the three *hypostases*, to assert that the Spirit proceeds from the *ousia* of the Father is necessarily to assert that the Spirit proceeds from himself. (Molnar in fact asserts this in terms in the second quotation above: "the Spirit ... proceeds ... from the being of God the Father in unity with the Son *and Spirit.*')

This is not problematic because we can somehow analyze divine relations and assert that this is impossible; we do not have that level of understanding of the eternal divine life; rather, it is problematic because we know from revelation that the three hypostases are distinguished by relations of origin and not otherwise. So it is imperative that the Spirit is the one who proceeds, not the one from whom the Spirit proceeds. The analogous argument is even clearer: if the Son is begotten of the *ousia* of the Father, then the Son is both the one begotten and the one who begets.

The clearest statement of this problem in the tradition comes in Calvin, who sees clearly that the Son's deity is the Son's own possession, not derived from the Father, because the Son is truly God — and similarly with the Holy Spirit. This claim that the Son and the Spirit are autotheotic seems to me simply necessary.

The format of this volume requires each author to criticize the others, and so I have offered my concerns about certain aspects, methodological and substantial, of Molnar's essay. In closing, however, I wish to reiterate that on almost every point he makes, I am in simple agreement; he exposes the dangers of projectionism in particular with great clarity, and I am grateful for this. My criticisms, such as they are, are no more than an invitation to tighten the critique so it will hit home with all the force it should carry.

THOMAS H. MCCALL

I have been the beneficiary of works by Paul D. Molnar for several years, and I expected a helpful essay from him. I have not been disappointed, and in this wide-ranging and sharply written essay there is much to affirm and appreciate. Molnar provides us with a summary of patristic doctrine (though largely as seen through the lens of Thomas F. Torrance), and he draws useful comparisons and contrasts with many theologians of the contemporary "renaissance" of trinitarian theology.

Molnar is critical—indeed, sharply critical—of much trinitarian theology of recent vintage. The "adoptionist" and "explicitly degree Christology" of John Macquarrie, the efforts of Daniel Migliore to find alternative theological language, the "relational" panentheism of Ted Peters and others, the "Social Trinitarianism" of Jürgen Moltmann and Leonardo Boff, the theological existentialism of Rudolph Bultmann, Paul Tillich, and others, as well as the imaginative efforts of Elizabeth Johnson and Catherine Mowry LaCugna all come in for heavy criticism. Indeed, much of Molnar's essay is taken up by polemical theology. I confess that I am sympathetic to many of Molnar's worries, and I think that much of what he says will offer a helpful corrective if heeded (even if at points it might benefit from nuance and more careful precision). When it comes to positive doctrinal statements, I agree with Molnar's affirmations that the three persons exist within relations that are inherent to God's being in a "*perichoresis* that nothing can disrupt" (p. 72), that God would have been triune *sans* creation and in no way is constituted by the divine economy, and that God's freely chosen actions in the economy of creation, redemption, and reconciliation accurately reveal who God is "inherently and eternally" — there is no God "behind the back of Jesus" somewhere.[100]

I agree with much of what Molnar says, but I do have a few questions and concerns (most of which are fairly minor). With respect to methodology, he follows Torrance in the assertion that we must simply "suspend our thought" (p. 74) at certain points. This bold claim is not explained, and in the absence of such explanation we are left to wonder exactly what this means as well as why we should think this. There is an important distinction between claims of *ineffability* (understood either as the claim that God cannot be known or as the claim that none of our concepts can apply to God) and *incomprehensibility* (where this is understood as mere recognition that finite creatures will not fully understand an infinite Creator). The latter should not even be controversial, but the former is problematic (among other problems, it is self-referentially incoherent). Sometimes "ineffability" is used merely as a synonym for "incomprehensibility"; this further muddies the waters. From what Molnar says, however, we don't know enough to know what he means. Moreover, it is fairly easy to say that theology should originate from a center in the triune God (rather than from a center in us), and it is also fairly easy to charge other views with failing to start from the proper center. It is somewhat harder to demonstrate that other views have in fact failed to do so, and it is perhaps somewhat harder yet to ensure that this is not happening with one's own favored theological formulation. It strikes me that this is something that should be a concern to all of us, and that we would do well to proceed prayerfully, carefully, and charitably here.

Molnar is critical of "social and relational" views. Much of what he says here is commendable, and (speaking as one who accepts the editor's label of "relational" for this exercise) I agree with some of his criticisms. There is, however, some critical ambiguity here. On one hand, Molnar seems leery of the kind of "relational trinitarianism" that I am defending. But on the other hand, Molnar does not deny the mutual love of the divine persons. With the tradition (and, I am convinced, with the angels!), Torrance insists that there is mutual love within the Trinity: "This is what the doctrine of the Holy Trinity supremely means, that God himself is Love ... for God's Being is an eternal movement in

---

100. Molnar and I are also together in agreement with Lewis Ayres's summary of "pro-Nicene" theology (e.g., p. 73 n19).

Love, and consists in the Love with which the Father, the Son and the Holy Spirit ceaselessly love one another."[101] I take it that Molnar would agree with Torrance here (as he does elsewhere). And he would do so for good reason — after all, Scripture itself plainly attests to this love (e.g., John 17:23–24). But is it possible to have mutual love without having mutual lovers? What, exactly, would be the problem with affirming that the Father can say "I love the Son"? Cannot the Son say to the Father, "I love you" and "you love me"? If so, then do we not have "I-Thou" relationality within the immanent Trinity? Indeed, is not this implied by what Molnar himself believes?

I do wonder what is distinctly "Catholic" about Molnar's essay (or even what makes his view more deserving of the label "classical," especially since he does not deal with any medieval developments, and even his reading of patristic theology relies so heavily on Torrance). It seems "catholic" enough, but it is hard to see anything that is unique to (Roman) "Catholic" theology. When discussing the most notable issue that has separated Orthodoxy from Catholicism (and from much traditional Protestant theology), Molnar says that "there is no need even to raise the question of the *filioque* at all" (p. 85). It may, of course, turn out that Molnar is right to follow Torrance in an effort to find a third way beyond the impasse, but he doesn't look all that "Catholic" here. Instead, it looks to me as though he is saying that *both* the Latin and Eastern traditions were wrong. This is only an observation (rather than a criticism), but it does make me wonder.

Despite these qualms and questions, it seems to me that Molnar's account is close to mine in some important ways. He is committed to creedally orthodox formulations of the doctrine. Molnar appears to believe that the Father and Son love one another within the triune life; their love for each other is supremely and maximally strong, and while it does not depend on us for its actuality, the love of the Father for the Son is the same love as the love that is extended to us by the incarnate Son and the Holy Spirit. He is convinced that the triune nature of God matters more than anything else in this world or any other, and on all these points we are fully agreed.

---

101. Torrance, *The Christian Doctrine of God* 1996), 162–63.

PAUL S. FIDDES

Paul Molnar most helpfully offers us a checklist of five ingredients of what he takes to be vital for the classical doctrine of the Trinity, expanding the classic formula of the triune God as we have received it from the bishops gathered at the Synod of Constantinople, namely, that God is "one divine substance in three persons." Four of the propositions he offers (p. 72) seem to me to be inherent to any approach to the Trinity as it has been held in the church in all ages, and I am grateful for the clarity with which Molnar has set them out.

One clause, however, is—I suggest—more contentious and is not necessarily entailed by the other four. That is, "that God is in no way ... constituted by what he does for us within the economy since all of God's actions *ad extra* are sovereign acts of grace expressing God's eternal love for us." If this is taken to mean that God is not constituted as *God* in three persons by God's work in creation, this is surely uncontentious. But if it is taken to mean that God is not in any way affected, shaped, or conditioned by activity in the created world, I want to suggest that this proposition is not inherent to a doctrine of the Trinity. It certainly blocks the kind of development of trinitarian theology that I am myself commending. Like Steve Holmes in his chapter, and ultimately Aquinas, Molnar here equates the "simplicity" of God with being totally unconditioned and unaffected by anything outside God

Molnar seems to recognize in a significant footnote (p. 81 n49) that some theologians have proposed holding together a theology of the sovereign grace of God with some dependence of God on human history for the "development" of the divine being, by affirming that God has, in God's own self, freely desired and chosen to be conditioned by the created world. He quotes Wolfhart Pannenberg to this effect (p. 72 n12), and among these theologians I would number myself. He rules this approach out on the grounds that it denies "God's free sovereign acts of grace" in history. However, he seems to be criticizing a theological model that makes God's very *existence* dependent on history. It is surely possible to maintain the self-existence (aseity) of God, *creatio ex nihilo*, and the power of God to take saving initiatives in history, while affirming that God adapts divine purposes to the response that God receives from creation. This implies that ongoing creativity is cooperative and God, by God's own desire, needs this creaturely cooperation for certain purposes to be fulfilled. It means that God can be self-existent while choosing not to be entirely self-sufficient. This is the kind of reciprocal model of God's activity in the world that is indicated by "panentheism" ("everything in God"), to which I will return in a moment.

A related conclusion that Molnar draws from his principles of classical trinitarianism similarly seems to me to be less than necessary. This is the proposition that human experiences of relationship can contribute *nothing* at all to our understanding of God. He rejects the social analogy of the Trinity because it "takes the human experience of life-in-relationship as the best clue to an understanding of the triune life of God" (p. 71), whereas we can know nothing of God that God does not reveal to us. Now, if this is a critique of social trinitarianism in which the intense relations of three centers of consciousness supposedly constitute the one God, so that God is a remarkable instance of "community" rather than "communion" (*koinonia*), I am entirely in sympathy with him. This idea merely conforms the uncreated God to created reality, makes God in our image, and undermines the divine ineffability. But he extends his critique to *any* theology in which the relations of created beings offer a valid way of talking about God. This would rule out my own "relational" approach, where I suggest that it is not human individual persons but relations between them, in all their diversity and depth, that offers a helpful analogy to what we call divine "persons." The quality of relations between parent and child, husband and wife, teacher and pupil, men and women, and members in the church can all, for example, enable us not just to talk about God but to discover places in everyday life where divine relations of love can be experienced.

Molnar appears to make his absolute critique for two reasons. First, he thinks that any contribution from human experience to an understanding of God begins from a "center in ourselves," rather than from the divine center of God's revelation, and this ends up as human self-justification. He assumes that reflection on human experience is being claimed as the *starting point* for knowing God, arguing rightly that a truly trinitarian theology always begins from God's own self-disclosure as Father, Son, and Holy Spirit. But it is surely possible to agree that there can be no knowledge of God by human beings unless God takes the initiative in self-revelation, while at the same time thinking that the experience of human life as created and indwelt by God can help us, with the inspiration of the Holy Spirit, to form concepts to express and understand the self-gifting of God. This is the kind of distinction that Karl Rahner makes between "transcendental revelation" (the self-opening of God) and "categorical revelation" (the inspired human activity of making concepts to respond to this revelation). Molnar himself seems to recognize the validity of this approach when he comments that Gregory of Nyssa believed that the relation of the three persons "cannot be read off from human experience apart from revelation" (p. 75); the qualification "apart from" surely concedes that human experience has a part to play within the context of revelation.

Second, Molnar rules out any analogies from the human sphere because he regards the terms "Father, Son, and Holy Spirit," and the relations between them, as purely revealed without any human contribution or cooperation involved. So he declares, God "is" the eternal Father, Son, and Holy Spirit; he (Molnar's use of gender) "is" a Trinity of persons and not "like" a Trinity of persons, or "like" a threefoldness of relations. Molnar does not, as does Steve Holmes, restrict the revealed relations to relations of origin, and implies that there is more to be said about the revealed relations of love between Father, Son, and Spirit than begetting and procession. However, these names and relations are to be sharply distinguished from any analogies drawn from the human sphere, which are merely a "symbolic" thinking about what "we take to be our relationship to God" projected onto God. At first he distinguishes between a "conceptual" thinking about God and a "symbolic" thinking, the first revealed and the second imagined, but he then criticizes "*conceptualizing* God using any number of notions" drawn from human experience; so perhaps he is actually distinguishing between a small class of revealed concepts and a larger group of invented concepts.

However, all concepts about God are surely symbolic, not univocal descriptions of God. While Molnar writes of "God's own self-revelation in his Word and Spirit" (p. 83), the very terms "Father, Son, and Spirit" are drawn from human experience, as is the term "word." Karl Barth, the most vigorous defender in modern times of the necessity of divine self-revelation for knowing God, transgresses Molnar's dictum that God is not "like" Trinity by affirming that "in this one God there is ... let us put it cautiously, something like fatherhood and sonship" (*CD* I/1, §9). Molnar quotes Barth as saying that "we cannot say anything higher or better of the 'inwardness of God' than that God is Father, Son, and Holy Spirit, and therefore that he is love in Himself" (p. 81). The affirmation that we can say nothing "better" is precisely about appropriateness of language to express the mystery of God, not a univocal sameness between the word and the reality.

Moreover, while Molnar denies that the eternal generation of the Son has *any* similarity to human generation, Barth rejoices that "begotten" here is "a figure of speech from the creaturely realm," meaning that Jesus Christ "in an eminent sense ... has come into being as all living things in creation have come into being ... as the worm has come into being ... as man comes into being" (*CD* I/1, §11). We must surely agree with Molnar that thinking about the meaning of the relation of the Creator to the created begins with the Father-Son relationship in God, and so with an "analogy of faith," without denying that the very language of Father and Son is a human formulation. Molnar seems to be reflecting Barth's dictum here that God as Father of Jesus Christ precedes the notion of God as Creator, but as Barth also affirms, "revelation seizes the language."

Revelation, we may say, is not the direct disclosing of propositions but the self-opening of God in Christ, which calls out and enables a new response from users of human words. The concepts and propositions themselves come from the created realm, however strangely they are being used. As we think of Christ as the eternal "Word" of God (John 1:1), we recall that the early church fathers moved toward formulating a doctrine of the Trinity by an imaginative playing with an analogy, the relation between a word "immanent" in the human mind and a word "expressed" from the mind.

The question then is not which concepts are revealed and which are human inventions, but what impact revelation is having on human words, and which human words are more appropriate than others for responding to the self-offering of God. Analogy is about likeness *and* unlikeness. The generation of the Son according to Athanasius is both *like* a human begetting because it is "from the very being" of the Father (against Arius, *gennetos* signifies not merely a making but a "natural" begetting), and it is *unlike* human begetting because it is not by the will of the Father (again against Arius). My own proposal is that language of human relations is appropriate for speaking about God and for understanding the reality of God given to us by God's own gift, but that language of human individual persons is not.

This brings us to Molnar's objection to any kind of "panentheism," which he sees as all of a piece with language about God centered on ourselves. The kind of "panentheism" I am commending is the belief that all relations, human and in the natural world, are held within the flowing and interweaving relationships of the Trinity; as God makes room within God's self for the world, so in God "we live and move and have our being" (Acts 17:28). The affirmation that everything is *in* God (panentheism) is by no means simply the same as pantheism (everything *as* God). Molnar's judgment that "in reality panentheism never escapes the dilemma of pantheism" (p. 89) seems little more than an assertion. He is right that all forms of panentheism "require that in some sense God's eternal being is dependent on the development of history," but wrong to conclude the sentence with, "for [his] own existence," which would certainly end in pantheism. As I have suggested, we can conceive of God as desiring that creation should contribute to God's satisfaction, bliss, and fulfillment of purposes, without supposing that God's existence is dependent on anything but God's self. Thus, I am completely sympathetic to his protest about confusion of the Holy Spirit with the human spirit, but want to say much more about the intimate intertwining of the two which the apostle Paul envisages (Rom 8:27; 1 Cor 2:10–13).

With Colin Gunton, who comes in for a good deal of criticism by Molnar, I want to affirm that the eternal relations of the persons constitute the "substance" of God; at the same time I think that this makes most sense when the persons are identical with relations (a position that Gunton himself rejected). It is in these triune relations that we participate as we live in our own relationships. The Logos is *asarkos* ("not-in-flesh") as well as *ensarkos* ("in-flesh"), as Molnar stresses, but in the sense that divine relations of giving and receiving in love are always inexhaustibly "more," always deeper and richer than we can know in our experience.

REJOINDER COMMENTS AND CLARIFICATION

PAUL D. MOLNAR

I will begin by addressing Steve Holmes's concerns. He seems to think that I was basing the church doctrine of the Trinity on one scriptural proof text, namely, Matthew 28:19. Nothing could have been further from my intentions as I believe the basis of the doctrine is the revelation of God attested in Scripture. The reason I mentioned that text was to stress how problematic it is when theologians confuse Christ with the church. He apparently confirmed his judgment by noting my reference to the baptismal formula with respect to my explanation of why Athanasius rejected the idea that the Spirit could be understood as brother of the Son, or grandson of the Father. The point was that one could not mythologically project limited human experiences into the Godhead without distorting who God really was and is. Further, it is a drastic oversimplification to assert that for me revelation is no more and no less or other than what T. F. Torrance taught. Torrance speaks for many because he was instrumental in drawing up the joint statement of agreement on the doctrine of the Trinity endorsed by Reformed and Orthodox theologians in 1991, with which I believe many Roman Catholics would agree.

With respect to creation being in the mind of God before he created, but not eternally in God's mind, I wanted to emphasize the priority of the Father/Son relation over the Creator/creature relation. This raises the issue of God's time and our time, which would need to be addressed in that context.[102] Also, I intended to argue that the procession of the Spirit from the being of the Father should be governed by the Nicene Council's statement that the Son is from the being of the Father in order to avoid any idea of a "derived" deity. Is it necessarily the case that the

---

102. See, e.g., Paul D. Molnar, *Thomas F. Torrance: Theologian of the Trinity* (Farnham, UK/ Burlington, VT: Ashgate, 2009), 253–59.

Spirit would proceed from himself if one holds that the Spirit proceeds from the being of the Father? Only if one confused the order of the persons with their being. The being of the Father is the same as that of the Spirit; but the Spirit eternally proceeds from the Father through the Son.

Let me address some of Tom McCall's concerns. First, my essay was supposed to offer a contrast between classical trinitarian theology, which developed during the patristic era, and social trinitarian thinking. Hence, I needed to state what I affirmed and rejected. I did not deal with medieval developments since I restricted my considerations to classical and contemporary views. Regarding the *filioque*, McCall seems unfamiliar with the fact that Yves Congar argued that the *filioque* was inappropriately added to the Creed by Western theologians.[103] I simply observed that if we followed Athanasius's thinking, then the issues that led to the perceived need for the *filioque* never would have arisen.

Second, McCall says I do not explain what it means to "suspend our thought" (p. 74). I explicitly stated, following Augustine, Barth, and Torrance, that I meant that we could not delimit the persons of the Trinity from one another and could not explain the *how* of the processions or *how* God could be one being, three persons. I was rejecting any rationalistic attempt to intrude into the divine being. I never claimed, as McCall assumes, that God cannot be known or that none of our concepts apply to God, but that God could only be known accurately from revelation *through* our concepts.

Third, McCall said that while it is easy to say we must think from a center in God and to charge others with failing to do so, it is harder to demonstrate this. Certainly, while I am not immune from this problem, it is easy to demonstrate when one fails to think from a center in God. The obvious indication is the attempt to understand the trinitarian relations from social psychology, history, or anthropology apart from faith in Jesus Christ. I demonstrated that by describing the thinking of those who, by not consistently thinking within faith, espoused a "dependent" deity. Finally, one might speak of an I and Thou within the Trinity, but not by obviating the divine simplicity as I believe McCall does.[104]

---

103. See Paul D. Molnar, "Theological Issues Involved in the *Filioque*," in *Ecumenical Perspectives on the* Filioque *for the 21st Century* (ed. Myk Habets; New York: Bloomsbury/T&T Clark, 2014), 20–39.

104. See, e.g., Karl Barth, *CD* III/2, 218–19.

Finally, let me address some of Paul Fiddes's concerns. First, he agrees that God is not constituted as *God* by acting as Creator, but claims this cannot mean that God is unaffected by creation. We agree that God is affected by creation since God is compassionate and merciful and takes the pain and suffering of sinful creatures upon himself in the incarnation, suffering, and death of Jesus in order to relieve our distress. But this is an act of grace, which cannot imply, as Fiddes suggests, that God is "shaped, or conditioned by activity in the created world" (p. 104). There is no mutual conditioning relationship between God and creation as proposed in all "panentheistic" conceptualizations of the God/world relation. The problem with panentheism, which Barth regarded as worse than pantheism,[105] is its claim that God is in some sense dependent on the world to enact his love for us. This undermines the sovereignty of God's grace and love. A dependent deity is surreptitiously identical with the world, and only so could God be said to need the cooperation of creatures to achieve his saving acts.

The difference between Fiddes and me concerns whether one can detach revelation in any respect from God's actions in his Word and Spirit. Fiddes believes he can. Rejecting this, I disallow nonobjective knowledge of God and Karl Rahner's notion of transcendental revelation — both concepts detach revelation from Jesus Christ and locate this in our experience of ourselves. Also, Fiddes says that Barth believes that God is *like* Trinity, but discounts Barth's point, namely, that while we use our terms *father* and *son* to speak of God, this language is "figurative" only as our language and not with respect to its object. Thus, these are not "freely chosen symbols" because "it is in God that the father-son relation, like all creaturely relations, has its original and proper reality."[106]

I sincerely thank my esteemed colleagues for their careful responses to my essay.

---

105. *CD* II/1, 312.
106. *CD* I/1, 432.

CHAPTER THREE

RELATIONAL TRINITY: CREEDAL PERSPECTIVE

THOMAS H. MCCALL[1]

Introduction

Orthodox Christians everywhere affirm the doctrine of the Trinity: there is one God, and there are three divine persons. But sometimes they disagree about some of the higher-resolution details of the doctrine. In this essay, I will argue that the divine persons of the Trinity are really and robustly distinct, that they are fully and thus equally divine, and that there is exactly one God. More specifically, I will argue for a *relational* understanding of the doctrine; by "relational" I mean that the Father, Son, and Holy Spirit live within a necessary relationship of mutual holy love (I *don't* mean that the triune God is necessarily related to creation).

A great deal of recent work in the development of trinitarian doctrine has gone the way of Karl Rahner and Karl Barth in holding to numerical sameness while also emphasizing a single divine subjectivity.[2] Many other recent theologians have followed the way of Jürgen Moltmann, Leonardo Boff, and others in emphasizing the distinction of the persons—but then rejecting numerical sameness. I offer something different from either of these—something that is, I think, much older and perhaps much stranger: I am convinced that we should affirm that the divine persons are really and relationally distinct while also affirming numerical sameness.

---

1. I wish to thank James R. Gordon, Shawn Graves, Aaron James, Adam Johnson, Michael Pahl, Ryan Peterson, Carl Smith, Doug Sweeney, Elizabeth Sung, Alan J. Torrance, and Kevin J. Vanhoozer for their helpful comments on an earlier draft of this essay.

2. At least the Karl Barth of *CD* I/1. I leave aside considerations of development (and coherence) of his theology.

Trinitarian Methodology

But first things first: I should lay my methodological cards on the table. While I cannot offer anything approaching a rigorous argument for any particular theological method in the short space of this essay, I can make my commitments explicit.

I believe that Scripture is finally and supremely authoritative in theology. If we know anything about God and God's works, it is only because God reveals to us something of himself and his ways. I take the Bible to be the inspired and authoritative witness to the self-revelation of God that culminates in Christ (indeed, there is an important sense in which we can affirm that the Bible *is* revelation).[3] As such, it is the "norming norm" (*norma normans*) that is authoritative above any other sources of authority and thus able to guide and correct our theological endeavors. As Oliver Crisp puts it, the Bible is the "final arbiter of matters theological for Christians as the particular place in which God reveals himself to his people," and the "first order authority in all matters of Christian doctrine."[4]

Scripture is never interpreted in a vacuum, however, and the Christian tradition is indispensable in good interpretation of divine revelation. As I see things, theological proposals should be in alignment with the major ecumenical creeds. This definitively rules out any views deemed heretical, such as all forms of modalism, Arianism, and other versions of subordinationism as well as all forms of polytheism. These creeds are a doctrinal authority as a "norm" that is "normed" (*norma normata*) by Holy Scripture, from which they derive authority. The confessions of particular ecclesial bodies are a third tier of authority (standing under the creeds and ultimately under Scripture). Beyond this, the work of the great theologians of the church catholic deserves our deep respect (while not being binding in the same way as creedal statements).

Here it is important for systematic theologians to listen carefully to the work of specialists in historical theology. While I do not believe that a constructive or systematic theologian earns a license to appeal to

---

3. For more on this point, see Thomas H. McCall, "On Understanding Scripture as the Word of God," in *Analytic Theology: New Essays in the Philosophy of Theology* (ed. Michael C. Rea and Oliver D. Crisp; Oxford: Oxford University Press, 2009), 171–86.

4. Oliver D. Crisp, *God Incarnate: Explorations in Christology* (New York: T&T Clark, 2009), 17.

some figure from the tradition only when she is actively adding to the scholarly literature on that figure, neither is the responsible theologian at liberty merely to trawl through the waters of Christian history hoping to net various quotations that can then be pressed into service. A better way forward, it seems, is for the theologian who hopes to appeal to the tradition to engage not only the relevant texts themselves (in translation where available but also, where appropriate, in the language in which the texts were originally composed) but also the pertinent scholarship.

When dealing with the doctrine of the Trinity, it is especially important to recognize that there is a both a stable core of trinitarian orthodoxy as well as some truly remarkable differences.[5] This core can be found in the ecumenical creeds, while the divergent perspectives can be seen not only in such obvious cases as the split between East and West over the *filioque* but also within, say, late medieval Latin formulations of the doctrine or the best definition for "person" in medieval trinitarian theology.[6] And at any rate, my goal is consistency with orthodoxy — not mere repetition of some particular theologian or school of thought.

Engagement with the Christian tradition reminds us that the use of reason is unavoidable in theology, and it also illustrates for us the reality that religious experience is a key element of theological construction. It is at this point that the tools of "analytic theology" are especially helpful. As I have argued elsewhere, use of the analytic tools does not entail commitment to a univocal view of religious language; to the contrary, the vast majority (perhaps all) of our language for God is analogical *at best*.[7] Nor does use of analytic theology imply that philosophical issues are the only ones that matter. To the contrary: theological desiderata first, metaphysical "fit" second.

---

5. We should be careful to avoid the deeply mistaken overgeneralizations that are still depressingly common in discussions of the history of the doctrine — with the tired old "Cappadocian vs. Augustinian" account being the chief of sinners in this respect.

6. For a helpful overview, see Richard A. Muller, *Post-Reformation Reformed Dogmatics: The Rise and Development of Reformed Orthodoxy, ca. 1520 – ca. 1725*; vol. 4: *The Triunity of God* (2nd ed.; Grand Rapids: Baker, 2003), 17 – 58.

7. Thomas H. McCall, "Theologians, Philosophers, and the Doctrine of the Trinity," in *Philosophical and Theological Essays on the Trinity* (ed. Thomas McCall and Michael C. Rea; Oxford: Oxford University Press, 2009), 341. For recent work in defense of univocity, see William P. Alston, *Divine Nature and Human Language: Essays in Philosophical Theology* (Ithaca, NY: Cornell University Press, 1989), 17 – 117; Richard Cross, "Where Angels Fear to Tread: Duns Scotus and Radical Orthodoxy," *Antonianum* 76 (2001): 1 – 36; and Thomas Williams, "The Doctrine of Univocity is True and Salutary," *MT* 21 (2005): 575 – 85.

Trinitarian Doctrine

Some Important Affirmations: An Initial Statement

Working from these theological sources, I am convinced that the doctrine of the Trinity has been divinely revealed and indeed is true. Although the doctrine is nowhere formally stated in Scripture (it isn't as though the Niceno-Constantinopolitan formula is embedded in some secret code in the text of the Bible), Scripture witnesses in multiple ways both to the personal distinctions and to the full divinity of the Father, Son, and Holy Spirit. When this witness is seen in light of the unwavering biblical commitment to monotheism, the creedal statements of the doctrine of the Trinity emerge. As David S. Yeago puts it, "the ancient theologians were right to hold that the Nicene *homoousion* is neither imposed *on* the New Testament texts, nor distantly deduced *from* the texts, but rather describes a pattern of judgments present *in* the texts, in the texture of scriptural discourse concerning Jesus and the God of Israel."[8] Or as C. Kavin Rowe concludes, there is an *"exegetical necessity"* to the doctrine of the Trinity, because "there is an organic continuity between the biblical testimony and the early creeds, and that the creeds can serve as hermeneutical guidelines to reading the Bible because it is in fact the biblical text itself that necessitated the creedal formulations."[9]

To summarize, I believe that divine revelation reveals that there is exactly one God who exists necessarily and who exists necessarily as triune; the Father, the Son, and the Holy Spirit are three fully divine persons who live in a perichoretic communion of holy love. By "fully divine" I mean that the divine persons are *homoousios*; each divine person has the complete divine essence and enjoys ontological equality with the other divine persons. By "divine persons" I mean necessarily existent entities who enjoy "I-Thou" relationships within the triune life. By "one God" I intend a wholehearted commitment to monotheism: there is exactly one God, and this one God exists as three persons. But I am aware that Christians sometimes disagree about exactly what this

---

8. David S. Yeago, "The New Testament and the Nicene Dogma: A Contribution to Recovery of Theological Exegesis," in *The Theological Interpretation of Scripture: Classic and Contemporary Readings* (ed. Stephen E. Fowl; Oxford: Blackwell, 1997), 88 (italics in original).

9. C. Kavin Rowe, "Luke and the Trinity: An Essay in Ecclesial Biblical Theology," *SJT* 56 (2003): 4 (italics in original).

means, so let me be more specific. In what follows I focus primarily on issues related to divine personhood (the "threeness issue") and issues related to monotheism (the "oneness issue").

The Divine Persons Are Really Distinct

I understand the divine persons to be "persons" in a rich and robust sense of the term. The divine persons are fully personal in the sense that they exist together as what may be called distinct speech-agents in what are sometimes referred to as "I-Thou relationships," and they exist only within their mutual relationships. Peter van Inwagen puts it well when he points out that "persons are those things to which personal pronouns are applicable: a person can use the word 'I' and be addressed as 'thou.'"[10] So even though there are important differences between divine and human personhood, I will argue that we should conclude that there are genuine interpersonal, "I-Thou" relationships within the triune life.

Some critics may worry that this just seems too anthropomorphic. Is this not simply another instance of using a human term, one loaded up with a distinctly modern understanding, and using it uncritically and univocally of God? Such critics do raise some legitimate worries, for surely it is all too easy to assume that we already "know" what "persons" are, and then conclude that the divine persons must fit our preconceptions and be just like human persons. While I cannot see how any presumptions of univocity are actually entailed here, or that problematic anthropomorphism is inevitable, the worry raises some important warnings. So we must do our best to proceed with a properly biblical and theological understanding of the divine persons. In other words, we should let divine revelation shape (and perhaps reshape) our understanding of divine personhood.

So what do we find when we look to the New Testament portrayals of the divine persons? We see the divine persons depicted in "I-Thou" relationships with one another (as well as with created agents).[11] Although a full consideration of the biblical witness to this is beyond the scope of this essay (and would be pedantic and unnecessary at any rate), consider

---

10. Peter van Inwagen, *God, Knowledge, and Mystery: Essays in Philosophical Theology* (Ithaca, NY: Cornell University Press, 1995), 265–67.

11. This summary draws heavily from Allan Coppedge, *The God Who Is Triune: Revisioning the Christian Doctrine of God* (Downers Grove, IL: InterVarsity Press, 2007), 26–33.

as examples these accounts of the relationship between the Father and the Son. The Gospels are replete with language reflecting robustly inter-personal relationships between Father and Son. Jesus' birth and child-hood fulfill the prophecy of Hosea 11:1: "Out of Egypt I called my son" (Matt 2:15), and thus the earthly ministry of the incarnate Son begins with such a depiction. At Jesus' baptism, his Father refers to him as one who is clearly distinct: "This is my Son, whom I love" (3:17). Jesus refers to his relationship with his Father—sometimes called his *Abba*—in the deepest relational terms (e.g., 7:21; 10:32–33; 12:50; 18:10; 20:23; 25:34; 26:29–42; Mark 14:36). Jesus coordinates his work with that of his Father (e.g., John 5:17–18; 6:27–40), and the prayers of Jesus can only be understood as reflective of a deeply intimate "I-Thou" relationship. The voice of the Father thunders forth at the transfiguration of Jesus: "This is my Son, whom I love" (Mark 9:7). The life of the crucified Jesus ends with his cry to his Father (Luke 23:46), and his ascension is to his Father.

Or consider these depictions of the relationship between the Father and the Spirit. Jesus promises that the Holy Spirit will come (John 14:16), and this is fulfilled "what my Father has promised" (Luke 24:48–49) at Pentecost (Acts 1–2). Paul echoes these themes; he closely relates the Father and the Spirit but without confusing them (e.g., Rom 5:5; 8:14–16; 1 Cor 2:4–5, 10–14; 3:16; 6:19; 14:2; 2 Cor. 5:5; Eph 6:17; 1 Thess 4:8).

The situation is similar with respect to the relationship of the Son and the Spirit. The Holy Spirit is the agent of the virginal conception of Jesus (Matt 1:18–20; Luke 1:35). The Spirit is present at the baptism of Jesus (Matt 3:17; Mark 1:9). The Spirit leads Jesus into the wilderness and sustains him there (Matt 4:1; Luke 4:1–14), and Jesus teaches and ministers in the Spirit's power (e.g., Luke 4:18; cf. Isa 61:1–2; 10:21–24; 11:13, 20; John 3:3–8; 7:37–39). Jesus promises the Spirit will be another Paraclete (John 14:16) and that he will send the Spirit from the Father (15:26). Paul also closely relates the Son and Holy Spirit (e.g., Rom 8:2; 9:1; 2 Cor. 3:17–18; Gal 3:14; 5:5–6, 22–24; Eph 1:13–14; 3:5–6; 1 Pet 1:11), but never in such a way that they are confused.[12]

Such considerations provide straightforward biblical support for a robustly relational view of divine personhood. Perhaps a critic will

---

12. See Gordon Fee, *Pauline Christology: An Exegetical-Theological Study* (Peabody, MA: Hendrickson, 2007), 586–93.

object to the above account on the ground that it is insufficiently chris-tological. More precisely, the objector might claim that this data refers to the *incarnate* Son in relation to the other divine persons. She might say that such an account of robust distinction should be understood as referring to the will of the *incarnate* Son; when Jesus says "not my will, but yours be done" (Luke 22:42), any distinction of will is to be attrib-uted to the *human* will of Christ.

Perhaps we should interpret the Gethsemane prayer in just this way (this is a deeply traditional move, and I have no objection to doing so), but I doubt that such a strategy can work to undermine my case for robust personal distinction. Do the biblical accounts of personal related-ness (in the sense of "I-Thou" relationships) refer only to the *incarnate* Son (and thus perhaps to the person of the Son *qua* human nature)? No, for at least three reasons. First, it does nothing to account for the robustly personal distinction of the Father and the Holy Spirit. As we have seen, the biblical account includes not only witness to the distinction of the Son from the Father, but it also reveals the distinction of the Holy Spirit in relation to the Father and the Son. Of course, since the Holy Spirit is not incarnate, this distinction cannot be ascribed to the humanity of the Spirit. And it is *the Father* who refers to his "beloved Son."

Second, while it is true that much of the biblical data refers to the economic Trinity, for this distinction to be real in the economy there must be robust distinction within the immanent Trinity.[13] The Son became incarnate—the Logos became human—by humbling himself and taking on himself the form of a servant (Phil 2:5–11; cf. John 1:1–18). *Someone* emptied himself and became incarnate, and this someone is the one who was already fully divine and with his Father. He did not become a distinct someone by becoming incarnate; he was already a "someone" who became incarnate. As Simon Gathercole observes, the Son "*acts* to take on human existence: though in the form of God, he *empties* himself to become a servant (v. 7)."[14]

---

13. This should not be confused with "Rahner's Rule" (that the immanent Trinity *is* the economic Trinity and vice versa), on which see Randal Rauser, "Rahner's Rule: An Emperor without Clothes?" *IJST* 7 (2005): 81–94, and Scott Harrower, *Trinitarian Self and Salvation: An Evangelical Engagement with Rahner's Rule* (Eugene, OR: Pickwick, 2012).

14. Simon Gathercole, *The Preexistent Son: Recovering the Christologies of Matthew, Mark, and Luke* (Grand Rapids: Eerdmans, 2006), 290 (italics in original).

Finally, what we do know of the immanent Trinity and the intra-trinitarian life from Scripture supports my claims. For instance, when Psalm 2:7 is interpreted traditionally (as a reference to the eternal generation of the Son and thus to the "immanent Trinity"), the use of personal indexicals clearly shows a robustly interpersonal relationship between the Father and Son: "*You are my Son.*" Similarly, John's Prologue testifies to preexistence that is not only real (the Logos is both God and "with" God) but also personal; that is, the preexistent Logos has an identity that is distinct, and it is distinct enough that the Logos and only the Logos "became flesh" (John 1:1, 14). In Jesus' famous prayer in John 17, he refers to the mutual glorification of the Father and Son that "I had with you before the world began" (17:5). What is this if not an "I-Thou" relation within the Trinity before (or *sans*) incarnation? Moreover, Paul tells us that the Holy Spirit "intercedes" for us (Rom 8:26). What is this if not intra-trinitarian communication?

Critics may, however, yet complain that the picture just sketched reflects a naive and modern reading of Scripture; they may worry that it is not adequately engaged with the history of theological interpretation of Scripture. "Look," they may say, "you are uncritically importing a problematic modern notion of personhood into the interpretation of the Bible." So let us look at some important affirmations made by theologians from the broad Christian tradition.

Let us begin with what is explicit and universal in the theology of pro-Nicene theologians. First, all theologians who are committed to (developing) orthodoxy agree that the divine persons are *distinct in action* in the economy of creation and redemption. This claim must not be misunderstood; I am not suggesting that we think of the divine persons as mere teammates, colleagues, or buddies. Khaled Anatolios offers a helpful clarification of Gregory of Nyssa's understanding: "Human co-activity and divine co-activity are radically and structurally different. When human beings cooperate, 'each one acts separately and by himself.'"[15] Divine activity, by contrast, "originates in the Father, proceeds through the Son, and is completed in the Holy Spirit" and is thus more deeply unified.[16] Indeed, it is so unified that there is a sense in which it

---

15. Khaled Anatolios, *Retrieving Nicaea: The Development and Meaning of Trinitarian Doctrine* (Grand Rapids: Baker, 2011), 231.
16. Ibid.

should be understood as one action. Nonetheless, there is an irreducible distinction in divine action as well, since "the notion of an altogether undifferentiated agency in which each of the persons partakes in exactly the same manner is also implicitly but very clearly ruled out."[17]

The work of creation is thus typically said to be the work of the triune God that reaches its *terminus* on the Father—and in this sense is said to be the special work of the Father. The Father sends the Son to be incarnate for the salvation of the world. The Father says—and *only* the Father says—"this is my beloved Son." The work of redemption and satisfaction is the work of the triune God that reaches its *terminus* on the Son—and in this sense is the unique work of the Son. Only the Son becomes incarnate. Only the Son suffers under Pontius Pilate and is crucified, dies, and is buried. Only the Son rises from death on the third day, and only the Son ascends to the right hand of the Father. Only the Holy Spirit is the agent of the virginal conception of Mary, only the Spirit descends in the form of a dove on the incarnate Son, and only the Spirit comes upon believers at Pentecost.

Traditional trinitarian theology has stoutly insisted that the works of the triune persons are never *divided*; to the contrary, the works of the Trinity are "always undivided" (*opera ad extra omnia sunt indivisa*). I fully agree with this traditional affirmation, but it need not (and it *should not*) be taken to imply that the agency of the divine persons in the economy is not genuinely distinct. To the contrary, we should agree with Maximus the Confessor that the Father and Holy Spirit "themselves did not become incarnate, but the Father approved and the Spirit cooperated when the Son himself effected his Incarnation."[18] The orthodox Christian tradition has agreed on these points universally and explicitly; indeed, they are woven into the fabric of the creeds themselves. Anything less was seen as a kind of modalism and accordingly was labeled as

---

17. Ibid.

18. Maximus the Confessor, *On the Lord's Prayer,* PG 90:876, quoted in Richard Swinburne, *The Christian God* (Oxford: Oxford University Press, 1994), 181 n7. Cf. John of Damascus: "the Father and the Holy Spirit take no part at all in the incarnation of the Word except in connection with the miracles, and in respect of good will and purpose" ("An Exact Exposition of the Orthodox Faith," III.11, in *NPNF²* 9:55). This is also a theme in medieval theology, e.g., Peter Lombard: "it was specifically in the hypostasis of the Son, not jointly in the three persons, that divine nature united the human one to itself," *Sentences, Book Three: On the Incarnation of the Word* (trans. Giulio Silano; Toronto: Pontifical Institute of Medieval Studies, 2008), 21 (PL 192:766).

heresy. One of the Trinity suffered in the flesh. The work of the triune God "outside of God" is always undivided, and in such a way that the divine persons operate distinctly in their relations to one another and to creation by the undivided divine power.

When we turn our attention to the "internal" works of God (the *opera ad intra*), however, the situation is much different. For the tradition, the works of the triune God *ad intra* or "on the inside" of the Trinity are (or can be) uniquely and completely the work of a particular divine person. As an example, consider the venerable doctrine of the eternal generation of the Son.[19] What we hear is a universal chorus:[20] *the Father* generates the Son, and *only the Father* generates the Son. To be clear: while the tradition of classical orthodoxy affirms that the *opera ad extra* are "always undivided," it has no similar affirmation about the *opera ad intra*. In point of fact, it denies that generation is an act of the divine essence or of all three persons, and takes such a denial to be part and parcel of Christian orthodoxy.[21] The person of the Father — and only the person of the Father — is rightly said to beget the Son.

So with respect to divine action in the economy, the works of the divine persons are always completely unified but nonetheless distinct in an important sense as well. Thus the Son becomes incarnate as he is sent by the Father and by the power of the Holy Spirit, but only the Son actually becomes incarnate. With respect to the works of the immanent Trinity, however, such works are uniquely and completely the work of one divine person. Thus the Father — and only the Father — generates the Son within the immanent Trinity. This much is explicit in the tradition of classical Christian orthodoxy, and it is universal within that tradition. What surely seems to be implied by what is explicit is this: the divine persons are distinct agents. If it is true that only the Son becomes incarnate, suffers, and dies under Pontius Pilate, then only the Son performs such actions and is the subject of these actions. Thus it

---

19. Criticisms of the doctrine of eternal generation are gaining strength, e.g., John S. Feinberg, *No One Like Him: The Doctrine of God* (Wheaton, IL: Crossway, 2001), 488–92. I think that such challenges deserve a serious hearing, but I am not convinced that they are decisive. Detailed discussion of the relevant issues is, however, beyond the scope of this essay.

20. It is universal with respect to the doctrine of eternal generation but not with respect to the doctrine of the procession of the Holy Spirit (as the debates over *filioque* illustrate).

21. Cf. the discussion of Peter Lombard and Thomas Aquinas by Gilles Emery, *Trinity in Aquinas* (Ypsilanti, MI: Ave Maria, 2003), 12, 191.

seems undeniable that the Son is a distinct agent—indeed, anything else would seem close to heresy. As William Lane Craig says:

> among the three persons of the Trinity there are three irreducible and exclusive first-person perspectives.... The Father knows, for example, that the Son dies on the cross, but He does not know and cannot know that He Himself dies on the cross—indeed, the view that He so knows even has the status of heresy: *patripassianism*.[22]

And if it is true that only the Father generates the Son, it is obvious and even platitudinous that only the Father performs such an action. Thus it seems undeniable that the personal agency of the Father is distinct in an important sense.

To summarize the argument thus far, I have argued that the broad tradition of classical, catholic orthodoxy sees the actions of the divine persons in both the economy of salvation and in the immanent Trinity as distinct. This much is both explicit and universal. I have argued further that it is not unreasonable to take what is explicit and universal to suggest that the divine persons are distinct agents (who interact with one another and with their creation). At the very least, my proposal is consistent with these emphases that were vital to Christian orthodoxy.

Indeed, some major theologians are explicit. While it is abundantly clear that modern notions of "centers of consciousness" are not central to the traditional understandings of "person," a closer look makes it fairly obvious that not all elements of relational views of divine personhood are foreign or antithetical to the views of some major theologians. The theology of Gregory of Nyssa has been the hotbed of controversy here, and it serves well as a case study of sorts. Sarah Coakley argues that Gregory was not a "social trinitarian," and she rightly notes that many claims made by social trinitarians about "the Cappadocians" (or, even worse, "the East") are unwarranted.[23] But her own claims (of a single divine subject) run too far in the other direction. Michel R. Barnes has argued that "personal relationship and consciousness are

---

22. William Lane Craig, "Does the Problem of Material Constitution Illuminate the Doctrine of the Trinity?" *Faith and Philosophy* 22 (2005): 83.

23. Sarah Coakley, "'Persons' in the 'Social' Doctrine of the Trinity: A Critique of the Current Analytic Discussion," in *The Trinity: An Interdisciplinary Symposium on the Trinity* (ed. Stephen T. Davis, Daniel Kendall, SJ, and Gerald O'Collins, SJ; Oxford: Oxford University Press, 1999), 123–44.

not important, substantial psychological concepts for Gregory," and he doubts that Gregory thinks of the divine persons as possessing separate wills.[24] But he argues that even though psychological notions are not *central* to Gregory, nonetheless Gregory "may indeed be said to have a psychology of the Individuals of the Trinity."[25] More specifically, for Gregory "what is at stake is not simply the 'separate reality' of the Holy Spirit, but the Spirit's status as what we would call a 'person': the Holy Spirit 'acts and says such and such things, and defines, and is grieved, and is angered.'"[26] Therefore, "there is reason to believe that he understood the need for stronger and clearer language on both the distinct and personal reality of the Spirit—language which made it clear that the Spirit *like the Son* was a psychological entity with a distinct existence."[27]

So on Barnes's reading, we should not import various modern notions of personhood (those derived from Descrates, Locke, and others) into patristic doctrines of the Trinity, but neither should we conclude that Gregory (and others) held to a view of single subjectivity. Similarly, Khaled Anatolios says that the divine persons display "distinct inflections of the one divine will" in Gregory's thought.[28] As he puts it,

> while Gregory clarifies elsewhere that there is one movement of will that encompasses divine being, he is equally clear ... that this one movement is appropriated by all three *hypostaseis* such that each becomes the subject of the divine will, agency, and power. This might not amount to "modern conceptions of personhood," but neither does it utterly exclude some of these conceptions.[29]

We could (if not constrained by space) examine further various other patristic, medieval, and Reformation/Post-Reformation accounts,

---

24. Michel R. Barnes, "Divine Unity and the Divided Self: Gregory of Nyssa's Trinitarian Theology in its Psychological Context," *MT* 18 (2002): 476.

25. Ibid., 487.

26. Ibid., 485.

27. Ibid. Cf. also Cornelius Plantinga Jr., "Gregory of Nyssa and the Social Analogy of the Trinity," *The Thomist* 50 (1986): 351–52.

28. Anatolios, *Retrieving Nicaea*, 220 n234. Anatolios offers gentle correction to Lewis Ayres here as well. For further discussion, see also Lucien Turcescu, *Gregory of Nyssa and the Concept of Divine Persons* (Oxford: Oxford University Press, 2005).

29. Anatolios, *Retrieving Nicaea*, 219–20. Richard Cross agrees that "Eastern and Western views of the divine essence are both consistent with social accounts of the Trinity" ("Two Models of the Trinity?" *HeyJ* 43 [2002]: 288).

where there is much that is consistent with what I have sketched here.[30] Scott Williams has identified a version of so-called "Latin Trinitarianism" according to which there are "three metaphysical agents."[31] Critics of the sort of robustly relational view that I am advocating will sometimes protest that the broad Christian tradition is a long way from the "Social Trinitarianism" of Moltmann, Boff, and others. Such critics are undoubtedly correct in this assessment, and we are indebted to the historians of doctrine who continue to drive home this point.[32]

But it should be clear as well that a deeply relational account of divine personhood is far from antithetical to orthodox trinitarian theology. On the contrary, such a relational view is consistent with orthodoxy. Does anyone in the tradition of orthodox Christian theology *deny* that the divine persons love one another? Karl Rahner is famous for his denial that the divine persons love one another; he exclaims that there is "properly no mutual love between the Father and Son, for this would presuppose two acts."[33] But here, as elsewhere, Rahner stands outside the mainstream catholic tradition. Even Thomas Aquinas, whose theology is often taken to be the "high water mark" of Latin scholasticism, agrees that the divine persons love one another.[34] "The Father and the

---

30. As an example (among many others), we could point to the Reformed doctrine of the *pactum salutis* (the covenant or contract between the divine persons for the salvation of the elect). This is, according to Richard A. Muller, based upon intra-trinitarian love: the Reformed "were very much in favor of describing the relation between the Father and the Son in the Godhead in terms of a mutual love" (*Post-Reformation Reformed Dogmatics*, vol. 4, *The Triunity of God*, 266). In turn, this doctrine earned scathing criticism from Karl Barth, precisely on the grounds that it entailed tritheism (*CD* IV/1, 65). Whatever we are to make of the notion of the *pactum salutis*, the historical point should be clear.

31. Scott Williams, "Indexicals and the Trinity: Two Non-Social Models," *Journal of Analytic Theology* 1 (2013): 84. He goes on to say that in "soft 'LT' [Latin Trinitarianism] each divine person is an agent," 87.

32. Among the most helpful critics are Lewis Ayres, *Nicaea and Its Legacy: An Approach to Fourth-Century Trinitarian Theology* (Oxford: Oxford University Press, 2004); Richard A. Muller, *Post-Reformation Reformed Dogmatics*, vol. 4; and Stephen R. Holmes, *The Quest for the Trinity: The Doctrine of God in Scripture, History and Modernity* (Downers Grove, IL: InterVarsity Press, 2012).

33. Karl Rahner, *The Trinity* (trans. Joseph Donceel with an introduction by Catherine Mowry LaCugna; New York: Crossroad, 1997), 106.

34. Cf. Emery, *Trinity in Aquinas*, 155, 216–17. Elsewhere, Emery says that "at the root of an action is a 'self' which engages with and knows itself as such because it is so constituted through its ontological principles: free action manifests the genuine nature of persons. So we need not contrast Thomas's metaphysical attitude to the topic with one which stresses 'psychological' elements of the person (such as the life of the mind: knowledge, freedom, action, and openness to another), because these elements are integrated into his own approach," Gilles Emery, OP, *The Trinitarian Theology of St. Thomas Aquinas* (Oxford: Oxford University Press, 2007), 106.

Son love each other and love us by the Holy Spirit."[35] Granted that not all traditional theologians emphasize the mutual love of the divine persons as much as, say, Richard of St. Victor (following Augustine) or John Duns Scotus,[36] but do any major theologians actually deny it? Does anyone traditionally orthodox deny that only the Father generates the Son? Does anyone deny that only the Son became incarnate?

We should think this through carefully. If God is perfect in love (and if God's perfection is not compromised by dependence on creation), then God must be loving within the triune life, or "on the inside." If the divine persons love one another, they must be capable of doing so. That is, they must be relationally *distinct* enough to do so, and thus we have reason to hold single-subject theology at arm's length.

Consider further: if only the Father eternally generates the Son, and if we work from the assumption (one that should be safe) that the Father does so knowingly, then it is not a stretch to think that the Father knows that only he eternally generates the Son. After all, "actions, as Aquinas reminds us, only come from actors."[37] Similarly, if only the Son becomes incarnate and suffers for us and our salvation, then the Son knows that only the Son becomes incarnate and suffers for us and our salvation (the Father, of course, also knows that only the Son becomes incarnate and endures the passion). If so, the doctrine of the Trinity should lead us to conclude that the divine persons are genuinely distinct, that they act (*ad extra*) in full concord, that they love another, and that they know it.

In summary, we can see that core theological beliefs about the works of God (with respect both to the "economic" and "immanent" works) cohere well indeed with the robustly relational view of the divine persons that I have proposed. These core claims are grounded in Scripture,

---

35. Aquinas, *ST* 1a.37.2. See the helpful discussion of Gilles Emery, "The Trinity," in *The Oxford Handbook of Aquinas*, (ed. Eleonore Stump and Brian Davies; Oxford: Oxford University Press, 2012), 423.

36. On Richard of St. Victor, see especially Nico DenBok, *Communicating the Most High: A Systematic Study of Person and Trinity in the Theology of Richard of St. Victor* (Paris: Brepols, 1996). Marilyn McCord Adams describes Scotus's view: "For Scotus, God is a maximally-organized lover. The persons of the Trinity love one another with friendship love (*amor amicitiae*), which is unselfish and so reaches out to desire other co-lovers for the Beloved" (*What Sort of Human Nature? Medieval Philosophy and the Systematics of Christology* [Milwaukee: Marquette University Press, 1999], 69).

37. Russell L. Friedman, *Medieval Trinitarian Thought from Aquinas to Ockham* (Cambridge: Cambridge University Press, 2010), 22.

they are explicit and universal in the tradition of Christian orthodoxy, and they imply that the divine persons are distinct agents who are necessarily related in a perichoretic communion of holy love. I conclude that there is good reason to think that there are genuine and robust relationships between the truly distinct divine persons.

The Distinct Persons Are Equally Divine

The divine persons are distinct from one another in their mutual relations, and they are also fully and equally divine. The Son and Spirit are not ontologically inferior to the Father; it is not as if the Father has A+ divinity while the Son and Spirit have A- divinity. After all, for the monotheist there is only one divinity, and one either is or is not divine.[38] It is true that Scripture testifies to the subordination of the incarnate Son (e.g., John 14:28). But such testimony has been rightly understood by the broad Christian tradition as a reference to the Son *as incarnate.* Aquinas (explicitly following Augustine) says,

> Not without reason does the Scripture say both that the Son is equal to the Father and that the Father is greater than the Son. The first expression refers to the divine nature; the second to the form of a servant; and this distinction removes any possibility of confusion. Now that which is less is subject to the greater. Consequently, Christ, in so far as he has the form of a servant, is subject to the Father.

Aquinas goes on:

> Christ must not be thought of as a creature in unqualified fashion [*simpliciter*], but only in so far as he possesses a human nature.... Equally, Christ must not be thought of in unqualified fashion [*simpliciter*] as being subject to the Father. This is true of him only in his

---

38. The doctrine of divine simplicity entails this conclusion (although one may hold it independently of the doctrine of simplicity). For an historic example of how the doctrine of simplicity is used in defense of the doctrine of the Trinity, see, e.g., Gregory of Nyssa, "Against Eumonius" 1.19, *NPNF²*, 5:57 (PG 45:321B-D); 1.24, *NPNF²*, 5:66 (PG 45:356B); "Ad Ablabium," *NPNF²*, 5:332 (PG 45:120B). See further Andrew Radde-Gallwitz, *Basil of Ceasarea, Gregory of Nyssa, and the Transformation of Divine Simplicity* (Oxford: Oxford University Press, 2009), 212–18; Thomas H. McCall, "Trinity Doctrine, Plain and Simple," *Advancing Trinitarian Theology: Explorations in Constructive Dogmatics* (ed. Oliver D. Crisp and Fred Sanders; Grand Rapids: Zondervan, 2014), 42–59.

human nature, even if this qualification is not always expressed. It is better to state the restrictive clause explicitly, thus avoiding even verbal agreement with Arius who taught that the Son is less than the Father.[39]

This is exactly the right way to understand such texts, and there is no room in orthodox Christian theology for any view that would diminish the full and equal divinity of the Son and Holy Spirit with the Father.[40]

There Is Only One God

So far I have argued for a robustly relational understanding of the divine persons. But what about monotheism? In my view, commitment to monotheism is demanded by both Christian tradition and Christian Scripture.[41] "Hear, O Israel: the LORD our God, the LORD is one" (Deut 6:4). Despite the protestations of Jürgen Moltmann, monotheism simply is not optional for trinitarians.[42] At the same time, we should be careful to make sure that we understand just what is demanded by Scripture and the tradition of creedal orthodoxy. There is no good reason to think that the Shema demands a unipersonal deity; indeed, the very term used for the Hebrew word "one" ('eḥād) is one that allows for personal interrelationship.[43] With respect to the New Testament (in its setting), the conclusion of Richard Bauckham is helpful:

> Jewish monotheism clearly distinguished the one God and all other reality, but the ways in which it distinguished the one God from all else did not prevent the early Christians [from] including Jesus in this unique divine identity. While this was a radically novel development ... the character of Jewish monotheism was such that this

---

39. Aquinas, ST 3a.20.1. (Blackfriars ed., 50:111–13).

40. For discussion of what is sometimes called "eternal functional subordinationism" (or, alternatively, "necessary role subordinationism"), see Thomas H. McCall and Keith E. Yandell, "On Trinitarian Subordinationism," *Philosophia Christi* 11 (2009): 339–58.

41. Stephen R. Holmes is right to point out that the Old Testament cannot be ignored, as it too often is in these discussions (*The Quest for the Trinity*, 34–48, 200).

42. Unfortunately, Moltmann actually critiques monotheism, e.g., *The Trinity and the Kingdom: The Doctrine of God* (Minneapolis: Fortress, 1993), 129–37.

43. For further discussion of this and related matters, see Thomas H. McCall, *Which Trinity? Whose Monotheism? Philosophical and Systematic Theologians on the Metaphysics of Trinitarian Theology* (Grand Rapids: Eerdmans, 2010), 56–72.

development did not require any repudiation of the ways in which Jewish monotheism understood the uniqueness of God.[44]

But what about the broad Christian tradition? Does my proposal run afoul of creedal orthodoxy? I have sketched an account of divine personhood that is relational: the divine *hypostases* are genuinely distinct, and they are related to one another in the interpersonal *perichoresis* of holy love. Does my position entail what Barth called the "worst and most extreme expression of tritheism?"[45] Or is there a way to "cling to respectability as monotheists?"[46] Many proponents of "Social Trinitarianism" insist that monotheism may be retained in two ways: the divine persons all share the same generic divine essence (they are all omnipotent, omniscient, omnibenevolent, and whatever else is included in the divine essence), and they all cooperate together perfectly and therefore function as one. Thus Cornelius Plantinga:

> The Holy Trinity is a divine, transcendent society or community of three fully personal and fully divine entities: the Father, the Son, and the Holy Spirit or Paraclete. These three are wonderfully united by their common divinity, that is, by the possession of the whole generic divine essence ... the persons are also unified by their joint redemptive purpose, revelation, and work. Their knowledge and love are directed not only to their creatures, but also primordially and archetypally to each other. The Father loves the Son and the Son loves the Father ... the Trinity is thus a zestful community of divine light, love, joy, mutuality, and verve.[47]

I agree with Plantinga that the divine persons are three fully personal and fully divine entities who know and love one another. I also agree with him that the divine persons share the divine essence; they are *homoousios*, and (going beyond Plantinga) they can even be said to share one divine "power pack."[48] I agree as well that the divine persons are

---

44. Richard Bauckham, *God Crucified: Monotheism and Christology in the New Testament* (Grand Rapids: Eerdmans, 1998), 4.

45. *CD* I/1, 351.

46. Cornelius Plantinga Jr., "Social Trinity and Tritheism," in *Trinity, Incarnation, and Atonement: Philosophical and Theological Essays* (ed. Ronald J. Feenstra and Cornelius Plantinga Jr.; Notre Dame, IN: University of Notre Dame Press, 1989), 31.

47. Ibid., 27–28.

48. Cf. J. T. Paasch, *Divine Production in Late Medieval Trinitarian Theology: Henry of Ghent, Duns Scotus, and William Ockham* (Oxford: Oxford University Press, 2012), 17.

fully unified in purpose and work—indeed, their agreement is so strong (even necessarily so) that we should affirm that there is one divine will in an important sense.

But can we say more? Can we affirm more than merely generic or cooperative oneness? I believe that we can, and indeed that we should do so. Recent work in analytic theology has done much to clarify matters here, and there are (at least) two routes that are open to the relational trinitarian at this point. The tradition of trinitarian orthodoxy has, in my view, basically affirmed numerical (rather than merely generic) sameness. But, in contrast to some modern theology, it has done so without losing the distinct identity of the divine persons. As we have seen, the traditional claim is that there *is* only one God: the Father *is* God, the Son *is* God, and the Holy Spirit *is* God. But how are we to understand the *is*, and how might we do so while maintaining numerical sameness without identity?

One option is to "relativize" identity claims. The most promising of such proposals follows a once-popular medieval strategy.[49] It is sometimes called "Constitution Trinitarianism" (partly because of its employment of the analogy of material constitution).[50] Jeffrey Brower and Michael Rea set the bar high: any acceptable doctrine of the Trinity should be consistent with the view that the divine persons are distinct individuals (but not parts) and that there is exactly one divine individual (rather than a society), should not come into conflict with the teachings of Scripture and the ecumenical creeds, and should carry no antirealist commitments in metaphysics (as with some versions of relative identity).[51] They suggest that the familiar puzzles about material constitution are

---

49. Cf. ibid., 31–38; also Paul Thom, *The Logic of the Trinity: Augustine to Ockham* (New York: Fordham University Press, 2012), 64–67. We should take care to note that "Constitutional Trinitarianism" (in its latter-day manifestations) does not follow Abelard in reducing the personal relations to nonrelational divine attributes.

50. Scott Williams points out that there is more than one version of "Constitutional Trinitarianism" (CT) in the Latin medieval tradition ("Indexicals and the Trinity," 74–94). In addition to Henry of Ghent and John Duns Scotus (the most prominent advocates of CT), Friedman lists Walter Bruges, Eustace of Arras, Matthew of Aquasparta, Roger Marston, and John Pecham as proponents (*Medieval Trinitarian Thought*, 30–31).

51. Jeffrey E. Brower and Michael C. Rea, "Material Constitution and the Trinity," in *Philosophical and Theological Essays on the Trinity* (ed. Thomas McCall and Michael C. Rea; Oxford: Oxford University Press, 2009), 263–82. It is important to realize that Rea and Brower don't deny that God is a society, but it is also important to understand that they deny that this is sufficient for monotheism, e.g., "Material Constitution and the Trinity," 266 n7.

instructive here; the divine persons may be conceived on analogy with form-matter compounds (such as the genuine differences between lumps and statues). They reject the mere "is" of predication (as in Social Trinitarianism) for the "is" of numerical sameness, but they also reject the "is" of identity. Instead, they argue, what we have is "numerical sameness without identity" (where this is understood as essential sameness rather than merely accidental sameness), and this is what is needed for trinitarian orthodoxy. Thus we have numerical sameness: one God, but three persons who are genuinely distinct rather than identical.

Alternatively, the relational trinitarian might appeal to (a version of) the doctrine of divine simplicity for support here but follow suggestions from John Duns Scotus. On Scotus's account of divine simplicity, the *formal distinction* plays a large role.[52] Earlier scholastic treatments of the doctrine of simplicity rejected *real* distinctions within the divine essence and allowed only for conceptual distinctions. Scotus, however, posits the formal distinction as something between merely conceptual distinctions and real distinctions. Real distinctions can be distinctions between different things of different essences, they can be distinctions between different things of the same (secondary or generic) essence, or they can be between different separable parts of the same thing. For Scotus, however, the formal distinction falls "between" real distinctions and conceptual distinctions, and it applies to entities that are both *really inseparable* (not, properly speaking, *parts*) and nonetheless *genuinely distinct*. Adopting the formal distinction, the trinitarian might hold that the divine persons are genuinely distinct; the personal distinctions between them can never be reduced to mere conceptions and thus modalism is avoided.[53] At the same time, however, the divine persons are *really inseparable*; their subsistence is (logically) possible only within their mutual relations. Thus polytheism is avoided.

Keith Yandell takes a route that is similar in some important respects.[54] He argues that the triune God indeed is complex (in one

---

52. Cf. Paul Thom, *The Logic of the Trinity*, 144–55 and Richard Cross, *Duns Scotus on God* (Burlington, VT: Ashgate, 2005), 99–114.

53. As for Scotus himself, he entertains the possibility that the divine persons are absolutely distinct, but (on common readings of Scotus) he settles with the more traditional view that they are relationally distinct. At any rate, however, for Scotus there are real distinctions between the divine persons. See Richard Cross, *Duns Scotus on God*, 153–55.

54. He does not relate his proposal to the work of Scotus.

sense, although, as we will see, simple in another important sense). In Yandell's precise sense of "complex," "X is complex if and only if there is a Y and a Z such that Y is not numerically identical to Z, it is logically impossible that Y exist and Z not exist, and Y and Z together are numerically identical to X in the sense of their together composing X."[55] The triune God is complex. But according to Yandell, this complex triune God has no parts. For on his understanding of parts, "if Y is a part of X, then Y can exist whether X exists or not. Further, if Y and Z are parts of X, then Y can exist without Z existing and Z can exist without Y existing." Put a bit differently, "X is a part of Y if and only if X exists, Y exists, X plus something else is all of Y, X is not all of Y, and it is logically possible that X exist and Y not exist or Y exist and X not exist (or both)." Yandell then denies that the divine persons are divine *parts*: it is logically impossible that any of the divine persons exist without the others. So something is "simple(i)" if and only if it has no parts, and he affirms that this is necessarily true of the Trinity. God is simple in just this sense: God has no parts. Yandell contrasts this with what he terms "simple(ii)," which is the denial of any complexity. Not surprisingly, he affirms that the triune God is necessarily simple(i) and necessarily not simple(ii).

So on this account of divine oneness, the doctrine of simplicity plays an important role: God is not composed of parts or pieces. At the same time, God is necessarily complex, for God is triune. The divine persons are "necessarily strongly internally related," and thus God is "necessarily particularly strongly internally complex." This yields the conclusion that there is exactly one triune God whose divine persons are necessarily related (thus not "parts" in any sense) in a perichoretic "relation of mutual profound love."

Summary: Relational and Classical Trinitarianism

These are some of the important features of a relational doctrine of the Trinity. As I understand the doctrine of the Trinity, the divine persons are internally and necessarily related within the communion of the

---

55. Keith E. Yandell, "An Essay in Particularist Philosophy of Religion: A Metaphysical Structure for the Doctrine of the Trinity," unpublished essay; cf. McCall, *Which Trinity?*, 168–70.

divine life. Working from what we see of the actions of the "economic" Trinity, as well as drawing from the fascinating and precious glimpses of the immanent Trinity that we see in Scripture, we should conclude that the divine persons are distinct speech-agents who know, glorify, and love one another. Their work in creation and redemption is perfectly unified, and this unity of action (*ad extra*) reflects — but does not exhaust or even constitute — the deeper unity of the immanent Trinity. This deeper unity goes beyond the oneness of a shared generic divine essence or mere cooperation: Father, Son, and Holy Spirit are not three gods who are much alike or who get along well. Instead, they are exactly *one God*.

I have argued that the elements of such a relational formulation of the doctrine of the Trinity (though not, of course, the formulation itself or details of the doctrine) flow from the biblical account. I am convinced that it reflects the biblical portrayals of the divine persons, and I am just as convinced that it falls within the boundaries of biblical monotheism. Is it also consistent with the tradition of trinitarian orthodoxy? The answer here should be positive. Surely it falls within the boundaries laid out by the major ecumenical creeds. It rejects both modalism as well as Arianism and other forms of subordinationism, and it avoids tritheism as well.

Similarly, it is hard to see how it might violate many major Protestant confessions. For instance, the model I propose does not violate the Thirty-Nine Articles (much the same could, I think, be said for major Roman Catholic statements; since I do not rely on merely generic accounts of divine oneness, my proposal does not run afoul of the statements produced at Lateran IV).[56] While I readily admit that what I propose does not draw slavishly or even strictly from any single theologian or from any school of theology (in the sense of being distinctly "Thomist," "Scotist, "Barthian," etc.), various elements of what I suggest indeed can be found in the work of major theologians from within the tradition.

For instance, while numerical sameness without identity clearly *is* the mainstream view of orthodox trinitarian theology, the same cannot

---

56. Cf. Emery, *Trinity in Aquinas*, 12–14, and Fiona Robb, "The Fourth Lateran Council's Definition of Trinitarian Orthodoxy," *JEH* 48 (1997): 22–43.

be said of the "Constitution" strategy *per se*. At the same time, however, we should remember that *no single strategy* can claim anything like universal support.[57] But the Constitution view does not trespass the boundaries of catholic orthodoxy, and it arguably has precursors within the tradition. Michael C. Rea argues that there are passages within the work of the Cappadocians that suggest this; Jeffrey E. Brower shows that Abelard held something like it; and J. T. Paasch mounts a strong case that many late medieval theologians follow Henry of Ghent in promoting just this view.[58] Moreover, my proposal is consistent with the doctrine of divine simplicity.[59] I conclude then, that the relational view that I have articulated flows from the biblical teaching, and it does so in a manner that is consistent with classical Christian orthodoxy.

Trinity and Creation: The "Relevance" of the Doctrine

Creation and redemption are, in Scripture, the work of the triune God. Indeed, the early Christian theologians began to articulate the doctrine while reflecting on the saving work of God. So it should come as no surprise to us that the doctrines are closely related.

Christians should affirm divine aseity, and, because God is triune, they can do so while still maintaining that God *is love* (1 John 4:8, 16). Because the loving relationships between the Father, Son, and Holy Spirit are essential to the triune life, there is no sense in which God can be said to "need" the world (to actualize himself, to display his glory, etc.). This affirmation of triune aseity renders otiose the kinds of theology that run downstream from Hegel, including not only process theology but also the versions that run through Moltmann and Barth (on some interpretations).[60]

---

57. For discussion of the diversity in medieval trinitarianism, see, e.g., Friedman, *Medieval Trinitarian Thought*, 169.

58. Michael C. Rea, "The Trinity," in *The Oxford Handbook of Philosophical Theology* (ed. Thomas P. Flint and Michael C. Rea; Oxford: Oxford University Press, 2009), 417–23; Jeffrey E. Brower, "Abelard on the Trinity," in *The Cambridge Companion to Abelard* (ed. Jeffrey E. Brower and K. Guilfoy; Cambridge: Cambridge University Press, 2004), 233–57; J. T. Paasch, *Divine Production*, 31–38. Cf. also Thom, *The Logic of the Trinity*, 64–67, and Friedman, *Medieval Trinitarian Thought*, 140.

59. At least some formulations of the doctrine.

60. Here I refer to the interpretation (and extension) of Barth's theology that is defended by Bruce L. McCormack, to which see especially *Trinity and Election in Contemporary Theology* (ed. Michael T. Dempsey; Grand Rapids: Eerdmans, 2011). An especially lucid and helpful

At the same time, however, we should see creation as the free expression *of the holy love of the triune God*. Creation *ex nihilo*, when considered within a trinitarian framework, is completely consistent with creation *ex amore*. As William Lane Craig reminds us, this is a "remarkable conclusion," for

> alone in the self-sufficiency of his own being, enjoying the time-less fullness of the intra-trinitarian love relationships, God had no need for the creation of finite persons.... He did this, not out of any deficit in Himself or His mode of existence, but in order that finite temporal creatures might come to share in the joy and blessedness of the inner life of God.[61]

So according to a biblically grounded and properly trinitarian doctrine of creation, human creatures are made to participate in the holy love of the divine life. We also find in Scripture that we have fallen into sin and stand in desperate need of redemption. Moreover, Scripture contains the wonderful news that the triune God has acted on our behalf. Indeed, as Fred Sanders says, "the gospel is trinitarian, and the Trinity is the gospel."[62] For just as we were created for nothing less than communion with the triune God, so also are we saved for nothing less. The entire *ordo* (or *via*) *salutis* is trinitarian: the Son becomes incarnate for us and our salvation as he is sent by the Father and empowered by the Holy Spirit, and the Spirit continues to work to transform God's children into the image of the only-begotten and to bring us home to the Father. The Son makes atonement for the sins of the world, and believers who are joined in union with Christ by the power of the Holy Spirit are then justified and counted righteous in God's sight. But more than our legal status is changed by the Trinity, for the same Spirit that unites us in justifying faith to the incarnate Son also truly sanctifies us as he transforms filthy and perverted rebels into saints of whom it can truly be said: "These are my beloved sons and daughters, in whom I am well pleased."[63]

---

discussion is found in Kevin Diller, "Is God *Necessarily* Who God Is? Alternatives for the Trinity and Election Debate," *SJT* 66 (2013): 209–20.

61. William Lane Craig, *Time and Eternity: Exploring God's Relationship to Time* (Wheaton, IL: Crossway, 2001), 241.

62. Fred Sanders, *The Deep Things of God: How the Trinity Changes Everything* (Wheaton, IL: Crossway, 2010), 10.

63. The burden of my little book, *Forsaken: The Trinity and the Cross, and Why It Matters* (Downers Grove, IL: InterVarsity Press, 2012) is precisely to explore these issues in more detail.

So we should conclude that the doctrine of the Trinity is incredibly relevant for life today. God created us to share in the divine life of holy love, and he has redeemed us so that we might be rescued from our sin and come home to that life. Beyond such biblically grounded (and historically affirmed) conclusions, however, we should exercise great care and caution in thinking about the "relevance" of the Trinity. The last few decades have witnessed an incredibly wide-ranging series of "trinitarian" pronouncements on theological and sociopolitical issues, many of which are only loosely related to serious trinitarian theology and some of which are actually contradictory. The flood of such competing pronouncements has led critics to call the entire enterprise of trinitarian ethics into question.[64]

The dangers of projection loom large. Indeed, some of these projects in trinitarian theology must be judged as striking confirmation of Feuerbach's own exaggerated claims. The sad irony is that much theology of recent vintage has "explored" all manner of areas of "relevance" even as it has largely ignored the genuine relevance as taught in Scripture. My own advice is this: while we should not dismiss all such considerations out of hand, we should proceed with caution as we work to distinguish genuine "implications" from spurious claims and we seek to understand what we might learn from Scripture about the issues under consideration.

Conclusion

Sometimes it seems to me that the lines are sharply drawn in contemporary trinitarian theology, and it sometimes seems to me that they are drawn in the wrong places. Some theologians, often following Moltmann's charge and waving the banner of "Social Trinitarianism," insist on robust personal distinctions between the divine persons — but then go on to downplay, ignore, or flat-out deny an adequate account of divine oneness. Other theologians, now (rightly) critiquing the "Social Trinitarianism" of Moltmann, Boff, and others at various points, follow the lead of Barth and Rahner in insisting on numerical sameness — but then go on to downplay, ignore, or flat-out deny robustly tripersonal

---

64. E.g., Karen Kilby, "Perichoresis and Projection: Problems with Social Doctrines of the Trinity," *New Blackfriars* 81 (2000): 432–45.

agency and the mutual love of the divine persons for one another. Meanwhile, partisans from both camps of modern theology often identify the "immanent Trinity" with the "economic Trinity" in problematic ways.

This is unfortunate at several levels. There is a sense in which both sides are largely correct in what they affirm but wrong in what they deny. The social trinitarians are right to recognize "I-Thou" relationships within God's own life, but they are wrong to deny a strong account of monotheism. The Barthian-Rahnerian counterattack is right (at least by traditional standards) to hold to numerical sameness, but such theologians are wrong to insist on a single divine subjectivity. Neither side can fully claim to be "the" traditional view, and (more importantly) both sides fail to account for the full biblical teaching.

I have argued for something different. I have made a case that the divine persons are genuinely and robustly distinct in their mutual relations, that they are each fully, completely, and equally divine, and that there is exactly one God. I am convinced that this doctrine is consistent with the commitments of catholic orthodoxy, and (even more importantly) it is grounded in Scripture. While I readily admit that there is much that is mysterious about the doctrine, I do not think that my account is incoherent. To the contrary, the doctrine of the Trinity is vitally important for helping us understand divine intention and action in creation and salvation in a coherent way. And while we should be cautious about extravagant claims about the "relevance" of trinitarian theology with respect to various issues, we should nonetheless be in a position to agree with C. S. Lewis: the doctrine of the Trinity "matters more than anything else in the world."[65]

---

65. C. S. Lewis, *Mere Christianity* (New York: Macmillan, 1943), 137.

STEPHEN R. HOLMES

Thomas McCall seeks to defend at length two theses in his essay: the genuine distinction and the genuine unity of Father, Son, and Holy Spirit. Of course, I agree with these two theses; as he notes in his own opening sentences, they seem minimum requirements of any doctrine of the Trinity seeking to represent itself as orthodox. Further, I do not see any major point of disagreement with McCall over his unpacking of these two theses: what he claims by way of distinction, I am happy to affirm; and what he insists on to safeguard the unity, I am equally happy to assert. I admire, as I always do, the analytic clarity and care that characterizes McCall's writing, and I cannot discover any significant gaps in his argument. This response essay, then, is in danger of being rather short.

Such as they are, my concerns with McCall's piece have more to do with mode of expression than with content. That is, by the time he has finished defining what he means by an "I-Thou" relationship, I am prepared to accept that this term might be used to speak of the relations of the three divine hypostases, but I cannot help thinking that the term is misleading, in that McCall's definition moves sufficiently far from a "plain sense" meaning of the term as to be in danger of being unrecognizable. At one level, this is not a great problem. He is clear in his definition, and if it seems to me to be a slightly eccentric use of words, this is of little moment. That said, reflecting on this issue does seem to take us to the heart of some crucial issues; thus, in the absence of any real disagreement, I will use my space here to offer such reflection.

First, the problems with the term. McCall rightly stresses the divine unity as being far more than just "sameness." He wants to go further than "merely generic or cooperative oneness," to "affirm that there is one divine will in an important sense" (p. 130) and to say that the three persons "share one divine 'power pack'" (p. 129). Unity of will and *ener-*

geia— what I assume is meant by "power pack"— is indeed a part of the traditional doctrine. It also, however, stretches the concept of an "I-Thou" relationship of the three persons significantly, or so it seems to me.

Why so? Because, on McCall's definition, these ascriptions of unity make the basic activity of an "I-Thou" relationship at least unnecessary and possibly impossible. McCall quotes Peter van Inwagen to begin to define what he means by "I-Thou" relationships: "a person can use the word 'I' and be addressed as 'thou'" (quoted on p. 117). Accepting, as McCall does, the contingency of creation ("God's perfection is not compromised by dependence on creation" [p. 126]), this definition presumably implies eternal address within the Trinity: the Father speaks to the Son and the Spirit, and so on.

But, if there is unity of will in the Trinity of Father, Son, and Spirit, we are perhaps entitled to ask, albeit slightly facetiously, what do they talk *about*? There is no discussion of purpose or desire to be had, no "I'd rather do this; what do you want to do?" What might be the content of the eternal triune conversation?

I can see several possible answers to this question, but none of them seem without problem. We might say, first, that there is no eternal conversation: van Inwagen's definition cites ability, not actuality ("a person can ... be addressed as 'thou.'"). I assume, however, that in the experience of a particular person it would be a fairly significant lack never to speak or to be spoken to. Given that creation gives rise to creatures— angels and humans, at least— who are addressed by the divine persons, and who do address the divine persons as "thou," it would seem that in this case God's life is made significantly better by creation, a point McCall rightly and specifically denies, as I have noted. (This argument, it will be observed, is a specific instance of a traditional argument that there can be no unactualized potential in God's life; I do not know if McCall holds to this position, but I suppose that the specific instance here sketched is convincing regardless of the broader position.)

Second, then, we might suggest an ecstatic eternal conversation. The analogy here would be "whispering sweet nothings" between lovers that is a cliché of poorly written romantic novels (or so I am told; my exposure to the genre is far from extensive). That there is no purposive discussion to be had might not eliminate the possibility of eternal divine address, repeated expressions of contentment in shared divine perfection that communicate nothing not already known and carry no perlocutionary or illocutionary force either, but which are true and are delighted in.

My worry here is twofold. On one hand, without denying the reality of such communication at all, I cannot but wonder whether it is somehow less significant, or at least less satisfying, than address that has locutionary (or illocutionary; or perlocutionary) force — in which case we would be back in the situation above, of creation bettering the divine life significantly. On the other hand, carrying the romantic analogy forward, there appears to be something immature in such communication; it dies in a lasting relationship, to be replaced largely by comfortable silence. Of course, pressing that analogy into the divine life is extraordinarily dangerous, but I note that I introduced the analogy to defend something apparently difficult; this point suggests it might well fail, and with it the defense.

Third, although he accepts unity of will, McCall clearly rejects unity of intellect. He approvingly cites William Lane Craig in saying: "The Father knows, for example, that the Son dies on the cross, but He does not know and cannot know that He Himself dies on the cross — indeed, the view that He so knows even has the status of heresy" (p. 123). This point is not quite so obvious as it seems for some reasons to do with developed christological formulae: the most that can possibly be said is the famous and controversial theopaschite proposal, that "one of the Trinity suffered in the flesh" (quoted by McCall on p. 122), where the qualification "in the flesh" is significant. Lane Craig's formula might be revised as follows: "The Father knows that the human nature which the Son has taken into personal subsistence with Himself dies on the cross, but He does not know and cannot know that a human nature which He, the Father, has taken into personal subsistence with Himself dies on the cross." But of course this is not so straightforward a demonstration of diversity of intellect as the formula presented. For the argument, I grant McCall his claims about diversity of intellect; the Father could say to the Son, "you died," and the Son to the Father, "I died."

This, obviously, is dependent on the prior fact of creation and incarnation, and so not necessarily helpful (in that Dr. McCall has affirmed the contingency of creation, and so cannot rest his arguments solely on created realities). A stronger argument would turn to the relations of origin: the Father says to the Son "I have begotten you," the Son to the Father, "You have begotten me," and the knowledge behind these two statements is irreducibly particular.

I accept this; an orthodox Trinitarian has to; but — crucially — I accept no more than this. McCall uses the relational distinctions as evidence of a distinction in personal agency (which I presume entails a distinction in intellect): "And if it is true that only the Father generates the Son, it is obvious and even platitudinous that only the Father performs such an action" (p. 123). This is right, but it overlooks the context of the statement in Cappadocian trinitarianism, which is the context for the assertion in McCall's discussion: the *only, single* act that the Father performs uniquely is the generation of the Son. Eternally, the Father can indeed say uniquely to the Son, "I have begotten you," but absolutely nothing else. At the risk of being facetious once again, on this telling the eternal divine conversation sounds somewhat tedious.

I can think of one or two other possible analyses of the eternal divine conversation, but they all end up in the same sort of place: eternally, God has nothing of significance to say to God. This might even be dogmatically important: speech is a mode of mediated presence, and the doctrine of the Trinity demands, I think, that the presence of the three persons one to another is immediate (this is a derivation, but I think a fairly straightforward one, from confessing *perichoresis*).

In the last few paragraphs of this response, I want to turn to Dr. McCall's reasons for assuming an "I-Thou" relationship of address between the three persons. They seem to me to be twofold. On one hand, he borrows this definition from van Inwagen without comment or criticism. On the other, he believes there are exegetical reasons to view an "I-Thou" mode of relating between the three persons to be affirmed in Scripture. I suggest that if the exegetical reasons do not hold, it would be easy to suggest that van Inwagen's definition is not the right one and so to have no need to assert these "I-Thou" relationships (which, I have argued, are in fact difficult to hold).

How strong is McCall's exegetical evidence, then? I fear it is rather weak: he makes extensive appeal to the New Testament, but precisely because of that almost every example of "I-Thou" speech he offers is an example of a relationship between the incarnate Son and the Father. A proposal that this form of relationship is generated by the event of incarnation would, if plausible (it does not even need to be proved), destroy almost all the exegetical evidential base on which McCall's thesis is built.

I happen to think that this destruction is more than plausible, for two reasons. First, most of the texts here appealed to are prayers (see the lists of texts on p. 168 of McCall's essay); I take it that prayer is necessarily a creaturely action. On the one hand, the act of bringing humble petition before God seems to me necessarily creaturely, but on the other, and more significantly, petitionary prayer must involve an at-least-potential diversity of volition, and McCall has asserted unity of volition within the Trinity, as I have explored. So when Jesus prays at Gethsemane, "not what I will, but what you will, be done," we must hear the volitional conflict as between the human will of the Jewish man Jesus of Nazareth and the shared divine will of Father and Son (and Holy Spirit).

Second, and following precisely from this example, the monoenergist and monothelite debates in patristic theology made this point strongly in that their conclusion asserted as matters of dogma that there was one divine "energy" (or "powerpack," as McCall puts it), and one divine will, and that in the incarnate Son there were two energies and wills — one human, one divine. Given this, and the exploration of potential forms of "I-Thou" discourse above, reading almost all McCall's exegetical evidence as pointing to incarnation, not Trinity, seems to me powerful.

Now, McCall anticipates this move and suggests it fails because of biblical data suggesting a personal distinction between Father and Spirit. But what data suggest a distinction that must be understood as "I-Thou" address? The single plausible text here is Romans 8:26, "the Spirit intercedes ..." (cited on p. 120). Is this convincing? There is not space here to engage in exegetical debate, but the context is our inability to pray and so to read this phrase as a somewhat loose way of speaking of the Spirit inspiring unarticulated, but nonetheless real, prayer within us (perhaps through the exercise of glossolalia) seems a plausible possibility, which removes this last exegetical support.

McCall insists on "I-Thou" relationships because he believes, on the basis of a definition proposed by van Inwagen, that this is what it is to be personal. I have argued elsewhere that this is a misunderstanding of the use of the term "person" in trinitarian theology.[66] It never meant "personal" in this, late modern/romantic, sense. Hypostases are existent instantiations, and that is all *personae* was ever meant to mean. McCall does a heroic job of redefining terms to make an "I-Thou" account of trinitarian relationships work, and as I said at the beginning of this piece, I think he essentially succeeds. But the effort was, I fear, unnecessary, based (as it is) on a misunderstanding of what "person" must imply in trinitarian doctrine.

---

66. Stephen R. Holmes, "Three Versus One? Some Problems of Social Trinitarianism," *JRT* 3 (2009): 77–89.

RESPONSE TO THOMAS H. MCCALL

PAUL D. MOLNAR

In his "robustly" relational view of the Trinity, Thomas McCall clearly wishes to espouse a biblically grounded and traditional (orthodox) view of the Trinity. On the one hand, he intends to distance himself from social trinitarians such as Moltmann, not so much because they espouse three distinct subjects in relation, but because they marginalize or even deny the divine unity. On the other hand, he explicitly intends to reject the thinking of those who uphold "a single divine subjectivity."

With social trinitarians, McCall believes we should ascribe "I-Thou" relations to God's inner life. This means that McCall is not simply advancing the idea that there are relations within the inner Trinity. Such a view would not only be noncontroversial; it would be thoroughly compatible with classical trinitarian theology. The fact that God is relational is an extremely important insight because it makes clear the fact that God is not a powerless and loveless monad incapable of living and acting as one who knows and loves within his own eternal being and freely creates us and enables us to have communion with him in knowledge and love. A monad cannot become incarnate and active in history in a real incarnation without ceasing to be God in himself, nor can a monad act to overcome our sin and alienation as the revealer and reconciler of humanity gone astray. I think McCall would accept this statement of the divine relations *ad intra* and *ad extra*, but with the proviso that the works of the Trinity *ad extra* are one while the inner trinitarian relations are distinct in such a way that they can be categorized as "necessarily existent entities who enjoy 'I-Thou' relationships within the triune life" (p. 116), such that "while there are important differences between divine and human personhood," there are indeed "genuine interpersonal, 'I-Thou' relationships within the triune life" (p. 117).

Now McCall says some critics may worry that this "seems too anthropomorphic" and says that they "have some legitimate worries" among which is the concern that the divine persons are here understood based on what we think we already know about "persons" from our own experience of human persons. He does not think this applies to his proposal because he says he is proceeding with "a properly biblical and theological understanding of the divine persons" that will "let divine revelation shape (and perhaps reshape) our understanding of divine personhood" (p. 117). At the same time, according to his stated methodology "religious experience is a key element of theological construction" (p. 115), so that as an analytic theologian he will use philosophy (metaphysics) to construct his analogies for speaking about God while maintaining the priority of theology over philosophy.

The only question is: Can one maintain the priority of theology over philosophy if, in addition to using reason within faith, one allows religious experience a key role in theological construction? While McCall says that "the vast majority (perhaps all) of our language for God is analogical *at best*" (p. 115; it is not clear which language he believes may not be analogical), and while he says his thinking will be shaped by "divine revelation," there is no clear and consistent indication in his essay that illustrates exactly what he means by divine revelation on the one hand; on the other hand, there is no clear and consistent indication that for him revelation is and remains identical with God's act in his Word and Spirit. At one point he equates revelation with the Bible (pp. 114–15), arguing that Scripture is the norm for "doctrinal authority" and that doctrines therefore receive their authority from Holy Scripture.

McCall also believes there is a "third tier of authority (standing under the creeds and ultimately under Scripture)," which is "particular ecclesial bodies" (p. 114). What is missing here, unfortunately, is a clear statement that the Bible is not revelation in itself but that it only becomes revelation when the Word of God, which is identical with the incarnate Jesus Christ who died and rose again for us, speaks through the power of his Holy Spirit and enables us to hear that Word through the witness of the biblical authors. This is an important distinction because if it is taken seriously, it means that we must allow all our knowledge of God (all our analogies) to begin and end with Jesus Christ himself as the Word of God, who continues to speak to us as the risen, ascended, and advent Lord through the power of his Holy Spirit. To put the matter directly, the question concerns whether theologians are thinking from a center in God or from a center in themselves.

It is clear that McCall does not want to think from a center in himself as many other social trinitarians do, even if some of them do that unwittingly. But while McCall is committed to the formal statements of classical trinitarianism—i.e., the fact that there is "exactly one God" and this God "exists as three persons" (pp. 113, 116) and that this means there can be no modalism, subordinationism, or tritheism since all of these errors would conflict with "orthodoxy" as he has described this—it appears that his thinking is not shaped by the unique relations of the Father with the Son and Holy Spirit in important ways. Thus, for example, McCall explicitly and frequently speaks of God's interpersonal relations in a manner that has the ring of tritheism to it.

According to the classical view of the Trinity, God is one being, three persons. There is little mention of God's being in McCall's essay, only a commitment to numerical unity. Christians are not committed simply to numerical unity but to the one God who *is* in the act of his eternal being as Father, Son, and Holy Spirit. Thus, there can be no knowledge of God's oneness without knowing the Father through his Son and in his Holy Spirit. When one is not bound to knowing God in this particular way, then one can construct a knowledge of God's "numerical" oneness by arguing that God is both simple *and* complex at the same time. This kind of reasoning, which in my view attempts to reconcile irreconcilable positions, allows one to make overtly tritheistic statements and so to speak of "three metaphysical agents" (p. 125), while insisting simultaneously that God is "exactly one." But everything depends on the kind of oneness that is being espoused.

For instance, McCall spends time citing Scripture to illustrate that the divine persons have "I-Thou" relations. But "I-Thou" relations presuppose two distinct "entities" even according to McCall's own presentation. Yet according to the classical view of the Trinity, there is only one "entity" because God *is* One Being, Three Persons. That is the mystery of the Trinity. It cannot be explained, not even with the notion of "I-Thou" relations, because, according to the tradition, no one can explain *how* God can be One Being, Three Persons. One can only acknowledge the mystery in faith based on the revelation of the Father in and through his Son and then come to an understanding of who God is in his uniquely personal being and who we are in our relations with this God as established and maintained in grace. The relations between the Father and Son and the relation of the Spirit to the Father and Son within the life of the Trinity thus are utterly unique precisely because they are in fact relations of one single subject within the immanent Trinity and acting as creator, reconciler, and redeemer *ad extra*.

Consequently, it appears to me that McCall's attempt to embrace the social trinitarian view that God is at once three "entities" and "numerically" one presents us with conflicting visions of divine oneness and threeness. On the one hand, the Christian God cannot be three "entities" or "three metaphysical agents." On the other, the doctrine of the Trinity was not advanced to solve a mathematical problem by espousing any sort of oneness or monotheism. The doctrine rather directs us to the mystery of God, whose oneness is inherent in his threeness and whose threeness is inherent in his oneness. In all the relations of the Father, Son, and Holy Spirit depicted in Scripture, we are not dealing therefore with "I-Thou" relations, that is, relations of different persons interacting together. Such thinking seems effectively tritheistic. It is one thing to speak of personal relations between the Father and the Son and of the Spirit in relation to the Father and Son. And it is perfectly proper to assert, as McCall does citing Maximus the Confessor, that "the Father and Holy Spirit 'themselves did not become incarnate, but the Father approved and the Spirit cooperated when the Son himself effected his Incarnation'" (p. 121). But it is quite another to say that in these actions three distinct entities are enacting "I-Thou" relations with each other.

God's actions *ad extra* are grounded in unique relations within the one being of God such that there are never three wills in God but only one will. Only the one God acts in the incarnation of the Son and the outpouring of the Spirit. So when God acts as creator, that action may be ascribed to the Father. But the Father acts through his Word and in his Spirit to create. When God acts as reconciler, the Father sends his Son and reconciles the world through the Son's life of obedience even to the cross. But the Father and Spirit are also involved, each in their own ways, with the actions of the Son.[67] In other words they are not

---

67. Here we may refer to the Eleventh Council of Toledo (AD 675), where it is said that "we must believe that the Son was sent not only by the Father but also by the Holy Spirit, for he himself says through the prophet: 'And now the Lord God and his Spirit has sent me' [Is 48:16]. He is also understood to be sent by himself, because not only the will but also the action of the whole Trinity is believed to be inseparable," *Compendium of Creeds, Definitions, and Declarations on Matters of Faith and Morals* (43rd ed.; ed. Heinrich Denzinger/Peter Hünermann, Robert Fastiggi and Anne Englund Nash; San Francisco: Ignatius, 2012), 187.

individual persons in "I-Thou" relations but three distinct persons who are inherently one in all their actions *ad intra* and *ad extra*.

McCall uses the example of the Father's eternal generation of the Son in order to support his position. Hence, he says, "the person of the Father—and only the person of the Father—is rightly said to beget the Son" (p. 122). From this he concludes that the works of the persons are always unified in the economy, but distinct as well since only the Son becomes incarnate. I certainly agree with that. McCall proceeds to say, "With respect to the works of the immanent Trinity, however, such works are uniquely and *completely* the work of one divine person" (p. 122, emphasis mine). This implies that "the divine persons are distinct agents" (p. 122). Hence, he insists that only the Son suffers and dies—*only* the Son is the subject of the incarnation. In my understanding, this implication is exactly what must be rejected according to the classical trinitarian view because it is just this conclusion that not only appears tritheistic, but could open the door to the very subordinationism McCall quite rightly and explicitly rejects.

Let us say for instance that the generation of the Son is "completely" the work of one divine person, the Father. Such a view would eliminate the crucial insight of the original Nicene Creed that the Son is from the being of the Father and not just from his person. While it is indeed only the Son who became incarnate and suffered and died on the cross, that cannot mean the exclusion of the Father and Spirit from those activities as well.[68] That is why we can say with T. F. Torrance that Jesus Christ, the incarnate Word, suffered and died both in his divinity and in his humanity and he fulfilled his priestly and mediatorial activity "only in unbroken oneness in being and activity with God."[69] But we must also say that the Father and Spirit were involved in the suffering and death of the incarnate Son since the Son was never separated from the other persons of the Trinity in his actions for us. Hence, there is "the pain of God the Father in giving up his beloved Son ... in atoning sacrifice for

---

68. It is thus in conflict, I believe, with the clear statement of the Eleventh Council of Toledo (675) that "we must also believe that the entire Trinity brought about the Incarnation of the Son of God, because the works of the Trinity are inseparable. However, only the Son took the form of a servant ... in the singleness of person, not in the unity of divine nature; he took it into what is proper to the Son, not into what is common to the Trinity" (ibid., 186).

69. Thomas F. Torrance, *The Christian Doctrine of God: One Being Three Persons* (Edinburgh: T&T Clark, 1996), 252.

the sin of the world and its redemption."[70] Consequently, "the whole undivided Trinity is involved in our salvation.... [each Person] in their different but coordinated ways"[71] so that "the whole undivided Trinity shares in the saving passion of the incarnate Son."[72]

I certainly agree with McCall that the doctrine of the Trinity matters more than anything else in the world. But I believe his rejection of a "single divine subjectivity" is in reality a rejection of the unique unity and simplicity of the triune God. How many divine subjects are there? The answer of the classical doctrine of the Trinity is that there is only one true God and that God is the eternal Father, Son, and Holy Spirit.

---

70. Ibid.
71. Ibid.
72. Ibid., 253.

PAUL S. FIDDES

Thomas McCall aims to set out a "relational" view of the Trinity that is consistent with the creeds of the church, which in themselves, he stresses, intended to be hermeneutic guidelines for reading Scripture. "By 'relational'" he writes, "I mean that the Father, Son, and Holy Spirit live within a necessary relationship of mutual holy love" (p. 113). In developing this view he proposes, in contrast to the previous chapters of Steve Holmes and Paul Molnar, that religious experience "is a key element of theological construction" (p. 115). He also admits that the vast majority (perhaps all) of our language for God is analogical *at best*. With all this I am completely in agreement, which perhaps explains why his account and mine are placed alongside each other as "relational" approaches to the Trinity.

However, where we part company is in McCall's setting out to show that by "divine persons" he means "necessarily existent entities" who are "fully personal in the sense that they exist together as what may be called distinct speech-agents in what are sometimes referred to as 'I-Thou' relationships" (p. 117). He explains that "even though there are important differences between divine and human personhood, I will argue that we should conclude that there are genuine interpersonal, 'I-Thou' relationships, within the triune life" (pp. 116–17). In conceiving these I-Thou relationships it appears from his chapter that he now sits more lightly to the idea of three "centers of consciousness" (p. 123) than he did in an earlier book, when he gave the notion some qualified consent. However, while declining to attribute to the Greek Fathers modern psychological views of the self, he still maintains that they regarded the persons as "psychological entities" displaying "distinct inflections of the one divine will" (p. 124). They are distinct agents who "know, glorify, and love one another" (p. 133).

My own "relational" account rejects the identification of divine persons with interpersonal "agents" or "actors," though for different reasons from the previous accounts of Holmes and Molnar. McCall's account in fact offers a strong challenge to the direction taken by Holmes and Molnar, who are suspicious not only of social trinitarianism but any relational accounts of the Trinity. Holmes argues that the only relations within the Trinity that are valid are those of the origin of the persons, and Molnar argues that the divine relations are not to be understood by analogies drawn from human experience. By contrast, McCall draws attention to the range of relations between the Father, Jesus, and the Spirit, which are presented in Scripture and which—he claims—are analogous to the inner life of the Trinity, not just belonging to the economy of God's work in the world.

The Gospels, he argues, are replete with language reflecting robustly interpersonal relationships between the Father and Son, such as the accounts of the baptism and transfiguration of Jesus and his cries to God in Gethsemane and on the cross. Similarly, the New Testament offers depictions of the relationship between the Father and the Spirit, such as the sending of the Spirit, and between the Son and the Spirit, such as the virginal conception of Jesus. These accounts, he maintains, cannot be simply ascribed to the incarnate Christ, or to the human nature of Christ (as does Holmes), and must reflect relations in God eternally.

Though McCall does not explicitly express the matter in this way, I suggest that these portrayals exceed being merely relations of origin (against Holmes) and are activities that invite comparison and positioning with general human experiences (against Molnar). I agree with McCall that if we take Scripture seriously, they must reflect eternal distinctions in the being of God. However, I cannot agree that they demonstrate that the divine persons have "I-Thou relationships." McCall seeks to defend himself against anthropomorphic projection onto God, admitting that "there are important differences between divine and human personhood" (p. 117), but it is not at all clear what he thinks these differences are. He does not, it seems to me, sufficiently recognize the mystery of God's inner being and fails to show where the "unlikeness" lies within analogies we use for God. However, he surely has a point that "we should let divine revelation shape (and perhaps reshape) our understanding of divine personhood" (p. 117). The fact that God has revealed God's self in human relationships, and that God always speaks the truth about God's self (as Karl Barth put it), leads us to find some analogy of these relationships in God's own being, rather than simply ascribing them to the human nature of Christ.

At the end of the first three chapters in this book, we are thus left with the interesting question of how we might reconcile the truth of God's self-revelation (as stressed by McCall) with the ineffability of God (stressed by Holmes) and with the difference of God's relations from created relations (stressed by Molnar). Must we say that the well-presented arguments of my three co-authors simply cancel each other out? The more convincing we find them, the more we are left in a quandary.

There is a clue to a way forward, I suggest, in McCall's own stress on "irreducible distinction in divine action" (p. 121) affirmed by Catholic theology, both in the economy of salvation and — even more clearly — in the immanent Trinity. McCall himself follows Aquinas in postulating that actions only come from actors, arguing that "it is not unreasonable to ... suggest that the divine persons are distinct agents (who interact with one another and with their creation)," and that "at the very least, my proposal is consistent with these emphases that were vital to Christian orthodoxy" (p. 123). I will allow that his move from actions to actors is not unreasonable and not inconsistent, but it is not the only move and, in my view, it is not the best one; it does not seem to do justice to mystery and ineffability.

My own account prefers to remain with the idea of *actions* in the life of God (internal and external), declining to draw the conclusion of actors or agents and understanding the "persons" to be nothing more or less than distinct movements of relationship that catch us up into their momentum and in which we participate. My own chapter explains this idea further, in what the editor has dubbed a "radical" relational account. However, it is worth making the point now that McCall is less convincing when he claims that the Gospel accounts of the relation of the *Holy Spirit* to the Father and the Son portray interpersonal agents in relationship. It is hard to make the Holy Spirit fit this category; perhaps this gives us a clue to the nature of all three divine persons.

McCall *is* convincing in his appeal to scriptural portrayals of the praying of the Son to the Father eternally, and to Paul's telling us that the Holy Spirit "intercedes" for us (Rom 8:26). "What is this," he asks, "if not intra-trinitarian communication?" (p. 120). It is a powerful point, but its effectiveness lies in the appeal to "communication," not to "communicators." The image of prayer, taken as an analogy, evokes a movement like speech or self-expression going on eternally in God, characterized by the giving and receiving of love. If conceived as a personal agent (the Son) praying to God the Father, then surely this situation belongs to the life of the earthly Jesus, as Holmes insists. McCall in fact seems to be a little unfair in proposing that the *only* alternative to individual speech-agents in relationships is conceiving God as a single subject.

In my view McCall unjustly ascribes this view to Barth, and — though he does not explicitly mention Holmes and Molnar — they should also not be pushed into this category of thinking either. They simply want to say, for example, "the Father begets the Son" without defining this as an eternal "I-Thou" relationship, just as I myself want to speak of "father-son relations" in God without implications of "I and Thou." I do agree with McCall, nevertheless, that when we speak of the Father and Son as "loving" each other, the analogy does require *some* content from what we experience as loving relations in our own created lives. In this way, both our accounts are "relational."

At the heart of McCall's account is a denial that his relational approach is a species of social trinitarianism, though I suggest that he stands closer to this approach than I do because of his stress on the persons as "individual speech-agents." Aiming to distance himself from social trinitarians, he explains that they "are right to recognize 'I-Thou' relationships within God's own life, but they are wrong to deny a strong account of monotheism" (p. 137). Whereas social trinitarians find the divine unity either in the perfect cooperation of the persons or in *generic* sameness of their substance, he argues for a *numerical* identity of substance while retaining distinct persons in an "I-Thou" relation. Any acceptable doctrine of the Trinity, he believes, "should be consistent with the view that the divine persons are distinct individuals (but not parts) and that there is exactly one divine individual (rather than a society)" (p. 130). He maintains it is possible to argue this by relying on the tools of analytic theology, which offers two options — either a "constitution" theory, in which identity claims for the divine persons are relativized and are conceived on analogy with form-matter compounds;

or else alternatively, a version of the doctrine of divine simplicity as modified by John Duns Scotus and given a modern form in the work of Keith Yandell.

The former approach seems to me to place too much reliance on the analogy of materiality, but the latter appears to have considerable potential for a doctrine of the Trinity. For Yandell, the triune God indeed is "simple" in one sense but "complex" in another important sense, and simplicity and complexity are seen as consistent with each other. God is necessarily simple in the sense that God "is not composed of parts or pieces," but also complex in the sense that the divine persons are "necessarily strongly internally related"; thus God is "necessarily particularly strongly internally complex" in a perichoretic "relation of mutual profound love" (p. 132).

I myself want to argue that a God who is "simple" in the sense of having no parts is also complex (as my chapter proposes), but I suggest that understanding the persons as "movements of relationship" rather than "speech-agents" in an I-Thou relationship makes it possible to conceive this simple-complexity without the convoluted logical formulation to which Yandell and McCall in turn are driven. A complex event of interweaving relations can be conceived as having no "parts" without resorting to a piece of analytic theology, by which only an analytic philosopher will probably be convinced. Three movements of love in complex relationship might also better accord with the theory of Scotus about "formal" distinctions between the persons of the Trinity, where persons are both really inseparable (not, properly speaking, parts) and nonetheless genuinely distinct.

Moreover, this conception of divine simplicity need not entail the conclusion drawn by McCall that "because the loving relationships between the Father, Son, and Holy Spirit are essential to the triune life, there is no sense in which God can be said to 'need' the world (to actualize himself, to display his glory, etc.)" (p. 134). In Christian tradition the "simplicity" of God has indeed been taken to mean that God cannot be affected by anything external to God's self, and the same implication has been drawn from the related idea of the aseity of God. But the affirmations that God has no parts and that God is self-existent need not stand against the conviction that God can — in humble love — choose not to be self-sufficient, but rather to be in need, and to allow the divine relations to be enhanced by relations with created beings. Indeed, such a vision of a God who chooses not to be complete without the world is consistent with One who opens the divine relational life for our participation in God.

REJOINDER COMMENTS AND CLARIFICATION

THOMAS H. MCCALL

I am pleased to see substantial agreement with colleagues on several important points. Rather than continuing to focus on areas of agreement (and at the risk of clouding those), in these final comments I shall address several issues of contention.

I have argued that we should think of the divine persons as co-inhering in "I-Thou" relationships. Holmes thinks that my efforts are successful (at least in avoiding tritheism) but also lacking sufficient support and ultimately unnecessary. He judges my conclusions under-supported because he thinks that the exegetical basis isn't really so broad or deep as I suppose. But he doesn't engage all the evidence that I adduce. The case from the discourse between the persons in the divine economy isn't "destroyed" by the admission that much of it pertains to the voice of the *incarnate* Son:[73] after all, the Father also addresses the Son (and sends the Spirit), the Son refers to the loving communion shared "before the world began" (John 17:24), and the Spirit addresses the Father. Holmes addresses only the latter (Rom 8:26), but he doesn't actually have all that much to say about it. He asserts that prayer is "necessarily a creaturely action," but he doesn't yet give us reason to think that the Spirit isn't addressing the Father. Holmes also seems to think that what I say is unnecessary because it is based on a misunderstanding of the tradition, for the divine hypostases are "existent instantiations" (apparently *rather than* persons who exist in "I-Thou" relations). But as I have argued, it is a mistake to pit such an account against what I propose (or to label it "late modern/romantic"). To the contrary, I agree with Gilles Emery when he says that "we need not contrast Thomas's metaphysical attitude to the topic with one which stresses the 'psychological' elements of the

---

73. Moreover, while it is true that much of this concerns the incarnate Son, it is also true that we should predicate agency to the *person* of the Son (even if it is the Son *qua* humanity) rather than to the human nature itself.

person (such as the life of the mind: knowledge, freedom, action, and openness to another), *because these elements are integrated into his own approach.*"[74]

Molnar, on the other hand, seems convinced that what I hold about the divine persons amounts to tritheism. Unfortunately, it isn't clear to me that he is working with the best understanding of my position. What is clear to me is an even more unfortunate tendency to substitute assertion for argument. He observes that I cite Scripture "to illustrate that the divine persons have 'I-Thou' relations." So far, so good; indeed, I do this. But Molnar doesn't really understand *why* I appeal to Scripture.[75] Moreover, he asserts that this cannot be true according to the "classical view of the Trinity," but he never demonstrates from classical sources that this is the wrong way to read Scripture. Nor does he actually engage the exegetical arguments.

Or consider Molnar's treatment of my argument from the *opera ad intra*. I argue that the eternal generation of the Son, for instance, is uniquely and completely the work of the Father (I do not, contra Molnar's "hence," confuse this with the *ad extra*). Somehow, Molnar disagrees and further claims that this doctrine "appears tritheistic" and "could open the door to subordinationism." We are left to wonder just what the alternative might be. The Son generates himself, or cogenerates himself? Perhaps so, for Molnar says that the singularity of divine agency includes "all their actions *ad intra*." *This* is supposed to be "classical" trinitarianism? More explanation would be helpful, as would a more developed argument for such a striking conclusion.

Things get even stranger when we consider the *opera ad extra*. Molnar makes many affirmations with which I agree wholeheartedly; for

---

74. Gilles Emery, *The Trinitarian Theology of St Thomas Aquinas* (Oxford: Oxford University Press, 2007), 106 (emphasis mine). See also M. William Ury, *Trinitarian Personhood: Investigating the Implications of a Relational Definition* (Eugene, OR: Wipf & Stock, 2002). Another clarification: as I should have made plainer, I don't *base* my view on van Inwagen's work, but only use it as a helpful summary of what I take to be an important (and biblically based) theological desideratum.

75. I say that there is "a sense" in which the Bible may rightly be said to be the Word of God, but I do not "equate" the Bible with divine revelation (in the sense of identity). In my essay (p. 114 n3) I mention my article "On Understanding Scripture as the Word of God," in *Analytic Theology: New Essays on the Philosophy of Theology* (ed. Michael C. Rea and Oliver D. Crisp; Oxford: Oxford University Press, 2009), 171–86. See also my essay, "Ronald Thiemann, Thomas Torrance and Epistemological Doctrines of Revelation," *IJST* 6 (2004): 148–68. Here I engage the very concern raised by Molnar.

instance, I agree that "the Son was never separated from the other persons" during his Passion. I have no idea why Molnar would suggest that I might think otherwise (indeed, I have written a book on the topic).[76] But he makes other claims as well, some of which are surprising (when offered as representative of historic orthodoxy). For instance, he refers to the "pain of the Father" in the passion of Christ. So now some version of *patripassianism* is said to be "the classical view"?

Throughout, Molnar charges my view with tritheism (or something close). But beyond the platitude that we are talking about God rather than a math problem, he offers no real engagement with what I actually say about monotheism. This is disappointing. I have deep respect for Professor Molnar, but without an argument it is hard either to be corrected or, alternatively, to show where he might be mistaken. I do, however, want to state my appreciation for Molnar's insistence that we should do theology in obedience to divine revelation. I have *tried* to let God's self-revelation "shape" my understanding of the Trinity. The realization that one might speak wrongly of such important matters is sobering and humbling. Though what I have said is surely incomplete, I trust that I have spoken rightly of God, and I hope that I have done so in a way that brings honor to the Lord of glory.[77]

---

76. Thomas H. McCall, *Forsaken: The Trinity and the Cross, and Why It Matters* (Downers Grove, IL: InterVarsity Press, 2012).

77. Thanks to Isaac McCall for his advice on this essay.

RELATIONAL TRINITY: RADICAL PERSPECTIVE

PAUL S. FIDDES

A Radical Proposal

"Candidates should attempt three questions, taking at least one from each section of the paper." This is a rubric that I have often written for an examination paper, and there is a sense in which I and my fellow contributors to this volume are facing a similar challenge, though under examination only (fortunately) from our readers. Our editor has proposed that we should follow a common threefold division of the subject of trinitarian theology: first, the method and sources on which we are drawing; second, the doctrine we are commending; third, its implications for the life of church and society today. In this way, readers should be able the more easily to compare our approaches within our conversation with each other.

But before I embark on these three questions, I judge that I should put up-front the kind of approach I am taking, which has been called — for the purpose of this book — a "radical relational account." This strategy is not as elegant as working up to my proposal gradually, first enticing and teasing readers with the problems and then unveiling my solution with a revelatory flourish, but for purposes of comparison it may work better to come clean right at the beginning. My proposal is briefly this: that the most adequate and appropriate language we have available to speak about the "persons" of the Holy Trinity is that they are *relations*. More dynamically, they are *movements* of life and love that have some resemblance to the relationships that we recognize between finite persons. When we speak of "divine persons," we are using an analogy with relations, but not an analogy with human persons who *have* relations. Of course, those who do draw an analogy with human persons *in* relationship—often called "social trinitarians"—will hasten to add that divine persons are *completely* constituted by their relations with each other, where this is an unrealizable ideal in human life. I am dissenting even from this intensification of human societies in God when I make an analogy with "relationships" themselves.

So my proposal is a "relational" model that is not that of a social Trinity, even in a modified form. God is the name for an event or happening of relationships in which we are engaged. My proposal certainly shares with social trinitarianism the conviction that human "life-in-relationship" is our best way into a vision of God as Trinity,[1] and here I differ from two of my fellow contributors, Paul Molnar[2] and Stephen Holmes.[3] But my proposal differs greatly from social trinitarianism in that it does not conceive of God as a divine "society" or fellowship of individual persons, even when it is rightly asserted that "individuals" exist only in relations. In this way I differ also from my fellow-writer on relationality, Thomas McCall, who is closer to a social trinitarianism insofar as he understands the persons in God as personal "speech-agents," "distinct centers of consciousness," or "necessarily existent entities who enjoy 'I-Thou' relationships within the Trinity,"[4] although he does not ground divine unity simply in intensity of communion and cooperation.[5]

---

1. Examples of this kind of social trinitarianism are Jürgen Moltmann, *The Trinity and the Kingdom of God: The Doctrine of God* (trans. M. Kohl; London: SCM, 1981), 171–78; Ted Peters, *GOD as Trinity: Relationality and Temporality in Divine Life* (Louisville: Westminster John Knox, 1993), 10–20; Leonardo Boff, *Trinity and Society* (trans. Paul Burns; London: Burns & Oates, 1988), 134–54.

2. See Paul D. Molnar, *Divine Freedom and the Doctrine of the Immanent Trinity* (London: T&T Clark, 2002), 125–66.

3. See Stephen R. Holmes, *The Quest for the Trinity: The Doctrine of God in Scripture, History and Modernity* (Downers Grove, IL: InterVarsity Press, 2012), 16–29, 199–200. UK: *The Holy Trinity: Understanding God's Life* (Milton Keynes, UK: Paternoster, 2012).

4. Thomas H. McCall, *Which Trinity? Whose Monotheism? Philosophical and Systematic Theologians on the Metaphysics of Trinitarian Theology* (Grand Rapids: Eerdmans, 2010), 57, 70–73, 236–40; see McCall's essay in this volume, "Relational Trinity: Creedal Perspective," 113–37.

5. McCall, *Which Trinity?* 241–43. Nor does he ground it alone in sharing the same divine essence, but rather in a "constitution Trinitarianism"; see McCall, *Which Trinity?* 45–49, 106–10, 243–44 and my comments on his essay in this volume (pp. 150–55).

Our editor has labeled my approach "Relational Trinity: Radical Perspective," and I am content to accept this as a convenient designation. It is not radical in the sense of sitting light either to Scripture or to the Christian tradition, as I hope will become clear. It may be called radical insofar as it makes relation the final available concept we have for thinking about God and so is taking relationality to a radical conclusion. It is also radical in trying to get to the *radix* or "root" of our experience of God, which I suggest is not at basis an experience of one or more superior beings or even agents without bodies, but an experience of participating in movements of life, an experience that is like participating in relationships. Stripping things down to the bare root, this is *all* we can say, and it is *enough* theologically and spiritually. Talk of God as "an event of relationships" is then not an objectifying but a participatory kind of speech. It only makes sense as an account of *participating* in divine life and communion, not as a description of an object of observation by a subject.[6]

In case this sounds impossibly abstract, let me draw attention to the experience of Christian prayer, as one place where this participation comes alive. The cry of *"Abba*, Father" in prayer fits into a movement of speech like that between a son and a father; our response of "yes" ("Amen") leans on a movement that is like a filial "yes" of humble obedience, glorifying the Father, a response that is already there before us. At the same time, we find ourselves involved in a movement of self-giving like that of a father sending out a son on a journey, a movement that the early theologians called "eternal generation" and that has its outworking in the mission ("sending") of the Son by the Father in history to achieve the reconciliation of all things. In this moment of participation we discover that these movements of response and mission are undergirded by movements of suffering, like the painful longing of a forsaken son toward a father and of a desolate father toward a lost son. Here is where Jürgen Moltmann speaks of God as "the event of Golgotha," and to the question whether one can pray "to an event," he rightly answers that one can pray "*in* this event."[7]

---

6. I have worked this out in detail in Paul S. Fiddes, *Participating in God: A Pastoral Doctrine of the Trinity* (London: Darton, Longman and Todd; Louisville: Westminster John Knox, 2000), 34–55, 71–88.

7. Jürgen Moltmann, *The Crucified God* (trans. M. Kohl; London: SCM, 1974), 247 (italics in original).

Moreover, these two directions of movement, sending and response, are interwoven by a third, as we find that they are continually opened up to new depths of relationship and to the new possibilities of the future by a movement for which Scripture offers impressionistic images — a wind blowing, breath stirring, wings beating, oil trickling, water flowing, fire burning. The traditional formulation that the Spirit "proceeds from the Father through the Son" points to a movement that renews all relations "from" and "to" the other. In the language of the New Testament, we are praying to the Father, through the Son, and in the Spirit.[8]

Thus, through our participation, we can identify three distinct movements that are all like speech, emotion, and action; they are like movements within relationships "from father to son" and "from son to father," together with a movement of "deepening relations." They are mutual relationships of ecstatic, outward-going love, giving and receiving. Actively they are such moments as originating, responding, and opening; passively they are moments of being glorified, being sent, and being breathed. So far in describing them I have followed the form of address that Jesus himself taught his disciples, "Our Father" (Matt 6:9; cf. "Abba, Father," Mark 14:36), offering the image "from son to father" for the movement of response that we lean on.

But these movements of giving and receiving cannot in themselves be restricted to a particular gender, as is quite clear with the images for the movement of Spirit. They will also, in appropriate contexts, give rise to feminine images; for instance, the experience of our participation may require us to say that we are engaging in a flow of relationships like those originating in a mother (cf. Isa 49:14–15), especially in experiences of being spiritually nurtured and fed. Or these movements may seem like those that we can only say are characterized by the response of a daughter; without type-casting what such a response would be, as distinct from that of a son, in some circumstances we can *recognize* the same kind of "daughterly" response in God as we know in human life.

Methodology and Sources

Like other contributors to this book, I give primary *written* authority in making Christian doctrine to the Holy Scriptures as the text that has

---

8. See Matt 6:6; John 14:16; Eph 6:18; Heb 7:25.

most formatively shaped the community of which I am a member. Ultimate authority, of course, belongs to Jesus Christ, as the incarnate Word of God to whom all Scripture witnesses.[9] Second in *written* authority to Scripture is the tradition of the church, which interprets Scripture, and especially the tradition of the early ecumenical councils. So for the source of trinitarian doctrine we must begin with the New Testament, whose writers are attempting—inspired by the Holy Spirit—to grasp a new and final disclosure of God in Jesus of Nazareth.

New Testament writers were searching for concepts and images to express an *experience* based in revelation. That is, they were trying to articulate the richness of the personality of God that they had found in the story of salvation and in their own experience. It was no longer sufficient to say "the LORD" when they spoke a blessing in worship (Num 6:24–26); they had to speak of the love of the Father, the grace of the Lord Jesus, and the fellowship of the Holy Spirit (1 Cor 13:14), although they knew that the ultimate demand on their lives must come from one Lord. They began with God at work in salvation, healing human life. They had encountered God in the actions and words of a human Son, Jesus Christ; they found God revealed and active in this Son, who welcomed outcasts into the kingdom of God the Father and spoke the word of forgiveness on God's behalf. They found God in a new energy and guidance they experienced within their community, opening up relationships beyond the accepted social boundaries and opening up a hope for a future new creation; they could only speak of this in terms of the "Holy Spirit" of God, and they associated this Spirit in some way with the ongoing presence of Jesus Christ, who had been crucified (2 Cor 3:17–18), though they were not completely clear about the relation of "the Spirit of God," the "Spirit of Christ," and "the Holy Spirit." So the early followers of Jesus had to rethink their understanding of the being of God because of their experience of God's self-disclosure and acts among them.

They experimented with a range of language, drawing largely on the Jewish images of their heritage. Already in Judaism there was a feeling after diversity in God: Israelite prophets and poets had found "extensions of the divine personality"[10] in images of word, name, wisdom,

---

9. Barth, *CD* I/1:111–20.

10. Aubrey R. Johnson, *The One and the Many in the Israelite Conception of God* (Cardiff, UK: University of Wales Press, 1942), 20–26.

and spirit, and this discovery was now accentuated by their experience of Christ. One important concept here was the "wisdom" of God, leading to the conviction that in some way the preexistence of wisdom must apply to Christ.[11] Another significant concept was that of the Israelite king in the Psalms as a human "son of God," "sitting at the right hand of God," leading to images of the exaltation and glorification of the risen Christ.[12] The New Testament writings display an experimental approach to what we can only call complexity and relationality in God.

These experiments in language are response to revelation, to the self-disclosure of God in Christ, and so I cannot regard "relationality" as a concept projected purely out of human experience.[13] I will have more to say about the portrayal of the unique relation of Christ to God his Father later. These aspects of complexity and relationality were to be given conceptual definition by the Church Fathers with the language of "one *ousia* (essence) and three *hypostases*." It is not possible to impose this matrix of terms on the New Testament text and to draw from it exact conclusions about the nature of divine *hypostases*, such as concluding them to be "subjects," or "agents," or even "centers of consciousness."

Nevertheless, the development of thought about Trinity in the church is in continuity with the New Testament evocation of complexity and relationality, and I suggest that the New Testament hints of Trinity are faithfully captured in understanding the divine "persons" as relations. This is a model of thinking that I believe to be also grounded in Christian tradition. I cannot claim that there are any *direct* sources for it in the tradition, in the sense of the whole concept being directly stated there, but I do suggest that for our present age, it takes up key elements in the past thinking of the church and does justice to both the thinking and the experience of the church. So here are five points of origin for this model.

Hypostasis Not the Modern Notion of "Person"

In the first place, when the Church Fathers spoke in Greek of "three *hypostases*," the word *hypostasis* did not have the modern sense of a per-

---

11. E.g., Prov 8:22–31; cf. John 1:1–18; 1 Cor 1:18–30; Col 1:15–20.

12. E.g., Ps 2:7; cf. Ps 110:1; Acts 13.3; Heb 1:5; also Acts 2:34; Rom 8:34; 1 Cor 15:25; Heb 8:1; Col 3:1.

13. Against Molnar, *Divine Freedom*, 146.

son as a psychological center of consciousness. It meant something like a distinct instantiation of being or a distinct identity. My partner in conversation Thomas McCall admits this as a historical datum, but he argues that it is still *appropriate* to understand "*hypostases*" from *our* perspective as three agents in an I-Thou relation (or in his earlier work, as three centers of consciousness).[14] I agree with Stephen Holmes and Paul Molnar that any thought of persons with their own will and consciousness is imposing a modern framework of thinking on the tradition, but they may not be pleased that I am *also* reading the tradition from a contemporary perspective and asking what might be appropriate. My argument is that it is *more* appropriate to understand this distinct identity as a relationship than as a center of consciousness or even a personal agent; I urge that relationships can have their own distinct manner of being and be different from each other.

Hypostasis Defined Relationally

Second, the Church Fathers and the Scholastic theologians defined *hypostasis* relationally; a *hypostasis* or person (corresponding to the Latin *persona*) was entirely constituted by its relation to the other *hypostases* in God. The *hypostases* of Father, Son, and Spirit were not isolated, individual realities but existed only in relation to each other; there is no hint here of the modern concept of the person as a self-sufficient individual choosing to join a society as a kind of extension of his or her existence.

Athanasius is a good example of this relational way of thinking. Although this church father finally consented to the formula "one *ousia*, three *hypostases*," he could not get enthusiastic about what the philosophical difference might be between a *hypostasis* and an *ousia*.[15] He was more captivated by the *relations* of Father, Son, and Spirit. To the skeptical Arian question as to what the difference could be between the persons if they are one in divine essence (*ousia*), he gave a different kind of answer than a philosophical concept: the Father is "other" (*heteros*), Athansasius asserted, in that he alone begets the Son, the Son is

---

14. Cf. McCall, *Which Trinity?* 70–71, 236–40; cf. also his essay in this volume.

15. In fact, in some usages he treated these terms as identical; see *Contra Ar.* 1.11 (*NPNF²* 4:327–33); *De decretis* 27 (*NPNF²* 4:168–69); *De synodis* 41 (*NPNF²* 4:472).

"other" in that he alone is begotten, and the Spirit is "other" in that he alone proceeds from the Father through the Son.[16] They are different in the way they are related to each other in their origins. This doctrine of relations was taken up by the Cappadocians in the East — who spoke of paternity, filiation, and spiration — and indeed by Augustine in the West.[17] This is probably what Gregory of Nazianzus means when he says that the term "Father" is not a name for being (*ousia*) but for the relation (*schesis*) between the Father and the Son.[18]

A radical relational trinitarianism builds on this perception in two ways. On the one hand, the persons are more than *constituted* by relations — they *are* nothing more or less than relations. Gregory, we might say, spoke truer than he intended. On the other hand, they can be characterized by more than their relations of *origin*. The movements of relation can be envisaged as being like many movements of relationship in the world; indeed the divine relations can be found *in* all the relations we know in the world. Working back from the economic Trinity, the immanent divine relations can be found displayed above all in the life of Jesus, in his relation to God his Father, and in his empowerment for his ministry by the Holy Spirit.

But we can also discern the nature of the divine relationships of giving and receiving in love in such relations as those between a mother and the baby in her womb, between children and parents, between wife and husband, and between members of the church community. Although I am not advocating a social trinitarianism, there is an insight here from this model that I want to affirm and commend. Here it is clear that I differ from Holmes, who asserts that "the three divine *hypostases* are distinguished by eternal relations of origin — begetting and proceeding — and not otherwise."[19] The difference between us derives finally, it seems, from an understanding about the relation of God to the world, and this is a point to which I intend to return.

---

16. Athanasius, *Contra Ar.* 3.4–6, cp. 1.9, 39, 58 (*NPNF²* 4:395–97; cf. 4:311, 329, 340).

17. See, e.g., Gregory Nazianzen, *Orationes* 29.16 (*NPNF²* 7:306–7); Augustine, *De Trinitate* 5.6–13 (*NPNF¹* 3:89–94).

18. Gregory Nazianzen, *Orationes*, 23.8 (cf. *St. Gregory of Nazianzus: Select Orations* [trans. Martha Vinson; The Fathers of the Church 107; Washington, DC: Catholic University of America Press, 2003], 137).

19. Holmes, *The Quest for the Trinity*, 200.

Subsistent Relations

Third, if my relational model radicalizes the relational nature of *hypostasis*, there are hints of this already in a tradition of what has been called "subsistent relations," that is, the view that relations in God are as real and "beingful" as anything that is created or uncreated, and that their ground of existence is in themselves. Augustine is at least moving toward this idea when he deals with the alternative presented to him by the Arians, that the persons of the Trinity must be distinguished either by their substance (hence ending in tritheism) or accident (hence without the enduring nature of divinity); he replies in an experimental, even playful, way, that "the names, Father and Son, do not refer to the substance but to the relation, and the relation is no accident."[20] Although J. N. D. Kelly suggests that we should understand this statement squarely in line with the belief of Porphyry and Plotinus that relations in themselves have real subsistence,[21] it would be better to recognize that the phrase "the names refer to the relations" has the character of thought in process. Augustine is struggling to find a language to express the revolutionary idea that God exists in the communion of "paternity, filiation and gift," a concept that challenged all philosophy of the time.

Thomas Aquinas later gave formality to the notion by creating the actual term "subsistent relation," stating that "'divine person' signifies relation as something subsisting ... 'person' signifies relation directly and nature indirectly, yet relation is signified, not as relation, but as hypostasis."[22] Aquinas helpfully begins his discussion with *actions* in God, that is, with the two processions of "begetting" and "breathing forth." Then he shows that two processions imply four kinds of "real relations" (begetting, being begotten, breathing out, being breathed), which in turn imply three unique relations: begetting (including breathing out), being begotten, and being breathed forth.[23] These are the subsistent relations that we call "Father, Son and Holy Spirit," and a key point is that Aquinas has begun with movements or actions within God

---

20. Augustine, *De Trinitate* 5.6; translation from *The Trinity* (trans. Stephen McKenna; The Fathers of the Church 45; Washington, DC: Catholic University of America Press, 1963), 180.

21. J. N. D. Kelly, *Early Christian Doctrines* (4th ed.; London: Black, 1968), 275.

22. Aquinas, *ST* 1a.29.4 (Blackfriars ed., 6:61).

23. Ibid., 1a.27.1; 28.4 (Blackfriars ed., 6:3–7, 35–41).

rather than subjects who act in various ways. Unfortunately the potential here for developing a dynamic concept of God based on action and relationship rather than agents is spoiled because Aquinas explains the self-existence or subsistence of the relationships by the fact that they are identical with the one essence of God. In his view, they subsist because they are *the same* as the one divine substance which itself has self-existence.[24] So they too must be self-existent. This identity with one substance gives inflammable fuel to the suspicion Eastern theologians have that talk of "subsistent relations" is simply in aid of the typical Western stress on the unity of God's essence: the "relations" seem to be swallowed up into the one essence with the loss of any real threeness and "otherness" of persons within God.

For those who are interested in how Aquinas arrived at this point, we may note that he was deeply influenced by the Aristotelian view that the divine essence must be "simple," or radically unified. If this is so, both the properties and the relations of the essence must be identical with it; so the relations in God will have the same reality as the one essence. Hence relations subsist. This argument appears to underplay the important insight of the early Eastern theologians, that the being of God is communion or fellowship.

Augustine has also been accused of losing a grasp on this truth by using a psychological analogy for the Trinity and so finding a correspondence in aspects of the human mind (memory, understanding, will). His playful idea that the divine persons are relations is read in the light of this image, and he has been reviled as the chief architect of the Western "modalistic" tendency of stressing the oneness of God at the expense of any real diversity of persons.[25] Admittedly, his concentration on the image of the Trinity within the human soul did leave the impression that he conceived of God as an absolute individual with different faculties. However, we should also notice that his interest in psychological analogies was driven by a deep sense of our participation in God, and he preferred to speak not just of memory, understanding, and will, but the actions of our mind's remembering *God*, understanding

---

24. Ibid., 1a.29.4 (Blackfriars ed., 6:57–63); cf. 1a.3.6 (2:39–41); and 1a.27.4 (6:15–19).

25. E.g., Colin Gunton, *The Promise of Trinitarian Theology* (Edinburgh: T&T Clark, 1991), 38–41.

God, and loving *God*.[26] Thus he associated the triune persons with our involvement in God.

We can take up this insight, together with Aquinas's strategy of beginning with processions (actions) in God, to put the idea of "subsistent relations" on quite a different basis from that of one, simple, divine essence. Augustine too, we notice, had also assumed the simplicity of the divine essence and used this as the reason why the relations should be understood as eternally necessary to the being of God and not merely accidental. "Relation," he thought, could indicate a distinction in the essence of God without infringing divine simplicity.[27] I myself will be arguing, as I go on, for a view of God as complex rather than simple being, and so I prefer to put subsistent relations on a different basis, for which I find a fourth clue from more recent thinking—that of Karl Barth.

Barth and God's Being in Act

I refer to Barth's insistence that, "with regard to the being of God, the word 'event' or 'act' is *final*."[28] According to Barth, if God's self-revelation is a "happening," then God must "happen" in God's own self. God always speaks the truth about God's self, so if God unveils God's self as an event, then in an *eternal* event of self-repetition, God is "thrice ... the divine I," and eludes being objectified as either a numerically single "I" or three individual "I's."[29] Barth avoids using the term "person" to denote what are thereby distinguished in God as Father, Son, and Spirit, as he believes the word to be inevitably bound up with modern notions of an individual self-consciousness and so an undermining of the one lordship of God.[30] His preference for "mode (or way) of being" (*Seinsweise*) does, however, give some hostages to those who accuse him of presenting God as the absolute Subject of the Idealist heritage, reflexively diversifying himself.[31]

---

26. Augustine, *De Trinitate* 14.15–20 (*NPNF¹* 3:192–94).

27. Augustine, *De Trinitate* 5.3–9 (*NPNF¹* 3:88–91).

28. Barth, *CD*, II/1:263.

29. Ibid., I/1:351.

30. Ibid., I/1:355–59.

31. So Moltmann, *Trinity and the Kingdom of God*, 142; Catherine Mowry LaCugna, *God for Us: The Trinity and Christian Life* (San Francisco: HarperSanFrancisco, 1991), 252–53.

In my view this is an unfair accusation, as it is clear that Barth conceives the "ways of being" to be always defined by their relationships.[32] But it would be better to take up his insight into the event character of God—and so to take up Aquinas's strategy of beginning with actions or processions in God—by speaking of three *"movements of being characterized by relationship,"* or more simply "movements of relationship." We can then build on the classical Western formula of "three relationships subsisting in one being," perhaps reformulating it as "three movements of relationship subsisting in one event." Robert Jenson has a similar intention when he speaks of God as "an event constituted in relations and personal in structure."[33]

Divine Ineffability

The final clue I take from the Christian tradition is its insistence on the ineffability of God. In the context of discussing persons as relations, Augustine exclaims that we only use the word person "in order that we may not remain wholly silent when asked 'three what?'"[34] For Aquinas, talk of three persons or relations is not a literal description of God, but the most appropriate language we have for an ultimate reality that is a supreme mystery.[35] The question is, at what point are we reduced to silence? What is the most appropriate language, given that all talk of God is metaphorical? Basil of Caesarea thinks that we *can* speak of one substance or essence of God, and of a plurality of names for God; but then silence intervenes—plurality of names cannot be pressed to imply plurality of divine essence, since the nature of the one divine being is unknowable.[36] My own approach is to speak about plurality of *relationships*, but to remain silent about any concept of them as an *object* of thought.

When the proposal is made that the persons *are* relationships, the objection is likely to be brought forward that talk of relations makes no

---

32. Barth, *CD*, I/1:364–67.

33. Robert W. Jenson, *The Triune Identity: God according to the Gospel* (Philadelphia: Fortress, 1982), 161.

34. Augustine, *De Trinitate*, 7.11 (*NPNF¹* 3:112). Cf. Athanasius, *Contra Ar.* 2.36 (*NPNF²* 4:367–68).

35. Aquinas, *ST* 1a.27.1 (Blackfriars ed., 6:3–7).

36. *Contra Eunomium* 1.19 (cf. St. Basil of Caesarea, *Against Eunomius* [trans. Mark Del-Cogliano and Andrew Radde-Gallwitz; The Fathers of the Church 122; Washington, DC: Catholic University of America Press, 2011], 119–20).

sense without *subjects* who have relations. How can there be relations without subjects or agents on each end of them? the critics ask. But this is where we have to be silent; *this* is the *apophasis*. Of course, it is not possible to visualize, paint on canvas, carve in stone, or etch in glass three interweaving relationships, or three movements of being characterized by their relations, without subjects exercising them. It is not even possible to visualize this reality in the mind. But then this ought to be a positive advantage in thinking about God, who cannot be objectified like other objects in the world.[37] This is where we employ appropriate talk and *also* fall silent. The triune God cannot be visualized as three individual subjects who *have* relationships. Talk about God as "an event of relationships" is not the language of a spectator or observer, but the language of a participant. It only makes sense in terms of our involvement in the network of relationships in which God happens.

What Kind of Analogy?

I am thus advocating an analogy between the uncreated God and creatures. It is an analogy based in creation itself, or being made in the image of God; it is based in revelation, since the Christian community believes that there have been moments of disclosure in which people have been impelled to talk of God in personal terms, and Scripture bears witness to these decisive, community-shaping events; and the analogy is finally based in the incarnation of Christ as a human person who fully reveals God to us. But the analogy, I am proposing, is not between persons themselves but between *relations*, human and divine.

Of course relationships in human life require individual persons, since we are finite beings, bounded by bodies that are essential to our identity. But God is infinite and cannot be categorized or placed in any class of being. God is unique, incomparable. God is not bound by the rule that relations need individual agents. Analogy is about a likeness and an unlikeness between terms; I am proposing that the likeness is in the relations, the unlikeness in whether the relations *have* to be conceived as exercised by subjects. The notion of analogy also makes clear that there can be no literal or univocal language about an ineffable God;

---

37. So also David B. Burrell, *Aquinas: God and Action* (London: Routledge and Kegan Paul, 1979), 143.

we are seeking for the most appropriate and least inadequate language; this, I am proposing, is about participating in relationships.

This refusal to classify God as either one subject or three subjects may provide some response to the postmodern protest against God as a dominating subject who supposedly validates human subjects in their attempts to control the world around them.[38] There has been a postmodern reaction against the Enlightenment view of the self that finds its identity in controlling its environment and in treating the world and others as objects to be used. However, this does not mean we need to subscribe to an extreme postmodern view of the human self where it is radically decentered and viewed only as the "whence" and the "whereto" of relationships. This might well happen if we were to apply unequivocally the idea of the divine persons as "relations without remainder" to *human* subjects; this would make it hard to affirm any individuality of human persons, even one that is inseparable from relationships with others. The human person would evaporate into a mere bundle of relationships and fragmentary experiences. This is where the aspect of "unlikeness" in the analogy is significant.

But as we experience participation in the communion of a God where there are no subjects to be discerned, we may be able to overcome *some* of the gap and even hostility between subjects and objects in the world, cease to treat others as objects to be manipulated, and develop a deeper sympathy with the natural world in which we are immersed.

It may be argued, nevertheless, that language of personal relations should be subordinated to another kind of language — that of being. This challenge may be mounted from two directions. In the first place, it may come from those who stand close to the Christian tradition and think that only its language of "one being" ("substance" or "essence") is sufficient to safeguard the unity of a triune God. Paul Molnar, for instance, proposes that talk of relationality is merely "symbolic," projected onto God from human experience, whereas talk of "being" — or who God *is* — is a kind of language shaped by revelation, or by "the objective reality of God revealed by the Word and Spirit."[39] I have

---

38. See Jacques Derrida, *Of Grammatology* (trans. G. C. Spivak; Baltimore, MD: Johns Hopkins University Press, 1976), 98.

39. Molnar, *Divine Freedom*, 24–25, 124, 135–36; cf. also his essay in this volume, 69–95.

already suggested that talk of relationality is actually response to revelation, no less than language of being, and that this is consistent with a vision of the whole world as participating in a self-disclosing God.

Second, talk of personal relations in God may be dismissed as a kind of second-order language about God not on grounds of revelation, but because it is seen as subordinate to a language that is supposedly more adequate for religious purposes, namely, that God is Being or "Being-itself." This is a modern, existential version of the medieval analogy of being, which Paul Tillich adopts,[40] and which has been presented in a more popular form by John Macquarrie, refashioning Martin Heidegger's distinction between Being and beings. Language of God as "Being" is claimed to be more capacious than language of persons, more capable of expressing both the transcendence of God over the world and the immanence of God in the world, since we cannot think of Being directly but only as that which supports and sustains beings, or which (as Macquarrie puts it) "lets beings be."[41] This in turn leads Macquarrie to a refashioning of trinitarian Persons as "Primordial Being, Expressive Being and Unitive Being."[42]

This approach has the advantage of beginning from experience, while developing an "ontology" from it. Macquarrie, for instance, points to experiences of awe and wonder that we can identify as encounters with "Holy Being," or negative experiences in which the world falls to "nothing" with which Being can be contrasted. I do not want to deny that the analogy of Being has a useful place in theology. If all talk about God is metaphorical, then we can draw on the metaphor of being as well as the metaphor of relations. I *do* want to resist the claim that the analogy of being is *superior* to that of relations, or that language about personal relationships in God is more restrictive than language of Being.[43] Those who maintain this do not usually think that personal language is *useless* in religion; it is admitted, for instance, to have an indispensable place in public and private prayers, where "Holy Father" seems more appropriate than "Holy Being." God, after all, is "not less than personal"

40. Paul Tillich, *Systematic Theology* (London: Nisbet, 1968), 1:261–71.

41. John Macquarrie, *Principles of Christian Theology* (rev. ed.; London: SCM, 1977), 115–22, 142–45.

42. Ibid., 200–202.

43. Macquarrie, *Principles*, 93–94.

because Being lets persons be and so (in the words of Tillich) Being has "the power of personality."[44] The claim I want to resist, however, is that when we set out to think as carefully as we can in theology, "Being which overcomes non-being" is more adequate.

This kind of theology is right to insist that God is unique and unclassifiable and therefore cannot be put in a class with other beings by being conceived either as "a" being or "three beings," even the most elevated. However, it assumes that speaking of God as "personal" must reduce God to one or three individual beings, a confusion of thought often condemned under the name of "ontotheology."[45] In fact there is something mysterious about personalness that makes it an apt image for the otherness of God; we can never get what it is to be personal under our control or objectify it, since it inhabits the space of the "between" of communication. If we are looking for traces of God as the mystery in our midst, then the area of the personal is most promising. The metaphor of relationality expresses both transcendence and immanence, in fact the one in the other.

We must therefore think the "personalness" of God in a way that does not reduce God in any way to one individual subject (that is, "*a* person") or three subjects. This does not seem to be achievable by drawing a close analogy with individual human persons, although the way that they are formed through relationships certainly points toward the *transcending* of individual subjectivity. The clue is to think of personal relations in a truly participatory way. Unlike the language of Being, this has the advantage of being consistent with the experience and words of worship and so has a place in the corporate life of a community.

Doctrine of the Trinity: The Distinction of Persons

We have already been moving from questions of method to the content of trinitarian theology. Traditionally this has aimed to distinguish Father, Son, and Spirit from each other. Three movements of relationship might be comprehensible enough as united in one overall movement, satisfying the oneness of God, but are "persons" conceived in this

---

44. Tillich, *Systematic Theology*, 1:271; Macquarrie, *Principles*, 204.

45. Martin Heidegger, "The Onto-theo-logical Constitution of Metaphysics," in *Identity and Difference* (trans. Joan Stambaugh; Chicago: University of Chicago Press, 2002), 58; Jacques Derrida, "Différance," in *Margins of Philosophy* (trans. Alan Bass; Chicago: University of Chicago Press, 1982), 6.

way truly distinct? In the first place, and in line with tradition, there is a distinction of origin: that is, in terms of my relational approach, there is a movement of generation, a movement of being generated, and a movement of being breathed out.

Though I want to add a range of other distinctions, these three remain controlling movements in the sense that they indicate a direction of flow in relations. The Father always remains the *archē*, or origin, or source of communion. There cannot be, for instance, any kind of distinctions that imply that an origin is being begotten or breathed out. Here I take issue with Leonardo Boff's indiscriminate use of the Latin image of reciprocal relations to assert that it is as true that the Father is breathed out by the Spirit as the Spirit by the Father.[46] The irreversible directions of relation derive from the revelation of God in the life of Christ and in his relations with the Father, as the begotten Son and as the *receiver* as well as giver of the Spirit. It thus maintains better the direction of flow to speak of the Spirit as proceeding "from the Father *through* the Son" rather than "and from the Son" (*filioque*).

We might say that there is a flow of a divine "dance," though "dance" can be only one metaphor for the interweaving and interpenetrating movements in God that have been traditionally expressed by *perichoresis*. First used for the doctrine of the Trinity, it seems, in the eighth century, the term *perichoresis* expresses the permeation of each person by the other, their coinherence without confusion.[47] It takes up and develops the words of Jesus in the Fourth Gospel: "Believe me when I say that I am in the Father and the Father is in me" (John 14:11). It does not, etymologically, *mean* a dance—but along with such images as the rhythm of music, or the to-and-fro of speech, or the intermingling of three streams of water—a dance can be an apt image for *perichoresis*.[48]

In *this* dance the partners not only encircle each other and weave in and out between each other as in human dancing; in the divine dance, so intimate is the communion that they move in and through each other so that the pattern is all-inclusive. In fact, the image of the dance makes

---

46. Boff, *Trinity and Society*, 146–47.

47. John of Damascus, *De Fide Orthodoxa* 1.14 (*NPNF²* 9b:17).

48. So Fiddes, *Participating in God*, 72–81; LaCugna, *God for Us*, 271; Elizabeth Johnson, *She Who Is: The Mystery of God in Feminist Theological Discourse* (New York: Crossroad, 1993), 220–21.

most sense when we understand the divine persons as movements of relationship, rather than as individual subjects who *have* relationships. The image of the divine dance is not so much about *dancers* as about the patterns of the dance itself, an interweaving of ecstatic movements. When we speak of parts played by divine persons in *perichoresis*— for example, the Son "indwells" the Father, the Father "contains" the Son, the Spirit "fills" the Father— we are telling a *story* that enables us to enter the personal currents of love within God; but the closest analogy is with perichoretic *movements* in human life, not with the *movers*. After all, the *actions* of love of two human lovers, or of members of a Christian congregation, can interpenetrate and occupy the same social space simultaneously in a way that the personal *subjects* cannot, even though they can put themselves "in each other's place" through empathy and imagination.

At the same time, when we address God, praying "Father, your will be done," or "Christ have mercy," or "Come, Holy Spirit," we are not envisaging *beings* who have these names; this vocative use is the only way that we can place ourselves into the flow of relations, or rather in cooperation with God we allow ourselves to be drawn in. When we say "Father" or "Mother" to God we are being enticed into a movement of speech that is already there before us.

God, in generous freedom, is making room for us to dwell within the communion of the divine life, or— to use a more dynamic image— is making space in the dance for us to move toward God and others in the world. As Paul is reported as quoting with approval from a Greek poet, "in him we live and move and have our being" (Acts 17:28). In fact, it is the idea of persons as relations that makes it possible to conceive of God's making space for the whole created universe to exist within and between the relational movements of the divine life. To say that everything is in God is not to envisage God as some kind of *receptacle* for relations in space and time; the relations in God are *making* the space in which beings can dwell and move. This does not mean, I hasten to add, that all created realities relate to God in the same way; as Hans Urs von Balthasar stresses, they can exist in God in a mode of resistance and rebellion, causing a "hard knot" in the relations between the Son and the Father that we see in the cross.[49]

---

49. Hans Urs von Balthasar, *Theo-Drama: Theological Dramatic Theory* (5 vols.; San Francisco: Ignatius, 1988–98); vol. 4, *The Action* (trans. G. Harrison), 229–30.

Such a vision of the relation of God and the world fits with the idea of divine persons as relations, and also explains why the distinctions between the persons can take on many forms within the overall flow of origins. Scripture itself witnesses to some of these distinctions that emerge from the interaction between God and the world: there is a "praying" of the Son to the Father, an "obeying" and a "glorifying" of the Father by the Son, a "sending" of the Son on mission into the world by the Father, a "witnessing" of the Spirit to the Father and the Son, a "uniting" of the world with God, and an "opening" of the future to God by the Spirit.

In the cross of Jesus we find yet another distinction disclosed: there is one movement of feeling and self-sacrifice that is like a father losing a son, and one like a son losing a father. In this way relations can "delimit" each other, or have their identity in differentiating themselves from each other[50] no less than agents do. Nor do questions of hierarchy or subordination between hypostases arise if these are not conceived as subjects. The only question is whether a movement of humility is *appropriate* for God. Using the metaphor of being (for which I have admitted a place), the movements of being, which are like sonship and spirit-ness, can each be confessed to be *homoousios* with the movement that is like fatherhood, though we can also say (in an early phrase of John Hick)[51] that they are *homo-agape* (same love).

The filial relation (and the adjective in English is not gender-specific) is the axis of intersection of relations because it is through the particular human sonship of Jesus of Nazareth expressed in his words, actions, and suffering that we enter the communion of God's being. The relationships in which he lived were perfectly one with the dynamic of God's relations of love in a way that ours are not and never will be; he was *homo-agape* with God with a numerical identity of love and not simply a generic sameness.[52] The Christian claim is that the "movement" of the life of Jesus fits more exactly into the movements in God than do other finite lives, but that all life shares to some extent in this same dynamic.

---

50. So Wolfhart Pannenberg, *Systematic Theology* (Grand Rapids: Eerdmans, 1991), 1:309–14, referring to "persons" as agents.

51. John Hick, *God and the Universe of Faiths* (London: Collins/Fount, 1977), 156–59, 164.

52. Ibid., 159. I differ from Hick in believing that this function of identical loving has ontological consequences.

So all the speech of Christ, all the ways he sees the world, all his acts fit exactly into the movement in the Trinity that we recognize as being like a son relating to a father. The relation of the human person Christ to the one whom he calls his heavenly Father can be mapped exactly onto the relation in God, which is like that between a son (or daughter) and a father (or mother). His prayer, saying *"Abba*, Father"; his hearing of a father's speech to him at the baptism and transfiguration, saying "This is my beloved Son"; his cry of desolation, "My God why have you forsaken me"; and his offering a welcome to the outcasts of society — all these fit into the preexisting movements of the Trinity that are like speech, suffering, and generous love. This human son is the same as the divine *sonship* and remains so forever, as signified by his bodily resurrection. It is appropriate to call this numerical sameness a unity of being, not just of function. Pannenberg argues that by his openness to the Father, to other persons, and to the future, Jesus shows himself to be "the same" as the eternal Son;[53] to avoid any suspicion of "two sons," I would rather say, "the same as the eternal sonship."

But when we recognize this, we can find similar patterns in all other bodily life. Wherever in the world people give themselves to others or sacrifice themselves for others, these actions will also match the movement in God that is like a son going forth on mission in response to the purpose of a father; their acts share in the patterns of love in God, and so in them we can discern the body of Christ. Wherever there is the movement of a measure of music, of a stroke of a brush, of a blow of a chisel, of a sequence of thought in the arts or sciences, which reflects God's truth and beauty, this too shares in the dynamic flow of the life of God.

Doctrine: The Relationship between Immanent and Economic Trinity

How can we conceive the relation between the immanent and economic Trinity, or between God in God's own self and God at work in the world? It will have become clear by now that I follow the general modern trend to work from what is disclosed in the economic Trinity to what is true in the immanent Trinity, and to this extent I am in accord

---

53. Wolfhart Pannenberg, *Jesus — God and Man* (trans. Lewis L. Wilkins and Duane A. Priebe; London: SCM, 1968), 334 – 35.

with Karl Rahner's famous dictum that "the economic is the immanent Trinity,"[54] at least in the sense that the economic Trinity corresponds to and is inseparable from the immanent Trinity.[55] Indeed, I believe this is not just a modern practice. When the early Church Fathers developed the doctrine of the Trinity, they were not painting by numbers; they were finding concepts to express an *experience*. As I have already suggested, they were trying to articulate the richness of the personality of God that they had found in the story of salvation and in their own experience.

I have, admittedly, offered a more radical version than many do of the move from economic to immanent Trinity. In a similar way to Robert Jenson, I am supposing not only that the triune God is to be *identified* from the acts and words of Jesus, but that God is *identical* with this story: the persons of Trinity *are* the relations by which Jesus lives, in openness to his Father, other people, and the future — or, as Jenson puts it, "God" is identical to "whatever happens between Jesus and his Father in their Spirit."[56] I dissent from what Jenson seems to be saying, however, in that I do not think that the immanent triune movements of relationship can be exhausted, without remainder, into a human life — even that of Jesus. The relations of Jesus fit exactly into the divine dance to a degree that ours do not, but the dance remains deeper, vaster, and fuller of possibilities — an infinite resource on which to rely. In the triune God there is always something more. Only by thinking of the persons as relations is it possible to celebrate this "more" (sometimes traditionally called *logos asarkos*, or the Word outside the flesh) while at the same time affirming that Jesus is fully one with God.

But, thinking more about the economic activity of God in the world, we might ask: *How can relationships act?* If persons are relations, then — objectors say — the acts of God in the world will surely be the unified act of a single divine subject.[57] Currents of relationship cannot, of course, have an impact in the sense of divine agents operating

54. Rahner, *The Trinity* (trans. Joseph Donceel; London: Burns & Oates, 1975), 21–22.

55. Cf. Barth, *CD* I/1:311, 383; II/1:657–60.

56. Robert Jenson, *Systematic Theology* (New York: Oxford University Press, 1997–99), 1:221.

57. So Miroslav Volf, opposing Joseph Cardinal Ratzinger, *After Our Likeness: The Church as the Image of the Trinity* (Grand Rapids: Eerdmans, 1998), 67–72.

on worldly objects, causing things to happen mechanically and coercively; but they *are* actions in the sense that when we are involved in their movement, we are persuaded and moved to certain ends, caught up in their momentum. They are actions that are not characterized by domination, but by cooperation. There is an attractiveness of *movements* of love, patterns of the dance into which we are swept up, so that our actions follow the same divine aim. We are offered, or presented with, aims through being engaged in the purposeful flow of the divine love.

All this means that a concept of *mediation* between God and the world is not needed and is positively anti-trinitarian. Christianity in its early years was strongly influenced by a narrative of mediation and developed a habit of mind which fell just short of being absorbed by it. I mean that the figure of Christ, in whom the New Testament writers find God to be uniquely disclosed and who acts as a mediator in *relationship* between a righteous God and sinful human beings, was reconfigured as a *cosmic* mediator. As early as Justin Martyr we find the assumption of a Platonic worldview in which there are two ontological spheres — a world of unchanging, intellectual Being and a world of transient, material Becoming (or a rewriting of the biblical heaven and earth). It was almost irresistible for early Christianity, moving out from Palestine into a Graeco-Roman milieu, to take up these popular philosophical ideas and put Christ into the available role of the Logos or World Soul, mediating between two ontological realms, or bridging an abyss between two worlds of reality.[58]

This image has persisted in Christian thinking ever since. It has resulted in an uncomfortable tension. On the one hand, theologians have ascribed to God the philosophical attributes proper to unchanging Being — impassibility, immutability, nontemporality, rooted in a philosophical concept of simplicity. On the other hand, most theologians have wanted to affirm the biblical picture of a God who is moved by a compassionate love for the world, and this is a state that implies complexity. Any number of compromises have been made between these two approaches, usually in some form of distinction between the economic

---

58. Justin Martyr, *First Apology* 60 (*ANF* 1:183); *Dialogue with Trypho* 60–61 (*ANF* 1:227–28).

and immanent Trinity. But as Keith Ward suggests, "it is quite coherent ... to suppose that God, while indivisible, is internally complex."[59]

To be God at all, to be Creator and not created, God must certainly exist *a se*—that is, God cannot owe God's being to anything or anybody else than God's own self. But the self-existence (aseity) of God has been traditionally understood as also implying a self-sufficiency, in which God as absolute Being is defined as being totally uncaused and unconditioned by any created reality. This notion is rooted in the doctrine of divine simplicity. As Aquinas states, quoting Augustine, "God is the most truly simple thing there is [*vere et summe simplex est*]."[60] Simplicity is not problematic if it simply means that God has no parts. But it has usually been taken to mean that God cannot be conditioned by any reality other than God's self, on the grounds that this would assume "parts" in God which are being moved. An alternative vision, however, is that by God's own desire, a complex God can (in Barth's words) "ordain that he should not be entirely self-sufficient," and can be free to be "conditioned" as well as "unconditioned" by the world.[61] Such a God can commit God's self to a journey of time, to being satisfied and fulfilled through the world, to being injured by the suffering of the world and to having an open future.

A God who exists in the differences of interweaving rhythms of relationships will allow for new possibilities to emerge in the future—not only possibilities created by God alone, but those arising in the creative interaction between God's self and the world. Such a God will be omniscient—in the sense of knowing everything there is to be known, perfectly related to all the reality there is at any moment.[62] This need not mean that God knows reality that has not yet come into being, which by definition cannot be known; yet unlike us, such a God will always be able to harmonize the past, the present, and the future. God is not at the mercy of time, since God can indwell the many time scales that belong to the many spaces in the universe and can always heal

59. Keith Ward, *Rational Theology and the Creativity of God* (Oxford: Blackwell, 1982), 216, cf. 71.

60. Aquinas, *ST*, 1a.3.7 (Blackfriars ed., 2:41–43).

61. So Barth, *CD* II/1:303; II/2:10, but without all the implications I am drawing.

62. So Richard Swinburne, *The Coherence of Theism* (Oxford: Clarendon, 1977), 175–78; Keith Ward, *Religion and Creation* (Oxford: Clarendon, 1996), 275–77.

their moments, but this does not mean that they are unreal to their Creator. There is testimony to this in the rhythmic movement of the Holy Spirit in God, opening up the other persons or relations in God to a new future.

While Christian thought broke free from a *rigid* separation of two worlds, it never quite detached itself from the idea of a Logos that is projected to span a gap, as if God has to speak out a word as a messenger from heaven to earth. That is, in the end, a narrative of domination, a story that validates oppression. It is not surprising that a late-modern philosopher like Derrida links the concepts of divine "simplicity" and "mediation" with a total "self-presence" in which subjectivity attempts to impose itself on others.[63] Indeed, if a cosmic mediator is needed, it is a short step to reproducing this mediator on the earthly scene in the person of an absolute monarch or a supreme ecclesiastical ruler.

What is embodied in the model of the Trinity I am presenting is a paradigm change in Christian theology, from mediation to participation. The Son or Logos comes forth from the Father, as does the Spirit, not to link a remote God with the world as in the mediation model, but so that the world can share in the movements of self-giving within God, participating in the flowing movement of love between the Father and the Son in the ever-surprising newness of the Spirit. So a God who is complex in relationships embraces a complex world and gives it space to be creative itself in partnership with its Creator. In this sense the immanent Trinity, God in God's self, can never be separated from the "economy" of God in the world, or if not in *our* world, in some created world.

Implications of the Doctrine

Our concern should not be with "applying" a doctrine of the Trinity to our contemporary world. It is not even enough to implement an "imitation" of God as Trinity within our life in society, or as David Cunningham puts it, a development of trinitarian "practices" that "inform and are informed by" the "trinitarian virtues" of "polyphony," "participation," and "particularity."[64] All this modeling can lead to a loss of

---

63. Derrida, *Grammatology*, 13–15.

64. David S. Cunningham, *These Three Are One: The Practice of Trinitarian Theology* (Oxford: Blackwell, 1998), 236; also see LaCugna, *God for Us*, 366–68.

the sense of the divine mystery and otherness as God is conformed to the human image of community. It is not enough to urge: "God is united and yet lives in relations, so we should be like this too." Rather we should augment the *imitation* of God with a thoroughgoing attempt to speak of *participation* in God in our experience. On the one hand, human experiences of relationship can become places where talk of God as Trinity comes alive, so that it makes sense in reference to them. On the other hand, these occasions are opportunities for sharing in divine relations of life and love and for becoming aware that these larger relations actually transform our experience. Here, in conclusion, there is space for only a few examples of such occasions.[65]

In living in community, we often find it difficult to hold together an integrity of our own self with an openness to others. There is need for a balance between a proper self-centering, which is not a destructive self-centeredness, and formation through our social relationships.[66] A vision of God as an event of relations alerts us to the reality that there are movements richer and deeper than our own relations. We can lean on a movement that is like a willing response of a son to a father, becoming co-actors and co-narrators with his "Yes, Amen" to the Father's purpose. Openness to others will not mean, then, mere conformity to the human other, which would be a loss of one's own will, but conformity to the body of the Christ whom we meet in and through the other.

Again, in many situations we need to cultivate a healthy sense of dependence that is not mere submission to domination by others.[67] In a network of inter-dependencies, we can discover our active responsibilities. Engaging in the relationships of the Trinity is the context in which that discovery can happen. We can recapture our early childlike sense of dependence and trustfulness, but now set in a very different context. Participating in relationships in God, we experience a sense of dependence on an uncreated origin as we lean on a son-like movement of being sent forth by a father. We take our experience of being a child into the communion of God's life and discover a motherly-fatherhood that is not oppressive and in which we can cultivate life with others.

---

65. I give an extensive account of these instances in *Participating in God*, chs. 2–7.

66. See Paul Tournier, *The Meaning of Persons* (London: SCM, 1957), 71–83.

67. See Wesley Carr, *The Pastor as Theologian* (London: SPCK, 1989), 176–78, 215–18.

Then there is the experience of intercessory prayer, as we find ourselves being pulled into a zone of mutual love and support within the triune God, into a communion of relations in which all persons participate to some extent. As we pray, we can add the persuasive power of our love to God's. That is, in praying for others we are expressing our love and concern for them, and God takes that desire into the divine desire for their well-being, wanting to exercise the influence of created as well as uncreated love. God wants to create a response within persons at every level (conscious and unconscious), to entice them into an openness to new possibilities that will promote healing, to woo them into cooperating with initiatives of grace. Our hopes, expectations, and longings for someone are assumed into God's own persuasion, augmenting and amplifying the urgings of God's Spirit, so that together God and the interceders begin to work transformation.

In a situation of suffering, the belief that God suffers with us can strengthen a "practical theodicy" of experiencing consolation, finding meaning in the stories of the suffering of others, and protesting against the causes of suffering. But each of these elements becomes more powerful as we find ourselves actually participating in the interweaving relations of a suffering God, in a place where God has made room for us. The belief that God is "alongside us" becomes concrete as we share in movements of tragedy, love, and hope that are like experiences between a father and son who have lost each other in face of death. We discover that we have become part of the story of Another, where even a cross can acquire meaning. We become aware of a vast movement of protest against suffering and evil in creation that comes from the heart of the Creator, in which we can be swept up and empowered.

Then there is the experience of forgiveness. This is no mere remission of debt, but taking a painful journey of empathy into the experience of those who have injured us, seeking to understand why they did or said what was hurtful and thus enabling them to accept pardon.[68] We can find that we are not taking this journey alone, but are sharing in a movement that is already there, which is like the voyaging of a son into the world at the initiative of a loving father, a journey that ends in

---

68. The image of a journey comes from H. R. Mackintosh, *The Christian Experience of Forgiveness* (London: Nisbet, 1934), 191.

the utter desolation of death, and yet in not being finally overwhelmed. Even where our forgiveness is not accepted or the offender is not present to us, we are making a journey in God, enhancing a persuasive divine love that will have incalculable effects in the lives of others. Because this relational movement of life and love is there, we cannot know what our own journey will achieve, either in the one with whom we desire to be reconciled, or in others who need to be reconciled and of whom we are quite unaware.

Let us take a final example: aptly of facing the finality of death. Those who offer care to the dying find themselves accompanying people who are in a "threshold" period when recognition of death and denial of it are mixed together. Both reactions seem to have a healthy place at this time of crisis, both acceptance and protest, and the art of negotiating them sensitively and moving forward into death has been compared by one expert in palliative care as like a "dance."[69] In this pastoral situation, both carers and the dying can find themselves sharing in the patterns of the "dance" of the Trinity, in interweaving movements of relation that are marked by agonizing loss and infinite hope. So the dance moves on into new and richer measures.

The model of Trinity I am commending will only convince, I suspect, if it is illuminating for the kind of critical moments of human life I have mentioned. An "event of relationships" is a participatory concept that makes sense only in actual events of daily life. This does not replace revelation with human experience, but locates the self-disclosure of God where God wants to be.

---

69. Richard Lamerton, *Care of the Dying* (rev. ed.; Harmondsworth, UK: Penguin, 1980), 163–65, 168.

STEPHEN R. HOLMES

Professor Fiddes's contribution to this book shows the deep erudition, intellectual brilliance, and pastoral sensitivity that have marked all his contributions to theological scholarship over several decades now. That said, it is the essay I have least agreement with. If I were to try to sum up both my appreciation and my concern about it in a sentence, it would be something like this: if I started from where Paul Fiddes starts, I like to hope I might have the intellectual equipment to get to somewhere near where he gets to; but I do not and cannot start there, and so, while I can admire enormously the journey he travels, it is not one I can follow.

As I read him, Fiddes begins his trinitarian reflection with three mutually reinforcing reflections:

1. that the experience of Christian discipleship, perhaps particularly prayer, feels like, or at least can be helpfully compared to, entering into certain sorts of personal relationship;
2. that we can hear in the New Testament an echo of similar experience, an (inspired) attempt to name what it feels like to participate in God, God known in a new way through the events of the life, death, resurrection, and ascension of Jesus;
3. that we can find language of relations, and even of "subsistent relations," in the theological tradition that can be pushed into service to express in a helpful and suggestive way this experience of participation we share with the apostles and New Testament authors.

I would like to say that if I accepted these three points, I would have written the same essay Fiddes has written; I fear the reality is that I would have written one far inferior, but groping in the same directions. Regardless, I accept without comment that his development is consistent with his premises. I will devote the remainder of this response, then, to a consideration of these three starting points.

On the first, it seems to me at best an assertion: How do we narrate "the experience of Christian prayer" with any confidence? We might, I suppose, do extensive ethnographic work, listening carefully to people from a wide variety of cultural and church backgrounds narrating their own experiences of prayer, and seek to name some common themes within those narrations. To the best of my knowledge that work has not been done — certainly Fiddes offers us no references to anything of the sort. We might defend the position by suggesting that the purest or most authoritative accounts of prayer are in the spiritual masters of the Christian tradition, and that reading the great classics and harmonizing what we find there gives us insight into the "proper" experience of Christian prayer/spirituality/discipleship. Most surveys of Christian spirituality, however, emphasize the diversity of spiritual paths and encourage each of us to find the path that suits our own personality/spirituality. This suggests strongly that "*the* experience of Christian discipleship" does not in fact exist, in which case it cannot be argued from.

This is, of course, a form of the standard argument that has been applied repeatedly against theologies based on experience since (at least) Feuerbach's critique of Schleiermacher. In recent years the form of argument has been deployed with great power by disempowered groups protesting against assumptions that their experience can be assimilated to that of a more enfranchised group (consider, classically, the womanist protest against feminist theologies). In saying this, I am not, of course, accusing Fiddes of totalizing or hegemonic positions so much as pointing out a danger that is sufficiently strong to give many of us pause before we consider offering any argument of this form.

The evidence Fiddes does offer us — in brief with this essay but in much greater depth in his book *Participating in God*, to which he refers us — is in the form of a beautiful narration of an experience of prayer/discipleship (I assume his own). The reader will be convinced to the extent that she finds her own experience illuminated by this narration. Yet without any reason to be convinced that this discovery will be general, this does not establish the basis for a doctrine.

This reflection brings me to the second point: the appeal to the New Testament as a "response to revelation, to the self-disclosure of

God in Christ" (p. 164). Now, I am unhappy at describing the biblical texts as "response to revelation" rather than directly as "revelation," but I am not sure that this unhappiness is to the point here. Fiddes grants primacy to the Scriptures and accepts that they should be normative for our doctrine of the Trinity. This makes his point about the Scriptures a potential response to my arguments against his point about experience: if it can be shown that Scripture normatively describes the experience of Christian discipleship/prayer like this, then the fact of variety in Christian experience is rendered irrelevant; can a scriptural principle justify Fiddes's position?

Unfortunately, I fear the answer must be no. Fiddes offers convincing — to me, at least — biblical reason to insist on an experienced plurality in God, there among the people of Israel and coming into prominence in the experience of followers of Jesus of Nazareth. But his biblical references do not, it seems to me, demand that we understand that plurality through the relational matrix he has sketched. The cry of *"Abba*, Father" (Rom 8:15; Gal 4:6) is certainly biblical, and centrally so, but so is the cry of "my Lord and my God!" which accompanies prostration before Jesus the Lord (John 20:28). The relational experience of the latter — utter subjection and surrender — would not seem to map easily onto Fiddes's model. This is not to say that his model could not be defended as *the* core New Testament experience of Christian discipleship, but the work is not yet done, and the point is not simply obvious.

Turning to the third premise, on the suggestive and helpful language of relations in the Christian tradition, I am content to grant Fiddes most of his points. I have some minor historical cavils that might perhaps be worth brief notice, and two more substantial differences. Starting with the first, when Gregory of Nazianzus is glossed with the comment, "On the other hand, [the three hypostases] can be characterized by more than their relations of *origin*" (p. 166), Gregory's own logic is being dealt with rather violently. It was intrinsic to Gregory's account of divine unity that the three were distinguished by relations of origin and not otherwise — this was not an incidental, disposable, or corrigible point in his doctrine. Similarly, when Fiddes tells us that "when the early Church Fathers developed the doctrine of the Trinity, they were not painting by numbers; they were finding concepts to express an *experience*" (p. 179), I disagree. I believe that, fundamentally, they were laying down conditions to allow good exegesis. These points are rather trivial though.

My more serious points are two. One concerns divine simplicity. Fiddes writes:

> For those who are interested in how Aquinas arrived at this point, we may note that he was deeply influenced by the Aristotelian view that the divine essence must be "simple," or radically unified. If this is so, both the properties and the relations of the essence must be identical with it; so the relations in God will have the same reality as the one essence. Hence relations subsist. This argument appears to underplay the important insight of the early Eastern theologians, that the being of God is communion or fellowship. (p. 168)

The positive points about the doctrine of St. Thomas are correct; the last sentence, however, is actively misleading. If we assume that "the early Eastern theologians" means the Cappadocian fathers, their commitment to simplicity was every bit as strong as Thomas's, and for the same reason: God must not be held to be composite. Gregory introduced the logical notion of relations of origin, borrowed by Augustine and developed by Thomas, as a single and extremely limited qualification to this to allow the threeness of God to be confessed. A "social" or "relational" account of the Trinity needs to take this seriously if it is to claim to stand in any significant continuity to the tradition.

This leads directly to my second substantial quibble. Here again I quote at length:

> the most adequate and appropriate language we have available to speak about the "persons" of the Holy Trinity is that they are *relations*. More dynamically, they are *movements* of life and love that have some resemblance to the relationships that we recognize between finite persons. When we speak of "divine persons," we are using an analogy with relations, but not an analogy with human persons who *have* relations. (pp. 159–60, italics in original)

"Relation" here, in this summary of Fiddes's position, is a term determined and defined by a particular description of personhood. This vision clearly drives the model as we read on and discover the rich and beautiful vision of the inclusion in movements of relation in prayer. However, to find an echo in the tradition of this in the use of the word "relation" seems to me to be stretching a point: "relation" is introduced into discourse, both West and East, as an alternative metaphysical term to run parallel to terms like "substance" and "accident." It is not irreducibly personal; probably it is best understood first as a logical term, which then acquires a certain "personal" gloss because it is being used of Father, Son, and Spirit.

Of course, neither of these points invalidate Fiddes's argument. They do make its connection to the tradition less secure than his essay suggests, I feel. This is not devastating to his position; it is probably not even seriously damaging, but it is at least discomforting.

For these various reasons, I cannot follow Professor Fiddes in his construction of the doctrine. I can admire it as a profound and beautiful illustration or reconstruction, convincing to anyone who finds an echo of their own experience in his narrations of what it is to participate in God. As a basis for a doctrine of the Trinity, though, I simply have to find it inadequate.

RESPONSE TO PAUL S. FIDDES

PAUL D. MOLNAR

I begin with two clear statements taken from Karl Barth. First:

> For even when we are occupied with God's revelation, when therefore we are concerned with giving an answer in faith to God's revelation, we are still not capable of ourselves of having fellowship with God, and therefore viewing and conceiving Him, and therefore realising our knowledge of God. At this very point it emerges that although the knowledge of God certainly does not come about without our work, it also does not come about through our work, or as the fruit of our work. At this very point the truth breaks imperiously and decisively before us: *God is known only by God; God can be known only by God.* At this very point, in faith itself, we know God in utter dependence, in pure discipleship and gratitude.[70]

Second, since God has made himself known in revelation objectively in Christ and subjectively through his Holy Spirit, Barth emphatically believed that "the lofty but simple lesson that it is by God that God is known ... was neither an axiom of reason nor a datum of experience."[71] For this reason he insisted, "In the measure that a doctrine of God draws on these sources, it betrays the fact that its subject is not really God."[72]

In these two statements we see clearly why it is a mistake to embrace Paul Fiddes's idea that "God is the name for an event or happening of relationships in which we are engaged," and where his proposal "certainly shares with social trinitarianism the conviction that human 'life-in-relationship' is our best way into a vision of God as

---

70. *CD* II/1, 182–83 (emphasis mine).
71. *CD* II/2, 3.
72. Ibid.

Trinity" (p. 160). Fiddes appeals to the "social trinitarianism" advanced by Jürgen Moltmann, Ted Peters, and Leonardo Boff for support of his position, which overtly makes "relation the final available concept we have for thinking about God," and so takes "relationality to a radical conclusion" (p. 161).

It was my contention in *Divine Freedom* that while the triune God is certainly relational, our experience of relationality can never become the starting point without becoming the norm for thinking about God's internal or external relations. When that happens, it becomes impossible to distinguish who God is from who we are because it opens the door to panentheistic thinking, which sees our relations with God as mutually conditioned and mutually conditioning.[73] While Fiddes claims that he is thinking about revelation, the fact is that he has substituted "relation" for the objective revelation of God in Christ and the subjective action of the Holy Spirit, enabling us to know God objectively in Christ through faith, which is itself a gift of the Holy Spirit uniting us to Christ and thus to the Father. He speaks a great deal about the Father, Son, and Holy Spirit, but these appear to be little more than freely chosen symbols (metaphors) of various experiences of relationality in the early church and today.

This is what I meant in my essay when I distinguished Torrance's idea of significative thinking, which thinks objectively from a center in Christ who is the incarnate Son of the Father, revealing God to us in our experience of faith and through the Spirit, from the Tillichian idea of symbolic thinking. For Tillich, people may speak of the depths of their own experience or of ultimate concern and thereby know much about God![74] Symbolic thinking in this sense is what I rejected because it assumes we can know God by constructing symbols of our own self-experience. In reality this approach confuses God with what we then project from our own self-experience; it ignores the need for God's reconciling grace to heal our minds by pointing us toward Christ as the only one who can, through his Spirit, actively enable us to know God truly. It obviates the need to turn exclusively to the one mediator even to know the true meaning of revelation. Most importantly it eliminates

---

73. *Divine Freedom*, ch. 7.
74. Paul Tillich, *The Shaking of the Foundations* (New York: Charles Scribner's Sons, 1948), 56–57.

any objectively true knowledge of God who *is* Father, Son, and Holy Spirit and is not just *like* a father or a mother who loves.

Fiddes shows an aversion to the idea that Christ is the one mediator between us and the Father since his degree Christology affirms that "the relations of Jesus fit exactly into the divine dance to a degree that ours do not" (p. 179). Thus, he says that the "'root' of our experience of God" is

> an experience of participating in movements of life, an experience that is like participating in relationships.... Talk of God as "an event of relationships" is then not an objectifying but a participatory kind of speech. It only makes sense as an account of *participating* in divine life and communion, not as a description of an object of observation by a subject. (p. 161)

But how can one distinguish divine life and communion from human life and communion? Fiddes certainly wishes to do so. But he cannot do so consistently because his method, which is indebted to key aspects of social trinitarian thinking, will not allow him to say with Barth that God can be known only through God.

No experience of relations can ever be the starting point for thinking truly about the eternal Father, Son, and Holy Spirit because when we do experience this God through his grace and revelation and therefore in faith, we know that the starting point for theology is and always remains God himself. The object of our reflection is not our experience of participation but the God who meets us in our experiences and enables such knowledge. Here, Fiddes's own thinking encounters a major problem: he speaks about the Trinity, but he concludes that we can never have any *objective* knowledge of God; essentially, in the name of apophaticism, he embraces the agnosticism that I rejected in *Divine Freedom*. As I argued there, agnosticism opens the door to the idea that we may reconceive the Father, Son, and Holy Spirit simply as relations.[75]

---

75. Thus Fiddes, "My own approach is to speak about plurality of *relationships*, but to remain silent about any concept of them as an *object* of thought" (p. 170). Following Barth, I maintain that unless the triune God is a genuine object of our thought, then we do not have any real knowledge of God in himself. Without such knowledge God is indistinguishable from our experiences of participation, as when Fiddes writes: "Talk about God as 'an event of relationships' is not the language of a spectator or observer, but the language of participant. It only makes sense in terms of our involvement in the network of relationships in which God happens" (ibid.).

What difference does this make? It leads Fiddes to assume that it is perfectly appropriate to think of God as mother if that is the participatory experience we have, since to speak of God is not to speak of a single unique and personal being who eternally is Father, Son, and Holy Spirit in himself quite apart from us, and who must be recognized in his uniqueness *before* being able to speak about our own supposed experiences of God. Fiddes's panentheistic description of participation represents a classic case of confusing the immanent and economic Trinity in a manner similar to Ted Peters, who claims that God is in the process of becoming relational by relating with us.

Strangely, Fiddes appeals to Barth to argue that God is a "complex rather than simple being" (p. 169), by taking Barth's statement that "with regard to the being of God, the word 'event' or 'act' is *final*" (p. 169). But here he forgot to mention that Barth insisted, "To its very deepest depths God's Godhead consists in the fact that it is an event — not any event, not events in general, but the event of His action, in which we have a share in God's revelation."[76] Barth had in mind the particular action of God in his incarnate Word, who as the revealer could not be bypassed in order to know God and our relation with God. The difference between Barth and Fiddes is that for Barth, God is one in being in his eternal act as Father, Son, and Holy Spirit, so that we cannot bypass Jesus himself in an attempt to know God because he himself in his revelation is the act of God for us within history — the only possibility for real knowledge of God. We participate in God's own self-knowledge only through the act of the Holy Spirit, which enables us to participate in Jesus' own knowledge and love of the Father. Thus, Barth insisted that knowledge of God was "an event enclosed in the mystery of the divine Trinity."[77]

Barth holds to the classical view that God is simple (one unique being) even as he exists in his eternal act as Father, Son, and Holy Spirit (three modes of being). So while for Barth there is only one divine subject, and that subject is the object of our faith and knowledge (the triune God), Fiddes refuses "to classify God as either one subject or three" (p. 172). He rejects tritheism, but by denying that we have

---

76. *CD* II/1, 263.
77. *CD* II/1, 181 and 205.

"objective" knowledge of God as the sole subject, Fiddes is, with Ted Peters, failing to stress the fact that there is equality of essence in the Father, Son, and Spirit at every point so that "identity of substance implies the equality of substance of 'the persons.'"[78] The result is a vision that presents God as fulfilling himself through relations with us, and which virtually identifies the Holy Spirit with the human spirit.[79] This unfortunately opens the door to a Pelagian view of our actions, such that they contribute to God's actions of drawing us into relationship with himself.[80]

Other difficulties can be seen in Fiddes's analysis that stem directly from his refusal to begin and end his thinking with the revelation of God in Jesus Christ. While he does say that his analogy of participation "is finally based in the incarnation of Christ as a human person who fully reveals God to us" (p. 171), his thinking does not begin and end with Jesus himself as the unique Son of God, who alone can reveal God to us because of who he is. It cannot because his view of Christ's uniqueness sees his difference from us as one of degree rather than one of kind, as the one and only mediator between Creator and creatures. He argues that "there can be no literal or univocal language about an ineffable God," and proposes that the most appropriate language "is about participating in relationships" (pp. 171–72).

But, which relationships is he talking about? That's the main problem with his confusing use of the "divine dance" as his most frequent image of participation. T. F. Torrance rightly claims that this idea is based on a confusion of two Greek terms: χωρέω ("to make room for, to contain, to move toward"—*perichoresis*) and χορεύω ("to dance"). When this image is used, it becomes virtually impossible to distinguish divine and human persons in relationship. Thus, *perichoresis*, which is supposed

---

78. *CD* I/1, 351. Also, Ted Peters, cited in my essay, says, "There is no inherent reason for assuming that the three persons have to be identical or equal in nature" (Peters, *GOD as Trinity*, 20).

79. See Fiddes, *Participating in God*, 260–61.

80. Thus Fiddes, "the possibilities with which God persuades us can emerge in creative interaction between God and the world. In God's life of communion there are held 'outline' possibilities for the future, which will become more and more detailed as created beings make their contribution to God's purpose" (*Participating in God*, 135), and so our "co-working with God comes to its positive climax with Jesus" (136). Here degree Christology goes together with a Pelagian view of our cooperation with God.

to describe the inner relations of the eternal Father, Son, and Spirit, comes to refer to God's relations with us.[81]

This confusion further encourages the thinking we meet in panentheistic attempts to understand God's relations with us and ours with God. For Ted Peters, as seen in my essay, God will not be fully relational until salvation is complete and God is realizing himself in and through history. For Fiddes, similarly, "if God desires to include created persons within the communion of divine life, the dance will not be complete until this has been achieved."[82] And, "God can commit God's self to a journey of time, to being satisfied and *fulfilled* through the world" (p. 181, italics mine). Moreover, "the moment of begetting and creating is thus one of humility, and an opening of the divine life to pain and suffering."[83] Here, additionally, the all-important distinction between the eternal begetting of the Son and the free act of creation, which cannot be properly envisaged as eternally concomitant with the generation of the Son, is conceptually lost.[84]

---

81. LaCugna, *God for Us*, mistakenly believes that *perichoresis* refers to "the divine dance" and argues that the term should not refer to God's inner life but rather to "divine life as all creatures partake and literally exist in it" (p. 274). Hence, "the exodus of all persons from God and the return of all to God is the divine dance in which God and we are eternal partners" (p. 304). There are many such statements in Paul Fiddes's presentation that I find confusing.

82. Fiddes, *Participating in God*, 96.

83. Ibid.

84. Following Moltmann, Fiddes argues that in thinking this way there is "no gap ... between God in God's own self and God for us, since there can be no other communion of persons than the one in which we are included; the dance returns to the Father carrying us with it" (*Participating in God*, 75–76). This thinking is almost identical with the pantheistic vision offered by LaCugna.

RESPONSE TO PAUL S. FIDDES

THOMAS H. MCCALL

Paul Fiddes has given us a beautifully crafted essay, one that is in many ways creative, original, and even profound. It is one that showcases a theology very different from mine. Our views share an editorially assigned label ("relational"), but beyond that it is hard for me to see what they have in common. As I will point out, some of what Fiddes says baffles me; in my judgment other elements are seriously mistaken.

Before moving to analysis, we need to appreciate the truly "radical" nature of his proposal. On his view, the "persons" of the Holy Trinity simply are relations. They are not persons-in-relation; they are mere relations. They are relations-without-remainder, relations-without-*relata*, relations-*without-persons-in-relation*. Apparently, "God" is not a personal agent any more than are the Father, Son, and Spirit: "God" is thus an "event or happening of relationships in which we are engaged" (p. 160). Fiddes's theology is not to be confused with traditional affirmations that the divine persons are who and what they are only *in* relation — not even with Aquinas's account of the divine persons as "subsistent relations." No, for Fiddes the divine "persons" just *are* relations (I would say "are the relations *themselves*," though this might "objectify" the relations as something too much like "selves," something Fiddes would reject).

Fiddes refers to the "unique relation of Christ to God his Father" (p. 164). If we were to assume a traditional Christology (according to which the eternal second person of the Holy Trinity is incarnate as Jesus Christ), we would be talking about "the unique relation of a relation to a relation." Whatever this might mean, it isn't relevant to Fiddes's view, for he rejects traditional Christology just as he rejects traditional trinitarian theology. According to traditional Christology, God the Son is incarnate as the man Jesus Christ, and Jesus Christ is a distinct agent (distinct from other humans, and distinct from the Father and Spirit).

This traditional Christology coheres well with traditional trinitarian theology but not with Fiddes's proposal, so it is not surprising that Fiddes rejects it.

In place of traditional Christology he posits an explicit "degree Christology"—"the 'movement' of the life of Jesus fits more exactly into the movements in God than do other finite lives, but that all life shares to some extent in this same dynamic ... [and] the relations of Jesus fit exactly into the divine dance to a degree that ours do not" (pp. 177, 179). So it isn't the case that the eternal *hypostasis* that *is* the Son of the Father has become uniquely incarnate as the man Jesus Christ at all; instead we are told that the man Jesus Christ enters into the "divine dance" more fully and completely than the rest of us.

The tradition has affirmed the doctrine of divine simplicity (in various forms of the doctrine). Fiddes rejects the doctrine of simplicity. The broad and deep Christian tradition insists that within the life of the one and only God there are three fully divine *hypostases* or persons, and that the Father, the Son, and the Holy Spirit exist only within their relationships of mutual communion. Fiddes rejects this consensus; in its place he suggests that instead of these three mutually-and-necessarily-related *hypostases* there are only the relationships ("themselves"). Traditional Christology has insisted that the eternal Son *is* the person of the Trinity who became incarnate for us and our salvation. Relationships cannot become human (since they are not agents and cannot actually do things), so Fiddes replaces this consensual view with the notion that the man Jesus Christ is more deeply involved in the divine relationality than we are (though clearly not so much as he could be). Traditional Christology has joyfully affirmed that Jesus Christ is the "mediator between God and humanity" (1 Tim 2:5). Not surprisingly, Fiddes rejects this as well; he insists that we need participation rather than a mediator.[85] Indeed, he goes so far as to say that a doctrine of mediation is "positively anti-trinitarian."

Seeing the truly radical nature of his proposal (and its distance from the tradition, despite his use of traditional terms and texts), it is rather surprising that he does not do more to argue for his view. Fiddes

---

85. Although perhaps he only refers to "cosmic" mediation rather than "soteriological" mediation.

does say that it is "not possible to impose this matrix of terms [creedal language] on the New Testament" and to conclude that the divine *hypostases* are "'subjects,' or 'agents,' or even 'centers of consciousness'" (p. 164). I concur that we should not *impose* these notions on the text, for we should do our best to let Scripture itself form (and re-form) our understandings. But as I have argued, Scripture itself portrays the divine persons as entities that speak and act, as persons who *do* things—i.e., as distinct speech-agents. Of course, merely pointing out that Fiddes's view is a long way from classical theology does not amount to an argument against it. His theology deserves consideration on its own merits.

Unfortunately, such consideration is not easy, since it isn't always exactly clear just what we are to make of Fiddes's claims when they are considered together. He clearly replaces persons-in-relation with relations-without-remainder; thus the divine "persons" are *not* agents. Fiddes will also say that our participation in the life of God involves us "in a movement of self-giving" that apparently precedes our involvement (p. 161). But what is *self*-giving without a *self*? When speaking of the relations, he says that "they" are "continually opened up" (by the "third movement"). But who are *they?* He refers to the "personality of God" that was experienced by the writers of the New Testament. But what sense can we make of this *personality* if in fact there are no divine persons-in-relation but only the relationships themselves?

Fiddes says that "talk of relationality is actually response to revelation" (p. 173). But how is there revelation if there is no *revealer?* What sense can we make of a revealer without *someone* doing the revealing? And what can it mean to say that "God, in generous freedom, is making room for us to dwell" unless there is at least one divine entity—a divine *person*—who is free and who is doing things like making room? We could pile up such examples, for Fiddes both cordons off language of divine personal agency as inappropriate for the triune God and then regularly helps himself to it. Putting it mildly, there are worries about coherence in the neighborhood.

Describing Aquinas's view, Russell Friedman says that actions "only come from actors."[86] Aquinas's view is intuitive, and Fiddes recognizes

---

86. Russell L. Friedman, *Medieval Trinitarian Thought from Aquinas to Ockham* (Cambridge: Cambridge University Press, 2010), 22.

that indeed there *is* a threat to his view in the neighborhood. As he puts it, "the objection is likely to be brought forward that talk of relations makes no sense without *subjects* who have relations. How can there be relations without subjects or agents on each end of them?" Fiddes's response is as refreshingly direct as it is disappointingly empty: "this is where we have to be silent; *this* is the *apophasis*" (p. 171, italics in original). He claims that all God-talk is metaphorical and insists that "there can be no literal or univocal language about an ineffable God." So at just the point where Fiddes's view seems incoherent, he appeals to divine ineffability and apophasis.

But so far as I can see, such an appeal only makes matters worse. Setting aside the apparent but unfortunate conflation of literality and univocity, consider Fiddes's claim that

(L) there can be no literal or univocal language about an ineffable God.[87]

Whatever else it may be, (L) *is* a claim about God. Furthermore, it seems plain that Fiddes wants us to take it straightforwardly and literally. So is (L) literally true? If it is, then — by its own strictures — (L) either cannot be true or cannot be about God after all. It is thus self-defeating and merely a distraction that does not deserve our attention. If, however, (L) is not literally true, then we can reasonably wonder why we should be bothered by it at all.

Perhaps Fiddes would appeal further to divine ineffability to support this claim; maybe the defender of Fiddes will protest that I am not taking his recognition of divine ineffability with full seriousness. But claims about God's ineffability are themselves ambiguous.[88] Consider the claim that

(E) God is ineffable;

(E) can be understood in various ways. Plausibly, it might be intended either as (something like):

(E*) God is incomprehensible, and finite creatures will never exhaust all that there is to know about an infinite Creator;

or as (something more like)

---

87. Fiddes also says that all God-talk must be metaphorical. But some proposition (P) could be expressed metaphorically and yet be literally true (or false).

88. See Keith E. Yandell, "On Not Confusing Incomprehensibility with Ineffability: Carl Henry on Literal Propositional Revelation," *Trinity Journal* 35 NS (2014): 61–74..

(E**) God is unknowable, and none of our words or concepts can rightly apply to God.

Note that (E*) and (E**) are distinct claims. Note as well that (E*) does not support (L); the defender of (L) will need (E**). Note further that (E*) does not entail (E**) (although (E**) entails (E*)). By my lights, (E*) should not even be controversial, but (E**) is a different matter entirely. Indeed, it is problematic *in excelsis*. If exactly none of our words or concepts rightly applies to God, then (E**) doesn't apply to God either. Thus we do not need to pay further attention to it. If God is unknowable, then we cannot so much as know that (E**) is true. (E**) would have to be false for us to know that it is true. So (E**) is self-referentially incoherent, self-defeating, "hoist on its own petard."[89] How, then, should we take the claims of Fiddes? If he intends (E**), then his claims are self-defeating and we need no further argument against them. Perhaps Fiddes only intends (E*) rather than (E**). In this case he would be on solid ground, but in such a case he has nothing to support (L).

At any rate, Fiddes is inconsistent with respect to (L). He seems quite certain that "God is the name for an event or happening of relationships" (p. 160). He is confident that this way of talking about God is "participatory" rather than "objectifying," and further that this is a good thing. Somehow he knows that "God is not bound by the rule that relations need individual agents." He does not hesitate to criticize Boff's theology; in response to Boff he confidently proclaims that the "directions of relation" are "irreversible." Somehow he has become convinced that the "divine dance" is "deeper, vaster, fuller of possibilities" than Jesus himself ever experienced. He speaks with confidence when he says that liturgical prayer is not really directed to distinct entities that have the names of "Father," "Son," and "Holy Spirit." He seems sure that when we address God as "Father" or "Mother," we are "being enticed into a movement of speech that is already there before us." But how could Fiddes know all these things about an unknowable deity? How does he speak so confidently—and so *literally*—about God when none of this talk can be ("literally") true? None of this is clear. But all of it seems important.

---

89. See Alvin Plantinga's discussion of similar claims in his *Warranted Christian Belief* (Oxford: Oxford University Press, 2000), 3–63.

Fiddes seems convinced that his view holds great promise for a theological ethics that avoids idolatry and domination. It is a good thing that "God . . . cannot be objectified like other objects in the world" (p. 171). I'm not so sanguine as Fiddes, for I worry that it is entirely possible to objectify, idealize, and make an idol out of "relationality." Moreover, I worry about the ethical issues at stake if we begin to value "relationality" over the actual, concrete persons with whom we may have relationships. Idolatry is no respecter of ideologies.

Fiddes says that his model of the Trinity will be convincing "if it is illuminating for . . . critical moments of human life" (p. 185). His ultimate appeal is to religious experience, and while it is difficult and risky to speak for others or to speculate here, it seems to me that his theology will be found wanting when weighed in the balances of religious adequacy. Fiddes says that his account makes sense of prayer as participation. When we pray, we enter "a zone of mutual love" and relationship (all humans are already in to some extent anyway), and we "add the persuasive power of our love to God's" (p. 184). I see this as exactly upside down, for according to Romans 8 we enter into the communion of the triune God by the work of Christ as the Spirit intercedes for us.[90] What matters not is the paltry "power" of my faltering and sometimes inchoate prayer; instead what really matters is the prayer of the Spirit for me and indeed for all creation!

In praise and thanksgiving we pray to divine *persons*— we pray to the God who is personal (as three persons) as we thank God for (among other things) actions that God has done on our behalf. In intercession we address the triune God who speaks and acts and does things— in intercession we are, after all, asking the God who is both omnicompetent and omnibenevolent to do things. We do not pray to a cosmic process that somehow includes us and all evil and horror already—we pray to the tripersonal God who, in the purity of divine simplicity, is utterly free from and sovereign over the evil and horror of this world and thus able to act in order to rescue us from it. We pray to the God who is, in the glory of divine aseity and omnipotence, neither limited by our finitude nor besmirched by our sin. We pray to the tripersonal God

---

90. See further James B. Torrance, *Worship, Community, and the Triune God of Grace* (Downers Grove, IL: InterVarsity Press, 1996).

who did not abandon us in our fragility and filth but who took radical and drastic action for us and our salvation. We place our hope in the Father, who *sent* his only-begotten Son and *gave* him for us; in the Son, who *emptied* himself, offered himself as the one *Mediator*, and *justifies* us freely; and in the Holy Spirit, who *cleanses* and *intercedes* today.

PAUL S. FIDDES

I am grateful to my three colleagues for their comments on my chapter, which have helped me to think my position through further. I believe that they feel with me, despite disagreements, that we are all aiming to speak faithfully and responsibly about God. I must say, however, that at times my colleagues have presented a picture of what they *suppose* I am trying to do, in which it is hard for me to recognize myself.

Steve Holmes, for instance, in his generous and sympathetic response, nevertheless presents me as beginning my thought about the Trinity from the experience of discipleship today (especially prayer), and then finding an "echo" of this in the New Testament as a secondary matter. The reader might think that I actually expressed myself like that, which is not, of course, the case. In a second stage of his response Holmes does acknowledge my actual concern to begin all doctrine of God from the witness of Scripture, but then suggests that what I am trying to find there is a human experience of discipleship that can be the sole basis for the doctrine of the Trinity. In fact I have argued that while Scripture *does* show us an experience of participating in God that is characterized by relationship (the letter to the Hebrews, for instance, offers a profound experience of praying with the risen Christ), it also sets out the objective uniqueness of a *life* lived in relation to God and others by Jesus, which enables our participation.

Paul Molnar, to my astonishment, presents me as a thinker whose method "will not allow him to say … that God can only be known through God" and as one who attempts to "bypass Jesus." Molnar alleges that in saying we cannot know God as an object, I deny any share in God's own self-knowledge; but this would only be so if God were like *human* self-consciousness in knowing one's own self as an object. I certainly affirm "objective revelation" in the sense of a revelation of God "over against us," not reducible to our feelings and experience; I deny that God is revealed as "object" of our knowing. In fact my whole method assumes that God's self-revelation is needed to get any talk about God started at all. The difference between the two of us seems to be about *where* that event of divine self-disclosure happens. For Molnar it seems to happen only in the history of Jesus of Nazareth, while I want to affirm that God unveils God's self to us, and so allows us to share in God's own self-knowledge, through a whole range of human relations. This is of course never without Jesus Christ, since the God who reveals God's self is the triune God, and we can never separate the risen Jesus from the movement of relationship in God that we call "sonship." I do not therefore deny that Christ is a mediator in the *biblical* sense that he mediates in relationship between us and God. My point is that the reality of participating in God means that there is no need for a *particular kind* of mediator—that is, mediation between two supposedly separate worlds of the spiritual and the material.

Thus I do not "confuse" God in God's self (the immanent Trinity) with God active in the world (the economic Trinity), but I do urge that these two aspects can never be separated to the extent that God cannot—in free choice and sovereign desire—be affected and enriched by a creation that participates in God's own life. This is not Pelagianism but an adoring recognition of God's humility. Nor is this a social trinitarianism of "God as community" from which I explicitly distance myself, despite Molnar's odd claim that I appeal to it.

Thomas McCall portrays me as basing my view of divine persons as relationships on the ground that "God is unknowable," and so thinks he has caught me out in an inconsistency since I do make certain positive affirmations about God. In fact, I never claim that the ineffable God is completely "unknowable"—God could hardly be so if made known in Jesus—only that our words cannot literally or univocally describe the very God who makes God's self known. Nor am I myself making literal claims about God when I state (for example) that there can be no literal language about God, or I speak about being drawn into the "dance" of divine relations. I make clear that this is simply the most "appropriate" talk about God that we have, using both negative and positive forms of speech, in the light of Scripture and experience. I altogether agree that "we do not pray to a cosmic process"; I affirmed in my account that we do not pray "to" the event of God but "in" the relations in which God happens.

McCall insists, against me, that we cannot think of relationships in God without realities (*hypostases*) that are *exercising* these relationships, and it seems that my other two colleagues agree with him. But all of us are using human words oddly, or playfully, in order to express the mystery of God. The real issue is what the most appropriate odd language might be in light of revelation. Holmes envisages three divine realities as having no relationships except their origin in each other. Nothing, it seems, can be said about their character as loving, or glorifying, or sending out on mission into the world. Molnar has to deny that the relationships between these realities are anything that we can recognize from our human experience of relations. McCall certainly envisages recognizable relations between individual "actors" in the Trinity, but his attempt to show they are still one God depends on a logical formula that is hardly part of everyday or biblical speech. I suggest that we are more likely to be driven to our knees in wonder when we simply recognize relations in God in which we can share in the midst of our own daily experience of living in relations with others.

CONCLUSION ▐███████████████

JASON S. SEXTON

The presentations and exchanges in this book offer explorations into the deepest ocean of Christian theology. The contributors have given substantial portions of their views on the doctrine of the Trinity, drawing heavily from Scripture and the wide ecclesial tradition and arguing their views on each matter with great care. The dialogue format of this book has allowed for critical responses engaging the other representatives' views on the Trinity, and then each author has briefly clarified critical points in their final responses.

In this brief conclusion to the volume I will summarize key features of the conversation, including the trinitarian views of the contributors in relationship to the questions each aimed to address. These will be followed by brief comments about the need for further work on the doctrine of the Trinity, along with considerations about its relevance for Christian witness in the present context. The doctrine of the Trinity and the way in which it shapes the rest of Christian theology and practice are of enormous significance. As J. I. Packer has pointedly observed, "All non-Trinitarian formulations of the Christian message are by biblical standards inadequate and indeed fundamentally false, and will naturally tend to pull Christian lives out of shape."[1]

Summarizing the Views

To reiterate, the two views under consideration here have been called "Classical Trinity" and "Relational Trinity." The contributors have presented their positions under these broad banners, utilizing an established rubric that has come into common parlance and that captures something important in the current moment of reflection on the doctrine. For the Classical Trinity, there has been a strong retrieval movement into the heart of how the trinitarian faith has been confessed in

---

1. J. I. Packer, *Concise Theology: A Guide to Historic Christian Beliefs* (Wheaton, IL: Tyndale, 1993), 42. Thanks to Fred Sanders for drawing my attention to this point in Packer.

its earliest formulations. By contrast, as theology always does, contemporary theologians have sought to harness available conceptual tools for understanding the doctrine better. This does not happen apart from, and may even impart great precision of, biblical exegesis and the sound appropriation of the best of the ecumenical creedal tradition (notwithstanding anachronistic temptations). The representatives of the Relational Trinity view also highlight how both analytic tools (from contemporary and earlier philosophy) and critical literary tools might be harnessed for potentially better ways of understanding the triune God in eternal and temporal relation.

The terms *Classical* and *Relational*, of course, may be deemed unhappy in some ways, as each can lay claim to classic features and sources, and each view says something about God's *relations* (internal and external). Also, we have two representatives of each view so that no one person's reading can be said to speak for everyone else who wants to espouse a similar position, nor is the view of each author representative of the entire ecclesial tradition of that author—for example, Molnar's view is not *the* view espoused by everyone in the Roman Catholic Church, nor is Holmes's view *the* view espoused by all evangelicals. The views and the traditions have commonality, and the views represented have overlapping features with the others throughout. In important ways, the radical and creedal perspectives on the Relational View have some major points of disagreement, and the Catholic and evangelical perspectives on the Classical View also differ at critical points. Without attempting to retell every feature of the views, and with risk of major oversimplification, a brief recounting is in order.

Classical Trinity

From an evangelical perspective, Steve Holmes continues the ground-clearing exercise he has become known for in recent years. Critical of de Régnon's thesis of a strong East-West distinction in early trinitarian theology, and affirming closer affinity between the Cappadocians and Augustine, he argues that the Trinity is a set of conceptual distinctions for understanding what Scripture says about God, the church's earliest practice of worship, and subsequent trinitarian doctrine. In this way, while borrowing other ontological presuppositions from which this construction makes sense (namely, that the divine being is incomposite and simple), a "relation" is understood as "a mode of distinction" denoting the simple unity of two distinct (not different) subsistences (p. 38). Holmes sees two logically ordered processions or relations in the ineffable divine life—begetting and proceeding. These relations in the divine life, the origins of persons, each have two directions (paternity and filiation; spiration and procession). On this point, he becomes apophatic, noting that the usage of terms may be one thing or another at any given time or culture, but nevertheless analogously "gestures" toward the divine triune reality, which manner of ordering he finds speculative for many things like, for example, matters surrounding the *filioque* clause.

Paul Molnar similarly sees the matter of the *filioque* as an issue unnecessarily raised when the Spirit is seen as proceeding or "flowing" from *the being* (not merely the person) of God the Father in unity with the Son (at one point summoning McCall's chide of *patripassionism*). Accordingly and by virtue of *perichoresis*, with the Spirit proceeding from the Father through the Son, the *filioque* clause is not needed since avoiding subordination is no longer an issue. Molnar spends much of his essay critical of panentheistic views in similar ways as he had done in his earlier work, and he stresses the need to draw trinitarian doctrine from revelation, all the while maintaining a strong distinction between the immanent and economic Trinity, without separation. This particular matter is one Holmes quibbles about, with Molnar looking very Catholic on the point, perhaps receiving "the developed tradition as an authentic hearing and amplifying of the biblical revelation" (p. 98). Whether this is the case, as something of an "evangelical" Catholic, Molnar finds much of his source material in T. F. Torrance, in "Reformed" fashion emphasizing the Father-Son relation over the Creator-creature relation, distinguishing the Holy Spirit (who is full divinity, *homoousion* with the Father and Son) from the human spirit.[2]

The Classical representatives were especially emphatic about distancing themselves from any forms of subordination (and potential modalism, pantheism, tritheism, or Arianism),[3] or the kind of

---

2. Along with the other excellent contributions in the volume, note Molnar's essay in *Ecumenical Perspectives on the* Filioque *for the 21st Century* (ed. Myk Habets; New York: Bloomsbury/T&T Clark, 2014).

3. See pp. 80 and 88.

social trinitarianism characteristically espoused by Moltmann, Boff, LaCugna, Miroslav Volf, and others. Holmes notes that nothing like the inter-trinitarian relations may serve as a model ordering any human community, and thereby have no instrumental use whatsoever.

Relational Trinity

Tom McCall is our first representative of the Relational view of the doctrine, employing the rigorous analytic philosophical reasoning he's become known for and giving careful exegesis of the Gospels for his account. Establishing a distinction between the indivisibility of the Trinity's external works and the inability to hold this for God's inner life (*opera ad intra*), McCall understands the divine persons as "co-inhering in 'I-Thou' relationships" (p. 156). Attending to the threeness-oneness issue, McCall understands the divine persons as necessarily existent entities, something that Holmes excludes on his reading of modern forms of social trinitarianism (p. 146). Of no surprise, Molnar treats this notion of three self-relations as carrying "the ring of tritheism" (cf. p. 146), and perhaps even conceiving a particular kind of oneness that is unnecessarily purported as problematic and easily solved when an understanding of the one divine being is "established and maintained in grace" (p. 146). This may be, however, too simple for McCall's view. In his somewhat flexible view of the matter, following Scotus and Yandell and informed by Scripture,[4] McCall allows some forms of the doctrine of simplicity for theology proper, which sets apart the strength of his attempt to develop his doctrine of the Trinity from biblical exegesis and the human religious experience.

Consistent with this focus on experience, Paul Fiddes develops his Relational account of participation, employing an analogy of relations where the persons of the Trinity are completely constituted by their relations with each other. This is a communion of relations into which all human persons participate to some degree, although it nevertheless represents an unobtainable ideal for humans in this life (p. 160). Fiddes's view of divine subsistent relations affirms divine ineffability, that God is *a se*; and yet rather than being simple (cf. McCall's expansive definition), he understands God as a complex being. In this way God may be

---

4. See the careful presentation in Thomas H. McCall, "Trinity Doctrine, Plain and Simple," in *Advancing Trinitarian Theology: Explorations in Constructive Dogmatics* (ed. Oliver D. Crisp and Fred Sanders; Grand Rapids: Zondervan, 2014), 42–59.

shaped and conditioned by the world, even in his own suffering and the hope held out for future healing in God, since on Fiddes's account God simply is these interweaving relations that cannot be fully described and which nevertheless humans actually find themselves participating in somehow by grace. Like the others, he holds that the divine revelation stands over and against us, not reducible to feeling and experience, but also that God is not revealed as an "object" of our knowing. Rather, this God is known by *participation* in his very life in relation, in something akin to a "dance," a dynamic, ongoing relationship with the Trinity.

Both of these Relational accounts identify trinitarian language for God as analogous ("at best," for McCall), a point that the Classical representatives would agree with. They are understood as distinct agents necessarily related in a *perichoretic communion of holy love* (McCall) or as metaphorical personal *relations* (Fiddes), being closely connected then to "perichoretic *movements* in human life" (p. 176) or through "an analogy with 'relationships' themselves" (p. 160) and thus unable to correspond one-for-one with human societal relations in this life.

Further Observations

The contributors in this volume agree on many points. The writing of this book itself and the day-long conference preceding it has given some helpful time for reflection, for questioning, for revision, and for the refinement of the views. Much of this has yielded helpful understanding, and still some areas of misunderstanding. Yet the conversations will continue as the church seeks to discern the best ways to articulate our confession of the one God, the Father, the Son, and the Holy Spirit. While there are many potential areas beckoning further exploration at the present moment, I'd like to reflect briefly on three of these: the relationship of the doctrine of the Trinity to Scripture, to the tradition, and to the church's mission.

The Doctrine of the Trinity and Holy Scripture

Along with a deep reverence for the Lord and genuine piety, each of the contributors in this volume maintains a firm commitment to Scripture as the norming norm for theological reflection, shaping each one's views on all matters, including how and what to think about the triune life. In this way, each is committed to Scripture's authority. Yet there are different views here, and different ways of appropriating Scripture's authority for understanding the doctrine of the Trinity. Questions have been raised about the extent to which there is direct and organic continuity between Scripture and the church's later formulation of the doctrine, a continuity perhaps seen most in Molnar's reflections. Put another way, one may ask whether the doctrine is derived directly from Scripture, with a clear exegetical basis, say in the Gospels (see McCall), as with any other doctrine that may be found in the Bible.[5] The alternative, as one biblical scholar crudely put it, is that the doctrine of the Trinity "arrives from esoteric philosophizing,"[6] or else comes together as a way of making sense of what Scripture says about God.

Critical to this discussion, of course, are the considerations of the fourth-century innovation and addition of *homoousios* to the Nicene Creed, as well as the reckoning with material from both Old and New Testaments and from the experience of the life of the early church. One recent effort, perhaps the most serious and potentially game-changing proposal on the table, has been set forth by R. Kendall Soulen and is rapidly working its way through the trinitarian consciousness of contemporary theologians. In his book, Soulen argues that the Hebrew Tetragrammaton sets the dimensions for the three distinct patterns of trinitarian naming, which come to full flower in the Name of Father, Son, and Spirit, each of which represents the different patterns of naming in salvation history. This proposal accounts for historical-critical issues in biblical scholarship and progressive revelation, as well as matters in the tradition and the early church's life, and it has much to commend it for understanding the "most appropriate" way/s of naming the persons of the Trinity.[7]

The Doctrine of the Trinity and Traditional Trinitarian Discourse

Related to the above matter about the Trinity and Scripture is the matter of the Trinity and our traditions. It is no secret that the evangeli-

5. Fred Sanders, "Trinitarian Theology's Exegetical Basis: A Dogmatic Survey," *MwJT* 8/9 (2010): 78–90.

6. Michael F. Bird, "The Biblical Foundations of the Trinity: Evaluating the Trinitarian Exegesis of Stephen Holmes," in *The Doctrine of the Holy Trinity Revisited: Essays in Response to Stephen R. Holmes* (ed. Thomas A. Noble and Jason S. Sexton; Milton Keynes, UK: Paternoster, forthcoming), ch. 8.

7. See R. Kendall Soulen, *The Divine Name(s) and the Holy Trinity: Distinguishing the Voices*, vol. 1 (Louisville: Westminster John Knox, 2011).

cal tradition, at least, has not been as explicitly and comprehensively trinitarian as it might have been for various reasons related to operative evangelical epistemologies of theology; or, at least, evangelicals have not been as robustly trinitarian as other traditions have been. This is a weakness, and evangelicals are beginning to do better, drawing from their own internal sources wherever possible as well as from other traditions. Yet there are resources in the wider evangelical tradition that leading theologians situated in the older ecclesial traditions (e.g., Paul Molnar, being a Catholic) are drawn to (e.g., T. F. Torrance). Of course, Torrance was shaped by Athanasius from Alexandria in Africa, representing a much wider tradition that fueled his creative reflections on the doctrine of the Trinity, and opened up avenues for wider dialogue with other traditions about the Trinity. This highlights the representative variegations within the traditions represented and demonstrates that it is virtually impossible to work with a stagnated doctrine of the Trinity that is not being constantly reshaped and reconsidered in light of better ways that may be available for understanding God's life in Trinity. The conversation between Holmes and McCall is interesting here, with the former thinking the Gospel texts that the latter exegetes refer only to Jesus' incarnate life and to matters in the salvation economy, and therefore do not necessarily grant insight into the internal, eternal trinitarian relations.

A strength of the conversation carried out in this book is found in the warm and cordial style of the exchanges and the genuine regard for each other, an effect that friendship can have on theological disputes, demonstrating each one's commitment and openness to the triune God and others. Of course, I suspect the initial meeting in the charming setting of St. Andrews has also done something to cultivate this. Having observed a number of debates like these in the past, especially among evangelicals, the different heretical labels often came out far too quickly, well before adequate understanding was obtained. I did not see this in the present discussion. This is not to give the impression that some of what has been articulated here might not either seem like (or even be guilty of!) things like so-called perfect being theology, or patripassionism, or tritheism, or modalism. But it seems that where this designation is used, it is done with greater care than it sometimes has been used and only where precisely necessary, and tentatively, and with consciousness to both anachronism and the potential emergence of a seizure with regard to our own theological reflection. Each of the writers places stress on revelation for shaping our understanding of these things, and descriptions of the divine being as analogous in one way or another. Significant reflections and clarifications were rendered in the rejoinders, especially by perhaps the most creative of the theologians in this volume, those representing the Relational View. It seems like all of the contributors are willing to be convinced of better ways for understanding God's own triune life.

It is at this point, however, that I wonder if recent insight from the late Stanley Grenz might be helpful. While he himself followed (albeit not uncritically) the somewhat fashionable models of the day and acknowledged the necessity of understanding the three internal differentiations or distinctions within the divine life, he nevertheless referred to God as "Person." In his exposition of trinitarian prayer, with reference to Old Testament prayer, Grenz noted that the one to whom the Israelites prayed "is the God who remains 'Person,'" which meant further that "he remains living and sovereign, and confronts as person alive in love and wrath."[8] Grenz's insight is that God confronts us as *person* in relation and we address and relate to God as *person*. Accordingly, the triune God never relates to or addresses us as "We-thou," nor do the creatures address the divine as "Thou-Three." And yet in the ways that Christians have understood throughout the ages — through debates with Islamic scholars, the polytheists, and the pantheists — God is internally differentiated in order to confront in love *from eternity*. As such, this internal differentiation neither denotes three who are not one being, nor any eternal subordination, even as the trinitarian Father-Son language of eternal generation becomes a way of talking about something that is both totally divine and altogether unlike anything known or shared in the creaturely arena.[9]

---

8. Stanley J. Grenz, unpublished lecture, "What Does it Mean to be Trinitarian in Prayer?" from "What Does it Mean to be Trinitarians?" Part 2, Bible and Theology Lectureship, Assemblies of God Theological Seminary, Springfield, MO, Jan. 19, 2005.

9. For a traditional defense of trinitarian Father-Son language for God in missionary perspective, including a brief discussion of the eighth-century Christian-Muslim dialogue, see Scott W. Sunquist, *Understanding Christian Mission: Participation in Suffering and Glory* (Grand Rapids: Baker, 2013), 189–92.

Without developing this insight further, it seems that at the least whatever kinds of "persons" the Father, Son, and Spirit are, for whatever reason (and we could speculate) there is no biblical account of the three speaking simultaneously as three distinct voices — either speaking in the same tone, pitch, and voice. Neither do we see prayer ever made in Scripture simultaneously directed to three distinct entities, or to a troika. Beyond these things, though, and with what significant form of agreement was found within the discourse of this volume, might there yet be some kind of convergence of Classical and Relational trinitarianism, at least on the major points, that is shaped strongly by Scripture, drawing carefully from the best of the tradition and seeking to draw on contemporary insights from the culture for some sort of renewed Classical *and* Relational doctrine of the Trinity? If such developments are to come about, not only will they likely be helpful in serving the church's mission in the contemporary world, but they just may come as a result of the church's dynamic engagement and articulation of the trinitarian gospel in today's world greatly in need of the promises found in Christ. This leads us to our final point.

The Doctrine of the Trinity and Christian Mission

Lesslie Newbigin has done as much as anyone to help the church understand the significance of the doctrine of the Trinity for Christian mission, as well as the historical significance of Christian mission for the doctrine of the Trinity. He observed that the doctrine itself was forged and formulated while the early church was carrying out its Great Commission task. This responsibility set the church out to proclaim salvation in Jesus Christ. And when matters of Jesus' identity were raised, they were addressed "in terms that embody the Trinitarian faith."[10]

As such, it should be understood not only that what may be taken as the two eternal movements within the divine life constitute God as the Trinity — Father, Son, and Spirit — but also that these movements are indeed reflected, or imaged, in the economy in bidirectional manner indicative of the reconciling (missionary) action of this God in whose life there is both an essential *sentness* and an essential *unsentness*. In this

---

10. Lesslie Newbigin, *The Open Secret: An Introduction to the Theology of Mission* (rev. ed., Grand Rapids: Eerdmans, 1995), 28.

way, the triune movement of begetting the Son and spirating the Spirit is not a claim made exclusively about God's own life, but also for the life of others with whom he has chosen to commune—by the work of the sent Spirit to unite believers into filial relationship with God the Father as sons and daughters who share in the image of the only begotten God. In this way and with the degree of seriousness displayed in the conversations in this book, even amid strong disagreement on points, and yet conducted with a massive degree of respect of engagement—it is with this same degree of hospitality and dialogue that we should look to insights from the majority world and from our wider globalized (and localized) society who are underrepresented in Western theology, and from alternatively operative epistemologies that may grant new insights for a yet better understanding of God's life in Trinity.[11]

With all now said, and all that has been said, we offer this book in service to the church and also before our triune God, in whose presence all of our words and reflections fall flat in comparison to the sublime beauty of the infinitely glorious triune majesty. As all in all, worthy of endless praise, "so when we do attain to you, there will be an end to these many things which we say and do not attain, and you will remain one, yet all in all, and we shall say one thing praising you in unison, even ourselves being also made one in you."[12] In light of this prayer of Augustine addressed to the Lord, the one God, God the Trinity, our hope is also that this book may be used by the Lord to move the church one step closer to better understanding the doctrine of the Trinity in order to love the triune God more, and hopefully to a more faithful, awe-inspiring, and wondrous confession of this doctrine of God's triunity that is at the core of the exposition of the gospel .

---

11. For one attempt at something like this see Veli-Matti Kärkkäinen, *Trinity and Revelation: A Constructive Christian Theology for the Pluralistic World*, vol. 2 (Grand Rapids: Eerdmans, 2014).

12. Saint Augustine Bishop of Hippo, *The Trinity* (trans. Edmund Hill; New York: New City Press, 1991), 437.

GLOSSARY

a se. A Latin term meaning, literally, "from self." In trinitarian theology this is often used to denote divine aseity or God's freedom to exist alone with dependence on nothing outside of God's own life.

apophasis. A transliteration of the Greek term ἀπόφασις, first used in the Trinity discussions in the sixth century. Today it is often used to represent a so-called negative theology, or a manner of referring to God that acknowledges that all of our concepts fail to properly represent God's incomprehensible nature. Extreme forms of this can lead to agnosticism and were used by early Gnostics. It may also refer to being silent before the divine life in reserve and reverence.

aseity. From the Latin term *a se*, referring to the self-sustaining power and freedom of God to be who God is in God's own life. In the present volume the meaning of this term is contested as either referring to divine self-sufficiency or to the more general notion of divine freedom (where God may choose to be dependent on things outside of God).

Cappadocians. Often referred to as the Cappadocian Fathers, this group of Greek theologians—Basil of Caesarea, c. 330–379; Gregory of Nyssa, c. 330–379; and Gregory of Nazianzus, c. 330–389—wrote during the period between the Council of Nicaea (AD 325) and the Council of Constantinople (AD 381). Their theology was largely against the Arian heresy and contributed significantly to the development of the orthodox doctrine of the Trinity.

creation *ex amore*. A term adapting a Latin phrase that means "creation out of love." In this book it designates the basis of God's creation not out of his own need (as if having a deficit in his life or mode of existence), but so that creatures are made to participate in the intra-trinitarian love relationships within the divine life.

creatio ex nihilo. A Latin term meaning, literally, "creation out of nothing." In the patristic era of the church, this idea was meant to contradict alternate understandings of the universe as being created out of materials already in existence. The doctrine maintains a strong distinction between God and creation, and also states creation's radical contingency and dependence on God, who alone is eternal and self-existent.

Economic Trinity. This refers to the Trinity's relationship to the world, or the outworking of the divine plan and the divine relations within history (as opposed to how these relations between the Father, Son, and Spirit exist within the Immanent Trinity).

Euthyphro dilemma. This refers to Plato's famous dialogue between Socrates and Euthyphro about whether a thing or an act is good because God says it is good or whether God says a thing or act is good because it simply is good. In this volume, Holmes proposes the doctrine of divine simplicity as the Christian solution to this dilemma.

filioque. This term comes from two Latin words that form this word, meaning "and from the son." Referring to the Holy Spirit's double procession from the Father *and the Son* and not merely the Father alone, this Western addition (which had been taught since Augustine) to the Niceno-Constantinopolitan Creed caused a mounting dispute between the Eastern and Western churches.

glossolalia. This term is a composition of the Greek terms γλῶσσα ("tongue") and λαλία ("talking"), which refers to the supernatural gift of speaking in tongues, the phenomenon reported in Acts 2; 1 Corinthians 14; and elsewhere.

heteros. A transliteration of a Greek term that means "other" or "another" (of a different kind).

homoousios. The transliteration of two Greek terms meaning of "one or the same substance" (ὁμός + οὐσία). It was the term used in the Nicene Creed (AD 325) to identify the relationship between the Father and the Son as that of distinction yet while possessing the same substance or essence. This term was used by Athanasius against Arius, and by its insertion into the Creed formally excluded Arianism from orthodoxy. The Latin term for this idea is *consubstantialis.*

hypostasis and *hypostases.* This term, transliterated here from the Greek (ὑπόστασις) in the singular (*hypostasis*) or plural (*hypostases* or *hypostaseis*), refers to the three distinctions in the Trinity: the Father, the Son, and the Holy Spirit. The Latin terms given for this Greek term are *persona* and *subsistentia.*

Immanent Trinity. This refers to the Trinity's internal (intra-trinitarian) relations, which have always existed in God's triune life for eternity, as opposed to how these triune relations exist within the outworking of affairs in the life of the Economic Trinity. In this way, the Immanent Trinity is the basis for the Economic Trinity.

ineffability. A contested term in this volume, this word carries the idea of having limits on human language to speak of God. Distinguished from the notion of incomprehensibility, that God is ineffable means either that he cannot be known or that no human concepts can apply to God. For Fiddes to say God is ineffable means he cannot be objectified like other created objects.

in se. This Latin term means, literally, "in self." In trinitarian theology, it carries the idea of what exists within the divine life eternally, "in Godself."

ipsissima verba. Literally, the Latin term meaning "the same words." In Jesus studies, this suggests that in the Gospels, the writers wrote down Jesus' actual words themselves as opposed to just the thoughts or ideas (*ipsissima vox*, "the same voice") that Jesus expressed.

koinonia. Transliterated from the Greek κοινωνία and meaning "communion," this term was used by Gregory of Nyssa to denote an inconceivable and ineffable communion while maintaining a distinction between the three persons of the Trinity and yet never compromising their singularity of nature.

Leibniz's law. Formulated by Wilhelm Gottfried Leibniz (AD 1646–1716) as a principle of analytic philosophy that states that no two distinct things exactly resemble each other, and that no two objects have the same properties. This idea is also known as the Indiscernibility of Identicals.

Logos asarkos. This is a transliteration of the Greek term λόγος ἄσαρκος, meaning, literally, "the word unfleshed," or conceived apart from the flesh. Compare *logos ensarkos*, "the word enfleshed."

Monoenergist. Preceding the Monothelite controversy, in a move challenging the Chalcedonian two-natures Christology established in AD 451, this highly political view led by Patriarch Sergius I of Constantinople and Emperor Heraclius arose in the early seventh century. While understanding that the Father, Son, and Spirit have one energy, this debate raised the question of whether Christ had one single power, energy (ἐνέργεια), or two; the Monoenergists ultimately concluded there is only one energy in Christ. This view did not get wide support and was abandoned.

Monothelite controversy. Following the Monoenergist debate over the nature of Christ, this late seventh-century controversy focused on whether Christ had one will ("*mono*" and "*thelos*") or two. Against the Monothelites, the orthodox position argued that in the incarnate Son there were two energies and wills—one human, one divine. Both Monoenergism as well as Monotheletism were condemned by the Sixth Ecumenical Council, held in Constantinople in AD 680.

Nestorianism. This view was held by Nestorius, Bishop of Constantinople (c. 351–c. 451), and argued that the two natures (divine and human) within Jesus' one person existed alongside one another and were thus able to be divided. An implication of this view says that Jesus suffered in his humanity but not in his deity.

norma normans. This Latin term, literally meaning "the norming norm," refers to the primary authority of Holy Scripture for the theological enterprise.

norma normata. This Latin term, literally meaning "the normed norm," refers to the secondary authority structure of tradition for the theological endeavor.

opera trinitatis ad extra. This Latin term, literally meaning, "the external works of the Trinity," refers to the relationship external to the inner divine life. This phrase is often accompanied with the verbal clause *sunt indivisa*, which together means that "the *external* works/actions of the Trinity are undivided/indivisible," which denotes a commonly held belief about the unity of the trinitarian action in the world, consistent with the unity of the divine being.

opera trinitatis ad intra. This Latin term refers to "the *internal* works of the Trinity" as opposed to *opera trinitatis ad extra*; it denotes the eternal actions within God's own triune life.

ordo salutis. This Latin term means "order of salvation," and came into use as sixteenth-century Reformed theologians sought to understand the outworking of God's eternal decrees within time and history. These features of salvation often include election, divine calling, conversion, repentance and faith, justification, sanctification, glorification, and others that are to be understood as thoroughly trinitarian.

ousia. This transliterated Greek term (οὐσία) means "existence, being" or "having substance." Referring to God, it makes reference to the divine "essence" or "being" and denotes the manner of the oneness or unity of the Father, Son, and Spirit. The Nicene formulation (AD 325) said that these three (*hypostases*) are *homoousion* (literally, "the same substance").

Pantokrator. A term coming from the Greek words meaning "all" (πᾶν) and "strength" or "power" (κράτος), it was commonly understood in the early church as referring to Jesus Christ as the Almighty. It was a significant term for Origen, who deemed that God and the created universe exist together necessarily and logically in eternal relation.

patripassianism. As a form of modalistic Monarchianism (or Sabellianism), which developed in the early third century, this view held that God the Father suffered on the cross as or in the mode of the Son; this view thus confounds the persons of the Father and the Son.

perichoresis. This transliteration of a Greek term (περιχώρεσις), often thought to have been first used in the sixth century, expresses the permeation of each person of the Trinity by the other or "in one another," denoting their coinherence without confusion. In Latin, the term, translated as circumincession, represented the way that each person of the Trinity shares the divine essence without blurring their distinctions. The first reference of the Greek term, once thought to be from Pseudo-Cyril (now known as a fourteenth-century text), nevertheless shows dependence on John of Damascus (c. 660–c. 750), one of the last of the church fathers.

persona/personae. The Latin term/s used to describe the three *hypostases* of the Trinity, or existent instantiations, commonly translated "person" in English, although such a translation is not without significant problems.

schesis. An Aristotelian Greek term (σχέσις) for "state, condition, attitude," from the category of relationship. It was used by John of Damascus (c. 660–c. 750), enabling him to distinguish an icon from that which it points to. But in trinitarian terms, Gregory of Nazianzus used this term earlier to denote "Father" as the name of the "relation" between the Father and the Son.

Sabellianism. This term comes from the view espoused in the early third century by Sabellius, denoting that God is one divine person (not three) who reveals himself successively throughout history as the Father, and then as the Son, and finally as the Holy Spirit. Also known as modalism or modalistic Monarchianism.

seinsweise. The German term used by Karl Barth in his *Church Dogmatics* to refer to the notion of "person" in the English-speaking tradition of trinitarian theology. The word *seinsweise* often translates into English as "mode (or way) of being" and is most often rendered "mode of being" by Geoffrey Bromiley in his English translation of Barth's theology. This term often received the superficial critique suggesting that this led Barth to a *modalistic* (or Sabellian) understanding of God. However, Barth acknowledged the Father, Son, and Spirit as distinguished by their distinctive relations to each other, and used the term *seinsweise* to refer to the mode of being of an existent.

The *Shema*. Recited by Jews twice a day according to the earliest rabbinic sources, this term borrows its name from the passage's first Hebrew word (שְׁמַע) meaning "hear" from Deuteronomy 6:4–9.

simplicity. A contested term in this volume, this notion relates to that of having an uncompounded or noncomposite nature (without parts). Related to the simplicity of the divine being, this understands God as free from all composition, whether physically or logically, and thereby guarantees the absolute ultimacy and perfection of God. Divine simplicity is not held universally by everyone in this volume and is highly nuanced especially in the work of McCall and that of analytic philosophy.

Theopaschite proposal. This refers to the view developed in the fifth and sixth centuries by those who in addressing the issue about which of the Trinity suffered in the flesh, and in virtue of the unity of Christ, stated that it could be said that God suffered.

Tropici. This refers to a late-fourth and early fifth-century anti-Nicene sect that, along with other semi-Arians, denied the deity of the Holy Spirit. They were part of what prompted the orthodox theologians to clarify that the Spirit also was *homoousion* with the Son and the Father.

SCRIPTURE INDEX

SUBJECT INDEX

AUTHOR INDEX